Higher
COMPUTING

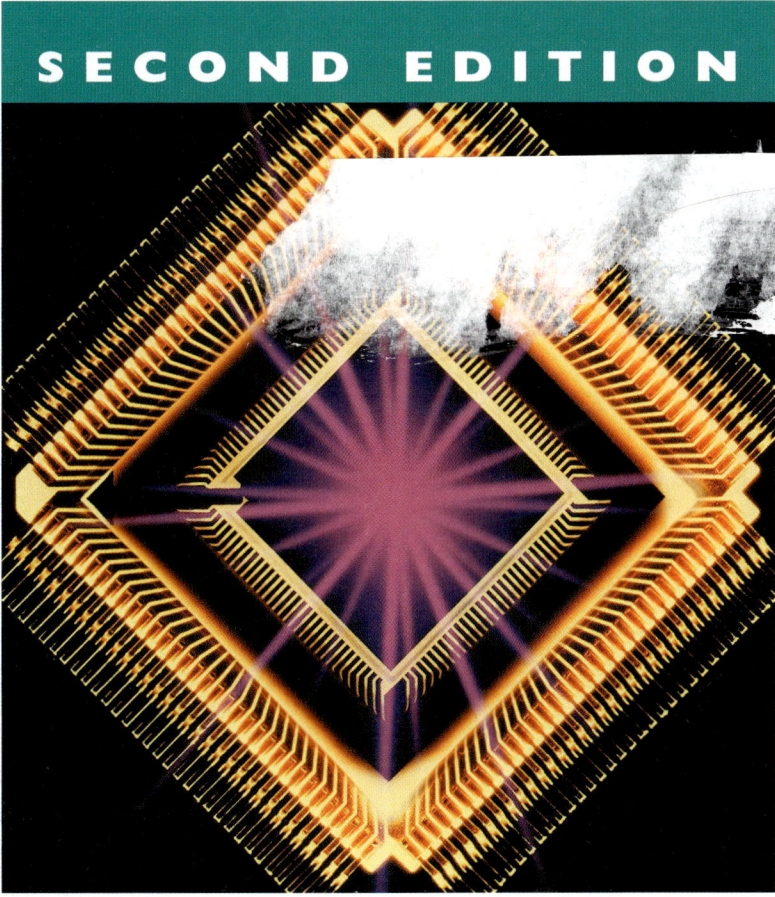

SECOND EDITION

John Walsh

Cover Photograph: the cover photograph shows a gold plated
chip connector reflecting light

Hodder Gibson

A MEMBER OF THE HODDER HEADLINE GROUP

Dedication

To Helen, Peter John, Mary, Sarah, Siobhan and Cecilia.
With thanks to Alice Shanks.

The publishers would like to thank the following for permission to reproduce any copyright material:
Naomi Tokita.

Photo credits
Page 11 Copyright © 1991–2006 Unicode, Inc. All rights reserved. Reproduced with permission of Unicode, Inc.; page 40 copyright © 2000–2005 www.TOP500.org; pages 43 and 54 reproduced courtesy of Apple; page 53 copyright © Kingston Technology Company, Inc.; the Bluetooth logo on page 57 is a licensed trademark of the Bluetooth SIG, reprinted by their permission; page 58 the Wi-Fi Logo is a trade mark of the Wi-Fi Alliance; figure 04.27 on page 78 is a trademark of Zigbee Alliance, Inc.; page 83 is the logo for the Honeynet Project. All Dilbert cartoons reproduced by permission of Knight Features.

Acknowledgements
Artworks by Tony Wilkins Design.
Cartoons by the Richard Duszczak Cartoon Studio Ltd.

Every effort has been made to trace all copyright holders, but if any have been inadvertently overlooked the Publishers will be pleased to make the necessary arrangements at the first opportunity.

Although every effort has been made to ensure that website addresses are correct at time of going to press, Hodder Gibson cannot be held responsible for the content of any website mentioned in this book. It is sometimes possible to find a relocated web page by typing in the address of the home page for a website in the URL window of your browser.

While every effort has been made to check the instructions of practical work in this book, it is still the duty and legal obligation of schools to carry out their own risk assessments.

Orders: Please contact Bookpoint Ltd, 130 Milton Park, Abingdon, Oxon OX14 4SB. Telephone: (44) 01235 827720, Fax: (44) 01235 400454. Lines are open from 9.00–17.00, Monday to Saturday, with a 24-hour message answering service. Visit our website www.hoddereducation.co.uk. Hodder Gibson can be contacted direct on: Tel: 0141 848 1609; Fax: 0141 889 6315; email: hoddergibson@hodder.co.uk

© John Walsh 2006
First Edition Published 2002 (entitled *New Higher Computing*)
Second Edition Published 2006
This Edition Published 2006 by
Hodder Gibson, a member of the Hodder Headline Group
2a Christie Street
Paisley PA1 1NB

ISBN 10: 0 340 905638
ISBN 13: 978 0 340 905630

Impression number   10 9 8 7 6 5 4 3 2 1
Year   2012 2011 2010 2009 2008 2007 2006

With answers
ISBN 10: 0 340 906588
ISBN 13: 978 0 340 906583

Copyright © 2006 John Walsh

Impression number   10 9 8 7 6 5 4 3 2 1
Year   2012 2011 2010 2009 2008 2007 2006

Cover photo © Royalty-Free/Corbis
Typeset in 10.5/13.5pt Plantin by Pantek Arts Ltd, Maidstone, Kent.
Printed in Italy for Hodder Gibson, a member of the Hodder Headline Group,
2A Christie Street, Paisley PA1 1NB.

A catalogue record for this title is available from the British Library.

Contents

Preface to the second edition

This book is based upon the Higher Computing arrangements document (First edition), published by the Scottish Qualifications Authority (SQA) in April 2004. It should be noted that this book is the author's own interpretation of the arrangements document.

This book covers the two mandatory units within the Higher Level Computing course, namely, Computer Systems and Software Development. The chapters match the grouping of the content for each unit as specified in the arrangements document. Hence, chapters 1 to 5 cover Computer Systems, and chapters 6 to 9, Software Development.

Short revision questions designed to focus the student's learning have been placed at the end of each chapter. Some longer questions of a more problem solving nature are also included in an appendix.

In chapters 6–9, examples are given in a range of programming languages and other software development environments. The programming language examples include Visual Basic, True BASIC and COMAL. Some of these program listings may be downloaded from the publisher's web site at *www.newhighercomputing.co.uk*.

Note that this book is *not* a programming manual. Your teacher or lecturer will provide support material tailored to your particular software development environment.

Note that the order of the chapters does not constitute a recommended teaching order.

John Walsh

February 2006

Unit 1

Computer Systems

This chapter, and the four which follow, are each dedicated to the Computer Systems unit. Each chapter is designed to cover the contents statements as they are grouped within the Arrangements document, namely Data representation, Computer structure, Peripherals, Networking and Computer software. The examples given in each chapter are based upon a range of hardware and software, which is current at the time of writing.

1

Data Representation

The method of data representation in a computer system depends upon the type of data which is being used. The types of data which we will consider in this chapter are:

1. Numbers
2. Text
3. Graphics

The binary system

Regardless of the type of data, all data is ultimately stored as binary numbers. Let's look at the binary system before we consider how these different types of data are represented.

The two-state machine

A computer system is known as a *two-state machine* because the processing and storage devices in a computer system have one feature in common – they have two states only. These two states are 'on' and 'off' and are represented using the digits 1 for 'on' and 0 for 'off'. This system of using only two numbers is called the **binary system** because the word binary means 'two states'. In the same way as a light bulb can have two states 'on' or 'off' a binary number has two values 1 or 0, 'on' or 'off'.

Why do computers use the binary system?

Computers use the binary system because it is easy to represent the two states 'on' and 'off' inside a computer. These two states are represented by voltages. Zero (0) volts is used to represent 0, and a voltage, usually between 1 and 5 volts, depending upon the type of computer, is used to represent 1.

Advantages of using the binary system

1. Fewer rules need to be built into the processor for the operations add, subtract, multiply and divide on two digits (0,1) than if all ten digits (0..9) were used.
2. Any slight drop in the voltage does not change the data, since any voltage above 0 volts is used to represent 1.
3. The two states are easy to represent in storage devices, for instance, the presence or absence of a pit on the surface of a CD-ROM.

Disadvantage of using the binary system

One disadvantage of using the binary system is that a large number of digits are required to represent numbers.

Bits

A single unit in binary is called a **bit**. The word bit is made up from the two words **BI**nary digi**T**.

Unlike computers, people use the decimal or **denary** system. Decimal means ten, so people count in units, followed by tens, hundreds, thousands and so on.

For example, the number 2407 is made up like this:

1000	100	10	1	these are the place values
2	4	0	7	these are the digits

This means $2 \times 1000 + 4 \times 100 + 0 \times 10 + 7 \times 1$. This is very easy for us to understand because we are familiar with the decimal system. Thinking about place values in this way will help us to understand the binary system.

Binary works in a similar way, except that binary place values do not go up in tens, they go up in twos. Let's look at a binary number made up of four bits:

8	4	2	1	these are the place values
1	1	0	1	these are the bits

Each bit has its own place value, starting with units, then twos, fours, eights and so on.

The binary number in the example is 1101. This means:

$1 \times 8 + 1 \times 4 + 0 \times 2 + 1 \times 1$ which is 13 in decimal.

Bytes

A binary number which is made up of eight bits (for instance 1101 0110) is called a **byte**. What is the largest number a byte can hold? Let's work it out. A byte has eight bits, so if each bit had the value 1, this would give 1111 1111. Now consider the place values for eight bits:

128	64	32	16	8	4	2	1	these are the place values
1	1	1	1	1	1	1	1	these are the bits

So we have $128 + 64 + 32 + 16 + 8 + 4 + 2 + 1$ which is 255 in decimal.

Note that a byte can have the value zero, so a byte can hold a range of values from zero (0000 0000) to 255 (1111 1111), making a total of 256 different numbers.

More and more bytes

One **Kilobyte** is **1024 bytes** (because $2^{10} = 1024$). One Kilobyte is also called one **Kb** for short. In the same way, one **Megabyte (Mb)** is 1024 Kilobytes (1024×1024 bytes) and one **Gigabyte (Gb)** is 1024 Megabytes ($1024 \times 1024 \times 1024$ bytes). A **Terabyte (Tb)** is 1024 Gigabytes ($1024 \times 1024 \times 1024 \times 1024$ bytes).

At the time of writing this book, the main memory of a microcomputer is measured in Megabytes, with 512 Megabytes being a typical amount for a normal desktop machine. The backing storage capacity is measured in Gigabytes, with typical hard disk capacities ranging from 100 to 500 Gigabytes.

Converting between units

To change:

bits to bytes, divide by 8
bytes to bits, multiply by 8
bytes to Kilobytes, divide by 1024
Kilobytes to bytes, multiply by 1024

All larger units are multiples of 1024.

Where do the place values come from?

The place values come from the number base which, in the case of the binary system, is the number 2. Each different place value can be created by starting from 2^0, like this:

Power of 2	10	9	8	7	6	5	4	3	2	1	0
Place value	1024	512	256	128	64	32	16	8	4	2	1

and so on ....

Note that the leftmost bit in a binary number is called the **most significant bit** (MSB) because it has the highest place value and that the rightmost bit with the smallest place value (1) is called the **least significant bit** (LSB).

A useful rule to remember is that 2^{10} bytes = 1024 (1 Kb); 2^{20} bytes = 1 Mb (1,048,576); 2^{30} bytes = 1 Gb (1,073,741,824), and 2^{40} bytes = 1 Tb (1,099,511,627,776).

It is easy to work out 2^{32} bytes, because 2^{32} bytes = $2^{30} \star 2^2$ = 1 Gb $\star$ 4 = 4 Gb

Table 1.1 *Binary place values up to 40 bits*

Power of 2	Place value	Notes
0	1	
1	2	
2	4	
3	8	
4	16	
5	32	
6	64	
7	128	
8	256	Range of numbers that may be represented by one byte
9	512	
10	1024	1024 bytes = 1 Kilobyte
11	2048	
12	4096	
13	8192	
14	16384	
15	32768	
16	65536	

Power of 2	Place value	Notes
17	131 072	
18	262 144	
19	524 288	
20	1 048 576	1024 Kilobytes = 1 Megabyte
21	2 097 152	
22	4 194 304	
23	8 388 608	
24	16 777 216	Number of colours in 'true' colour
25	33 554 432	
26	67 108 864	
27	134 217 728	
28	268 435 456	
29	536 870 912	
30	1 073 741 824	1024 Megabytes = 1 Gigabyte
31	2 147 483 648	
32	4 294 967 296	
33	8 589 934 592	
34	17 179 869 184	
35	34 359 738 368	
36	68 719 476 736	
37	137 438 953 472	
38	274 877 906 944	
39	549 755 813 888	
40	1 099 511 627 776	1024 Gigabytes = 1 Terabyte

Therefore, we can say that, using 32 bits, the largest number that may be represented is:

1111 1111 1111 1111 1111 1111 1111 1111 in binary or 4,294,967,295 in decimal.

and, if we include 0, a total range of 4,294,967,296 different numbers.

Changing between binary and decimal representations

It is easy to change a binary number into decimal, just write down the place values and add them up like this:

place values	128	64	32	16	8	4	2	1	
binary number	0	1	0	0	0	0	1	1	
decimal	0	+64	+0	+0	+0	+0	+2	+1	= 67

The easiest way to change a decimal number into binary is to write down the place values and then subtract each place value from the number in turn, like this:

Suppose the number is 99, then look at the place values: 128 is larger than 99, so put a 0 at place value 128

Now subtract 64 from 99, so that 99 – 64 = 35, put a 1 at place value 64

Now subtract 32 from 35, so that 35 – 32 = 3, put a 1 at place value 32

Now move to the next suitable place value which is 2, 3 – 2 = 1, so put a 1 at place value 2

Now we are left with 1 – 1 = 0, so put a 1 at place value 1

Result:

place values	128	64	32	16	8	4	2	1	
binary number	0	1	1	0	0	0	1	1	= 99

Numbers

Numbers may be classified as **real numbers** or **integer numbers**. Real numbers include ALL numbers, both whole and fractional. Integer numbers are a subset of real numbers which include only whole numbers, either positive or negative. The distinction is important because the method used to represent integer numbers is different from the method used to represent real numbers.

Representing integers

Positive numbers

Positive numbers are represented in the binary system as described above, using a set number of places.

Size of integers

The **size of the number** which may be represented depends on the number of bytes which are available in the computer's memory to store it. If the computer designer or programmer has allocated two bytes to store a number, then numbers from 0000 0000 0000 0000 up to 1111 1111 1111 1111 may be stored (0 to 65,535 in decimal – a total of 65,536 different numbers).

Negative numbers

Representing negative numbers in a computer system makes it necessary to store the sign of the number, i.e. whether the number is positive (+) or negative (–). Taking the previous example, one of the 16 bits available would have to be used to store the sign, leaving 15 bits for the actual number. This would reduce the size of the numbers that could be represented to a range of:

1111 1111 1111 1111 to 0111 1111 1111 1111
or $-(2^{15} - 1)$ to $+ 2^{15} - 1$
or   –32767   to   +32767   (in decimal)
where 1 represents the negative sign and 0 represents the positive sign.

As a general rule, when using this **signed bit** representation, for the number of bits n, the range of numbers would be:

$-(2^{n-1} - 1)$ to $+2^{n-1} - 1$

This signed bit system has a number of disadvantages, not least of which are the two values for zero: 1000 0000 0000 0000 (negative zero) and 0000 0000 0000 0000 (positive zero).

A system of representation which avoids this problem is called **two's complement**. It is easy to obtain the two's complement of a number by following these steps:

positive number in 8 bits	0000 0111	+7
change all the ones to zeros and	1111 1000	
vice versa, then add 1	+1	
negative number	1111 1001	–7

Two's complement has several advantages: there is only one value for zero; arithmetic carried out using two's complement numbers is correct and to change a number back from two's complement you just repeat the same process as you followed to create it.

Notice that two's complement representation also retains the leftmost bit as the sign bit.

Example

negative number in 8 bits	1111 1001	–7
change all the ones to zeros and	0000 0110	
vice versa, then add 1	+1	
positive number	0000 0111	+7

Note: While answering any questions about number representation it is important to be aware of which particular system of representation is in use, for example the number 1000 0000 could mean +128 or –128, depending on whether or not two's complement representation is used. If a question does not tell you which system of representation to use, then you should choose a system and write down what system you have used as part of your answer.

Representing real numbers

Fractions

Fractions in denary (decimal) use a decimal point and look like this:

fraction	1/10	1/100	1/1000	1/10000	1/100000
decimal	0.1	0.01	0.001	0.0001	0.00001

Fractions in binary use a binary point and look like this:

fraction	1/2	1/4	1/8	1/16	1/32	1/64	1/128
decimal	0.5	0.25	0.125	0.0625	0.03125	0.015625	0.0078125
binary fraction	0.1	0.01	0.001	0.0001	0.00001	0.000001	0.0000001

Floating point representation

Let's start by looking at real numbers in decimal. Any decimal number can be represented with the decimal point in a fixed position and a multiplier, which is a power of 10. For example:

$$20.125 = .20125 \times 100 = .20125 \times 10^2$$

This is a decimal number and so uses powers of ten. Ten is the base. Any number can be represented in any number base in the form:

m $\times$ **base^e**

Where m is called the **mantissa** and e is the **exponent**. The mantissa is the actual number and the exponent is the power to which the base is raised. For the binary system, the base would be 2. Furthermore, since the base is *always* 2, the base can be ignored and does not need to be stored in the computer alongside each number.

Taking the above example of decimal 20.125, in binary or base two this would be:

$$10100.001 = .10100001 \times 2^5 = .10100001 \times 2^{101}$$

(Remember 101 in binary = 5 in decimal)

If the position of the point is always kept the same and the number base is always two, then all that need be stored is the mantissa and the exponent. So using the above example:

10100.001 can be stored as	1010 0001	101
	mantissa	exponent

Therefore any number can be stored in a computer's memory as two binary numbers, the mantissa and the exponent. This way of representing numbers is called **floating point representation**.

Precision and range of floating point representation

Just as the computer designer or programmer has to make a decision about how many bytes in memory should be used to store integers, a similar decision has to be made for real numbers stored in floating point representation.

Using the example above, and ignoring two's complement, if 16 bits were used to store the mantissa, and 8 bits were used to store the exponent, then the number would be stored in the following way:

.1010 0001 0000 0000	0000 0101
mantissa	exponent

Increasing the number of bytes for the mantissa would increase the **precision**, since this would allow more digits of the numbers to be stored. Some computer programming languages have the option of doubling the number of bytes used to store a number. This is called **double precision arithmetic**.

Again, because the number of bytes is fixed, the precision is limited, and calculations carried out using numbers represented by floating point may not always give an accurate answer.

Increasing the number of bytes for the exponent would increase the **range** of numbers which could be stored.

Recalling our previous example of storing numbers using 16 bits for the mantissa and 8 bits for the exponent, and ignoring both two's complement and signed bit, the largest number that could be stored is:

$$.1111\ 1111\ 1111\ 1111 \times 2^{1111\ 1111} = 1 \times 2^{255}$$

and the smallest positive number that could be stored is:

$$.0000\ 0000\ 0000\ 0000 \times 2^{0000\ 0000} = .0 \times 2^0 = 0 \times 1 = 0$$

You should note that the above example has been deliberately simplified to make it easy to understand the basic principle involved in floating point representation of numbers. There is insufficient time available in this unit and space in this book to give a complete and detailed account of floating point representation.

Text

A byte is the space in a computer's memory which is used to hold one character. A **character** is a symbol or letter on the computer keyboard. Characters include the digits 0 to 9, letters and punctuation marks. They are called numeric, alphabetic and special characters respectively. A mixture of alphabetic and numeric characters is called alphanumeric. A, B, C, a, b, c, 0, 1, 2, 9, &, £, * are all characters.

The computer must be able to represent all the characters we may wish to use. A list of all the characters which a computer can process and store is called the character set. Different types of computer may have slightly different **character sets**. To allow a computer to represent all the characters, a different code number is given to each character.

The most popular form of this code is the **American Standard Code for Information Interchange** or **ASCII**. ASCII is a seven-bit code. Using a seven bit code allows 2^7 or 128 different codes, so ASCII can represent 128 characters. If more than 128 characters are required, then eight bits can be used, giving 2^8 or 256 possible characters. This is called **extended ASCII**, and allows additional characters, such as those with accents é, ç, or special symbols, like ™ and © to be represented.

Many different computers use ASCII to represent text. This makes it easier for text to be transferred between different computer systems.

Some ASCII characters do not print on the screen in the normal way. They are known as **control characters** because they control certain operations of the computer system. In ASCII, codes from 0 to 31 are used as control characters. The origin of control characters is found in the history of computers when output was obtained on a mechanical *Teletype* printer rather than a screen. Control characters were used to control the movement of the print head and the paper, for example a carriage return character moved the paper up one line and also moved the print head to the left-hand side.

Table 1.2 *Sample of ASCII*

Character	Binary	Decimal
enable printer	000 0010	2
disable printer	000 0011	3
bell	000 0111	7
tab	000 1001	9
Cursor down	000 1010	10
Cursor up	000 1011	11
Clear screen	000 1100	12
Return	000 1101	13

Character	Binary	Decimal
space	010 0000	32
!	010 0001	33
'	010 0010	34
0	011 0000	48
1	011 0001	49
2	011 0010	50
3	011 0011	51
?	011 1111	63
@	100 0000	64
A	100 0001	65
B	100 0010	66
C	100 0011	67
W	101 0111	87
X	101 1000	88
Y	101 1001	89
Z	101 1010	90
a	110 0001	97
b	110 0010	98

Unicode (Universal Character Set)

This book is written in English, and uses characters from the Roman or Latin character set. Many other languages, such as Japanese, use completely different types of characters.

The Unicode character set is designed to represent the writing schemes of all of the world's major languages. The first 128 characters of Unicode are identical to ASCII. This allows for compatibility between Unicode and ASCII. Unicode is a 16 bit code and can represent 65,536 different characters.

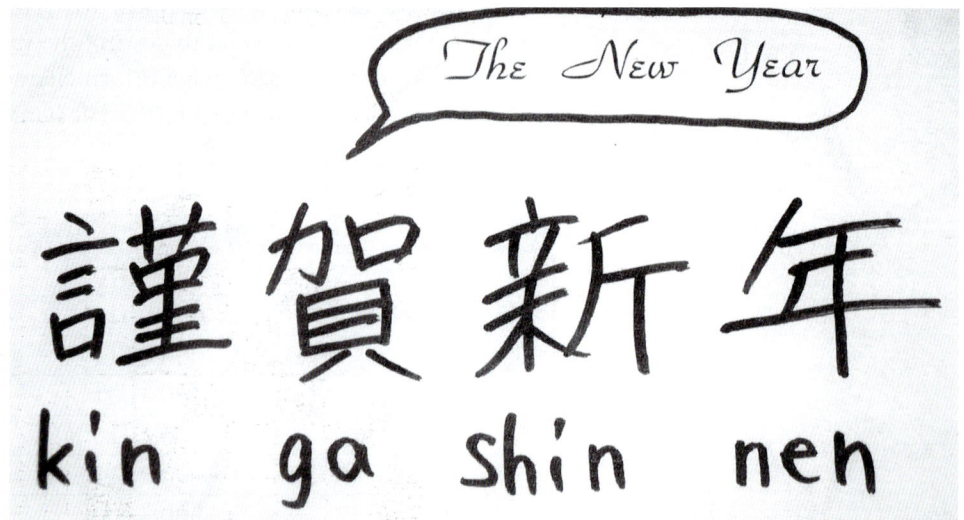

Figure 1.1 *A seasonal greeting from Japan*

It's not just computers that use Unicode. Your mobile phone may also use Unicode when sending certain kinds of text messages. Normal text messages are known as SMS. SMS stands for Short Message Service. A standard SMS text message can be up to 160 characters, where each character is 7 bits. 8-bit messages (with a maximum length of 140 characters) are not usually viewable by phones as text messages, they are used to send images and ring tones. A Unicode text message on a mobile phone is known as a UCS2 16-bit message (maximum length 70 characters), and is viewable by most phones. On some phones the message will appear as a Flash SMS (blinking or alert) message.

The Unicode standard continues to be developed, and is at version 4.01 at the time of writing this book. Early versions of Unicode contained fewer than 65,536 characters, and so all of the characters could be represented by 16 bits (remember that $2^{16} = 65,536$). Unicode now contains more than 96,000 characters and therefore more than 16 bits are required to represent all of these characters. It is thought that at least 21 or 22 bits may eventually be required.

The advantage that Unicode has over ASCII is that many more characters (or every possible character) may be represented. A disadvantage is that Unicode takes up at least twice as much storage space as ASCII (16 bits compared to 8 bits).

The development of a universal character code has implications for most computer software companies. Examples include those who create typefaces and companies who write General Purpose Packages.

There is a great deal more to Unicode than can be described in a few lines in this book. You can find out more about Unicode at http://www.unicode.org/ and http://en.wikipedia.org/wiki/unicode.

Figure 1.2 *Unicode logo*

Graphics

Graphics, like any information displayed on a computer screen, are made up of tiny dots called **pixels**. Pixel is short for picture element. Imagine the whole of the computer screen being made up of many thousands of pixels. Each pixel may be set to 'on' or 'off' depending on whether the value of the pixel in the computer's memory is 1 or 0.

Screen   **Memory**

1	0	0	0	0	0	1
0	1	0	0	0	1	0
0	0	1	0	1	0	0
0	0	0	1	0	0	0
0	0	1	0	1	0	0
0	1	0	0	0	1	0
1	0	0	0	0	0	1

Figure 1.3 *How graphics are stored in the computer's memory*

Look at figure 1.3, which shows how graphics are stored in the computer's memory. The picture is drawn on a 7×7 grid. Grid squares which are 'on' are represented by a '1' and grid squares which are 'off' are represented by '0'. The amount of memory required to store this graphic would be 7×7 bits, which is 49 bits.

Graphics resolution

The quality of the picture is determined by the **resolution** of the graphics available. The smaller the size of the pixels, the finer the detail that can be displayed on the screen. Small pixels mean high resolution. See figure 1.4 (a high resolution graphic). Large pixels mean low resolution. One way of describing the resolution of the screen is to give the number of pixels horizontally and vertically. For instance, a screen display operating at 800×600 pixels (SVGA) is a lower resolution than 1024×768 pixels (XGA). Another way of describing the resolution is to give the total number of pixels available, although this description is usually applied to devices such as digital cameras, as in 'a *7 Megapixel camera*'.

Figure 1.4 *A high resolution graphic*

Increasing the resolution of a graphic has consequences. As the number of pixels increases, so does the storage space that will be required to store the graphic. You can read more about the calculation of backing storage space for bit mapped graphic images later in this chapter.

Bit mapped and vector graphics

Graphics packages can be classified into two main types, **bit mapped** and **vector**. Both types of package are used to produce pictures, but they store the graphics in a different way. Bit mapped packages paint pictures by changing the colour of the pixels which make up the screen display. Vector packages work by drawing objects on the screen. Bit mapped packages and vector graphics packages are commonly known as *Paint* and *Draw* packages respectively. Vector packages are sometimes also called *object-oriented* graphics.

Other differences between bit mapped and vector graphics

(i)   When two shapes overlap on the screen in a bit mapped package, the shape which is on top rubs out the shape underneath. When the same thing is done in a vector graphics package, the shapes remain as separate objects. They can be separated again and both shapes stay the same. See figure 1.5.

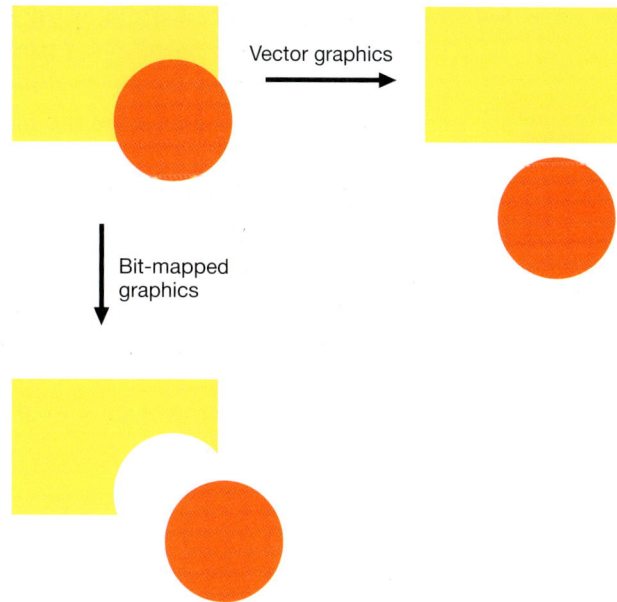

Figure 1.5 *Bit mapped and vector graphics*

(ii) When you save a file created by a bit mapped package, then the whole screen is saved, whether or not it contains any images. This results in a relatively large file size being produced. The objects produced by a vector graphics package have their descriptions stored as a file of data called object attributes. These object attributes take up far less backing storage space than a file created by a bit mapped package, since only the object attributes rather than the whole screen need be stored. Figure 1.6 shows an object and its attributes.

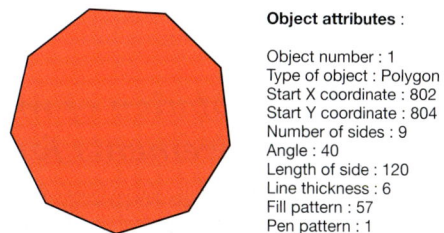

Object attributes :

Object number : 1
Type of object : Polygon
Start X coordinate : 802
Start Y coordinate : 804
Number of sides : 9
Angle : 40
Length of side : 120
Line thickness : 6
Fill pattern : 57
Pen pattern : 1

Figure 1.6 *Object attributes*

(iii) When you create a picture using a bit mapped package, its resolution is fixed at that time. If you then go on to print the picture, the original resolution will be maintained in the printout. The resolution of a printer is measured in dots per inch (dpi). For the purpose of comparison, we will also refer to screen resolution as dots per inch rather than pixels. Suppose the resolution of the microcomputer screen is 72 dpi in two dimensions and the printer which you are using is an ink jet, set at its default value of 360 dpi. When your picture is printed it will be at the screen resolution of 72 dpi, because in order to print, the processor sends the bit map to the printer.

When a picture is created using a vector graphics package, the resolution of the screen has no effect on the resolution of the printout. The picture will be printed out at the full resolution available on the printer. This feature is called **resolution independence**. Resolution independence is possible using vector graphics because when the picture is printed, the processor sends the file of object attributes which represent the picture to the printer.

Some printers have their own processor and high level language interpreter which can translate *page description languages* such as *Postscript*™ or *HP PCL*™. Page description languages are so called because their programs describe the page set up and each of the objects which will appear on the printed page.

Here is an example of a program in a page description language:

```
0       0       moveto
72      0       lineto
0       72      lineto
closepath   fill
showpage
```

If this program was sent to a *Postscript*™ printer, it would print a one inch black square in the bottom left corner of the page. Look closely at the code. Can you work out what is happening? Clue – there are 72 points in an inch.

(iv) When editing a picture created by a bit mapped graphics package, it is possible to zoom in as far as the individual pixels and make changes. When editing a picture produced by a vector graphics package, it is possible to zoom in to enlarge portions of the picture on the screen, but it is not possible to edit any pixels. It is possible to edit the individual objects which make up the picture, and alter any of the attributes, such as line width.

Calculation of memory and backing storage requirements for bit mapped images

The storage requirements of bitmapped images can be calculated using the formula:

*Storage requirements = total number of pixels used in the image * number of bits used to represent colours or shades of grey for each pixel*

The number of bits used to represent colours or shades of grey used in the graphic is known as the **bit depth** or the **colour depth** of the image.

Example 1

Suppose the size of the graphic to be stored is 1 inch by 2 inches, and the resolution is 90 dpi in 256 colours. The reason why dots per *inch* are used is because the United States has not (yet) changed over to the metric system.

The total number of pixels used in the image is 1 * 90 * 2 * 90 = 16200 pixels

Always remember to multiply by the dpi twice, once for each dimension.

The number of bits used to represent 256 colours would be 8 bits because 256 is 2^8

The storage requirements would therefore be 16200 ∗ 8 which is 129600 bits, 16200 bytes or *15.82 Kilobytes*.

Example 2

An A4 page (10×8) is to be scanned at 300 dpi in 65,536 colours.

The total number of pixels used in the image is 10 ∗ 300 ∗ 8 ∗ 300 = 7200000 pixels

The number of bits used to represent 65,536 colours would be 16 bits because 65536 is 2^{16}

The storage requirements would therefore be 7200000 ∗ 16 which is 115200000 bits, 14400000 bytes or 13.73 Megabytes

Comparing these two examples shows clearly *the effect that increasing the size and bit depth of the graphic has on its memory and backing storage requirements.*

You should also now understand why a computer system which is used for graphics may require a large amount of main memory and backing storage space.

True colour

True colour is represented on a computer system using 24 bits per pixel, giving a total range of 16,777,216 different colours.

Are there only 16,777,216 different colours in real life? No, because nature is an analogue system with infinite varieties. Digital devices like computers can only work with separate, stepped values. In order to simulate reality, analogue quantities, like colour and sound are chopped into millions of separate values. This technique, known as sampling, produces a more realistic result by using finer 'chops'. The trick is to chop finely enough for the desired effect. Music CDs sample the analogue sound from the original performance 44,100 times a second in order to fool us into thinking we're hearing the original music.

Figure 1.7 *A colour gradient*

Where does the figure of 24 bits per pixel come from? Imagine a line which is black at one end and white at the other, which becomes gradually lighter as you move along it. If you had to pick separate shades of grey in order to make up such a line, how many would you need? It is generally accepted that the human eye cannot distinguish between adjacent shades of grey when looking at a picture which contains more than 200 shades between black and white. The figure 200 is conveniently close to 256, which requires 8 bits per pixel to store. A colour picture on a computer screen is made by combining the three primary colours Red, Green and Blue. True colour uses 8 bits (256 shades) for each colour, making a total of 24 bits (3×8). Figure 1.8 shows how Red, Green and Blue combine to form a range of colours.

RGB model

A large percentage of the visible spectrum can be represented by mixing **red, green and blue (RGB)** coloured light in various proportions and intensities. Where the colours overlap, they create cyan, magenta, yellow and white. Because the RGB colours combine to create white, they are also called **additive** colours. Adding all colours together creates white – that is, all light is transmitted back to the eye. Additive colours are used for lighting, video and monitors.

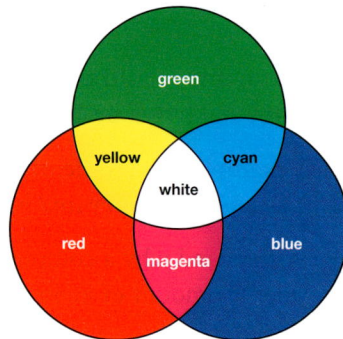

Figure 1.8 *The RGB model*

True colour is often called 24 bit RGB colour. Each of the three colours can have 256 possible values, ranging from 0 to 255. Figure 1.9 shows how the values Red = 255, Green = 255 and Blue = 0 result in the colour yellow being displayed on the screen.

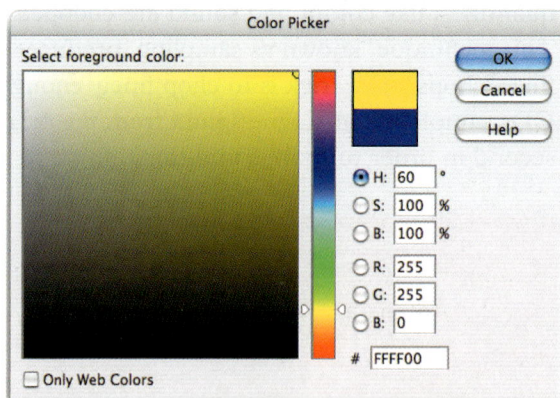

Figure 1.9 *The RGB Color Picker from Photoshop Elements*

Example 3

A photographic negative which is 345×675 pixels in size, is to be scanned in true colour.

The total number of pixels used in the image is $345 \times 675 = 232875$ pixels

The number of bits used to represent true colour is 24 bits

The storage requirements would therefore be 232875 * 24, which is 5589000 bits, 698625 bytes or 682.25 Kilobytes

Truer than true colour

Just because our eyes cannot detect more than 16,777,216 different colours, it does not mean that machines are so limited. Many scanners can produce images which have 36 or 48 bit colour depth. How many different colours could be represented by 36 bits or by 48 bits?

Explanation of the need for data compression

Data Compression means reducing the size of a file in order to save backing storage space. There are two types of data compression. They are **lossy** and **lossless**.

Lossless compression

Lossless compression means that none of the original data is lost. One method of lossless compression involves counting repeating pixels. This is shown in Figure 1.10.

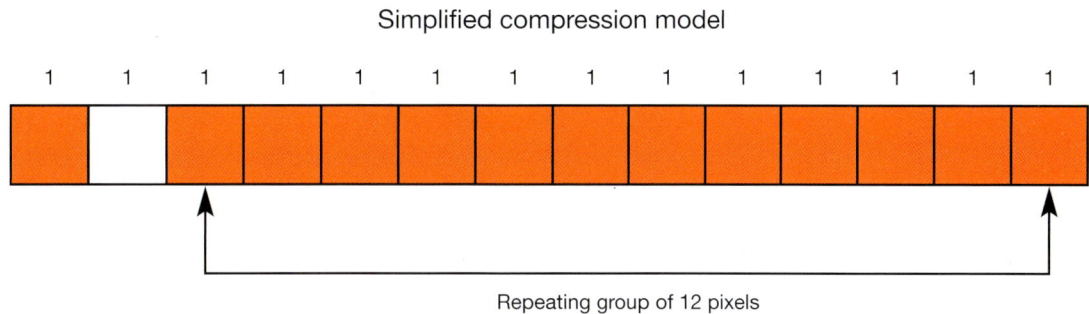

Simplified compression model

Repeating group of 12 pixels

Figure 1.10 *One method of lossless compression*

Look at figure 1.10, which shows part of a bit mapped graphic, which has a repeating group of 12 identical pixels. For the sake of this example, we will assume that it is monochrome graphics, i.e. one bit per pixel, but this technique works equally well for any number of bits per pixel.

Storage of this group of 12 pixels, at 1 bit per pixel = 1111 1111 1111

However, since all of the 12 pixels are the same, then all that need be stored is the colour of the pixel and the fact that there are 12 pixels.

Storage of the number 12 in binary = 1100. Storage of the colour of the pixel = 1. Total storage requirements = 5 bits.

Saving = 12 – 5 = 7 bits.

More storage space may be saved when a larger number of bits per pixel is used. A repeating group of 12 pixels in true colour (24 bits per pixel) would require a storage space of 12 * 24 = 288 bits. Compressing this repeating group would require 4 bits for the number 12 (1100) and 24 bits to store the colour of the pixel, total 28 bits. Saving = 288 – 28 = 260 bits.

Lossy compression

Lossy compression involves sacrificing some of the data in order to reduce the file size. Lossy compression techniques reduce the quantity of data in two ways: firstly by using complex mathematical encoding and secondly by deliberately losing some types of information that our eyes and brain usually ignore. Lossy compression is able to save more space than lossless compression. Lossy compression is only suitable if the loss of data will not cause the file to become useless. For instance, a program file cannot be stored using lossy compression, but a graphic or an audio file could be stored in this manner.

If lossy compression is taken to an extreme, it can result in a significant loss of picture quality. The higher the compression ratio, the worse the resulting image.

JPEG (Joint Photographic Experts Group)

JPEG is a file format commonly used for data compression of bit mapped graphic files. JPEG uses lossy compression which means that some data is lost. Most digital cameras use JPEG compression to store images on flash card memory. In figures 1.11 and 1.12 you can see the effect of compression on image quality and file size.

Figures 1.11 *and* **1.12** *JPEG compression*

Both of the above images are 24 bit JPEG files, 288 × 531 pixels in size. The left hand image has been saved at the maximum quality setting (least JPEG compression) and has a storage space of 192 Kilobytes. The right hand image has been saved at the lowest quality JPEG setting (highest compression) and requires a storage space of 80 Kilobytes.

The difference in picture quality is noticeable if you look at the fine detail, such as the edges of the windmill blades. You can see that the greater JPEG compression has had little or no effect on the quality of the blue sky.

The original photograph from which these images were taken, is shown here for comparison in figure 1.13.

Figure 1.13 *Original photograph for comparison*

More about JPEG
- JPEG is designed for either full colour or greyscale images of natural scenes.
- JPEG works well on photographs, but not so well on line drawings.
- JPEG handles only still images, MPEG is used for motion pictures.
- JPEG is lossy, which means that some detail is lost from the image.
- The amount of compression used may be changed, allowing a trade-off between file size and image quality.
- JPEG uses 24 bits per pixel for RGB colour images.

Advantages of data compression on bit mapped graphic files
- Bit mapped images can take up a great deal of backing storage space. Using data compression can save backing storage space. Compression is important when saving images on a backing storage medium which has limited capacity, like a flash ROM card in a camera.
- The smaller the storage space taken up by the image, the less time it will take to transmit as an email attachment, for example.
- Smaller images are faster to load in web pages. Users with a slow dial-up Internet connection can lose patience with a web site that takes a long time to load.

Disadvantages of data compression on bit mapped graphic files
- If lossy compression is used, then detail may be lost from the images.
- Sometimes lossy compression can lead to changes in the images, with the introduction of artefacts which were not present in the original image.
- It can take a significant amount of time to compress large image files. You may have noticed that when using a digital camera, there is a delay between taking successive shots. This happens because of the time taken to compress the image for storage in the camera's memory.

- Repeated compression can reduce image quality. If an uncompressed image file is re-compressed, especially when a different compression method is used, then the overall quality of the image can deteriorate. Artefacts (see above) may be introduced.

Figure 1.14 *Zeros are round and fat...*

Questions

1. Convert the following binary numbers into denary (decimal – all positive numbers):
   a. 1011
   b. 1001 1111
   c. 1010 1010
   d. 1111 1110

2. Convert the following denary (decimal) numbers into binary:
   a. 122
   b. 193
   c. 256
   d. 1023

3. Express the following denary numbers in binary using 8 bit two's complement notation:
   a. −6
   b. −25
   c. −92
   d. −120

4. Express the following denary (decimal) numbers as binary using a binary point:
   a. 0.25
   b. 7.375
   c. 15.53125

5. Convert the following real numbers into binary using floating point representation. Assume that 16 bits is available for the mantissa and 8 bits for the exponent.

   a. 27.5
   b. 134.125
   c. 4200.25

6. A binary number made up of only four bits is called a nibble. It is called this because it is half of a byte.
   a. What is the largest binary number a nibble can hold?
   b. What range of numbers may be held in a nibble?

7. Why is it possible to say that '*calculations carried out using numbers represented by floating point may not always give an accurate answer*'?

8. In floating point representation, what will be the effect of increasing the number of bits used to store the exponent?

9. What range of numbers can be represented in floating point if 4 bytes is available for the mantissa and one byte for the exponent? State any assumptions you make, for example, whether or not you are using two's complement representation.

10. If you have access to a high level programming language like TrueBASIC or COMAL, try out some calculations using real numbers and compare the answers with those you have calculated yourself. Look at the documentation

for the language and note the range and precision of the numbers which can be stored. Repeat the process using an application package which can handle numbers (like a spreadsheet). Note any differences in precision or range.

11. What is a:
    a. character?
    b. character set?
    c. control character?

12. a. What does ASCII stand for?
    b. How many characters can ASCII represent?
    c. Give a reason for your answer to **b**.
    d. Describe one method of increasing the number of characters that may be represented by ASCII.
    e. What is the ASCII for:
       i. 'e'?
       ii. 'E'?
       Express your answers in decimal or binary.

13. a. What is Unicode?
    b. State one advantage of Unicode over ASCII.

14. The character shown in figure 1.15 has been stored using.
    a. a bit map
    b. ASCII
    c. Unicode.
    In each case calculate (or show) the number of bits required for representing the character by each method.
    d. Which method is most efficient (uses least storage space)?

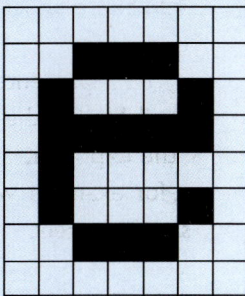

Figure 1.15 *Character bitmap*

15. Why are bit mapped graphics so called?
16. How are vector graphics stored?

17. a. What is true colour?
    b. How many bits are used to represent true colour?

18. With respect to graphics, what is:
    a. resolution?
    b. resolution independence?
    c. Which type of graphics package provides resolution independence?

19. Which of the following statements are true of:
    a. bit mapped?
    b. vector images?
       i. pixels can be edited
       ii. pixels cannot be edited
       iii. resolution independent
       iv. resolution dependent
       v. overlapping parts of the image may be separated cleanly
       vi. file size is constant regardless of the complexity of the image
       vii. file size increases as the complexity of the image increases

20. You buy a computer magazine with a DVD containing demo software. You install one of the programs, a graphics package, to try out on your computer at home. The graphics package has on-line help facilities, but it does not indicate whether it is a bit mapped or vector package. Describe two tests you could carry out while using the graphics package in order to find out whether you are using a bit mapped or vector graphics package.

21. What is a page description language?

22. Look at the example *Postscript*™ program on page 14. The program draws a square of size one inch. Write a new version of the program which would draw a square of size two inches.

23. Calculate the backing storage requirements for the following bit mapped images:
    a. a 640 × 480 screen shot in 256 colours
    b. a 1 megapixel image from a digital camera in 16 bit colour
    c. a 16 colour scan of a 10 × 8 page at 150 dpi
    d. a monochrome 4 × 6 image at 600 dpi.
    Express your answers in Kilobytes or Megabytes as appropriate.

24. Why does a grey scale image in 8 bits have the same storage requirements as a colour image?

25. Look back at figures 1.8 and 1.9 showing the RGB colour model. If the colour red may be represented by an RGB value of (255, 0, 0), which colours are represented by:
    a. (0, 255, 0)?
    b. (0, 0, 255)?
    c. (0, 0, 0)?
    d. (255, 255, 255)?

26. A given bit mapped image is 256 colours and takes up a backing storage space of 512 Kilobytes. What would the storage requirements be for this same image if it was
    a. changed to 65,536 colours (and in all other respects kept the same)?
    b. changed to greyscale with 256 levels?
    c. changed to true colour?

27. What is data compression?

28. Why is data compression used on bit mapped graphics files?

29. What is meant by the terms:
    a. lossy compression?
    b. lossless compression?
    c. Which type of compression gives the smaller file size?
    d. Which type of compression is suitable for a:
       i. computer program?
       ii. photograph taken with a digital camera?

30. Name one standard file format which uses:
    a. lossy compression
    b. lossless compression.

31. Look back at figures 1.11 and 1.12. Each image is 288 × 531 pixels in 24 bit colour.
    a. Calculate the storage requirement for the original image before compression. Express your answer in Kilobytes.
    b. Both of the images are stored as JPEG. Figure 1.11 has a compressed file size of 192 Kilobytes and figure 1.12 has a compressed file size of 80 Kilobytes. Using your answer from part (a), calculate the compression ratio (e.g. 4 : 1) which has been applied to each image.

32. Some digital cameras can output images in RAW format. RAW format takes the data directly from the camera's sensor without any compression being applied.
    a. Calculate the storage requirement for a RAW format image of 1567 pixels by 1807 pixels in true colour.
    b. State the approximate number of megapixels in this camera's sensor.
    c. When this image is transferred from the camera, it now takes up 1.51 Mb of backing storage space on disk. Compare this with the storage requirement you calculated in (a) and explain any difference.

• Key points •

- The internal representation of data in a computer system is in binary.
- Types of data which are represented in a computer system include numbers, text and graphics.
- Numbers may be stored as integer or floating point (real numbers).
  - Negative numbers are stored using two's complement representation.
- Fractions in binary use a binary point.
- Floating point uses a mantissa and an exponent.
- The mantissa holds the number and the exponent holds the power.
- Increasing the number of bytes used for the mantissa will increase the precision of the number being stored.

- Increasing the number of bytes used for the exponent will increase the range of the number being stored.
  - To change:
    - bits to bytes, divide by 8
    - bytes to bits, multiply by 8
    - bytes to Kilobytes, divide by 1024
    - Kilobytes to bytes, multiply by 1024
    - All larger units are multiples of 1024
- Text may be stored as integer values using the American Standard Code for Information Interchange (ASCII).
  - ASCII is a seven-bit code.
  - A character is a symbol or letter on the computer keyboard.
  - Control characters control certain operations of the computer system.
  - Unicode is a 16 bit system which can represent 65,536 characters.
  - The advantage that Unicode has over ASCII is that many more characters (or every possible character) may be represented.
- Graphics may be either bit mapped or vector.
  - Graphics are made up of tiny dots called pixels.
  - The quality of the picture is determined by the resolution of the graphics available.
  - The smaller the size of the pixels, the finer the detail that can be displayed on the screen.
- Bit mapped packages paint pictures by changing the colour of the pixels which make up the screen display.
- Vector packages work by drawing objects on the screen.
- Differences between bitmap and vector:
  - Overlapping shapes may be separated in vector
  - Bit map saves the whole screen
  - Bit map resolution is fixed, vector is resolution independent
  - Bit map can zoom to show and edit pixels
- Storage requirements of bit map = total number of pixels used in the image * number of bits used to represent colours or shades of grey for each pixel.
- True colour is represented on a computer system using 24 bits per pixel, giving a total range of 16,777,216 different colours.
- Data Compression means reducing the size of a file in order to save backing storage space.
- There are two types of data compression, lossy and lossless.
- Lossless compression means that none of the original data is lost.
- Lossy compression involves sacrificing some of the data in order to reduce the file size.
- JPEG is a file format commonly used for data compression of bit mapped graphic files.
- JPEG uses lossy compression which means that some data is lost.

2 Computer Structure

The **processor** is the main part of the computer, consisting of the **control unit**, the **arithmetic and logic unit** and the **registers**.

A computer may have more than one processor. This can help improve the performance of the computer by increasing its processing power.

Figure 2.1 shows how a processor connects to the input, output and backing storage devices of the computer.

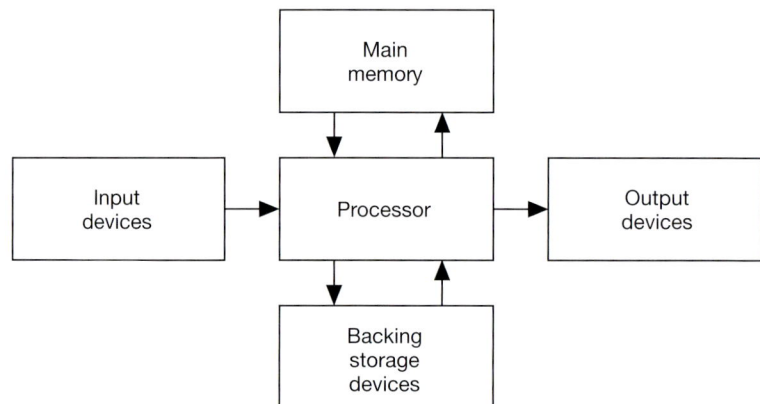

Figure 2.1 *Block diagram of a computer system*

The control unit in the processor controls all the other parts of the processor and makes sure that the program instructions of the computer are carried out in the correct order. The control unit makes sure everything happens in the correct place at the correct time.

The arithmetic and logic unit or ALU carries out the calculations (arithmetic) and performs the logical operations.

The registers are a group of *storage locations in the processor*. The precise details of what these registers are and how they function is not required for this unit on Computer Systems at Higher level. However, two of these registers are named in figure 2.2 to help with the explanation of the fetch-execute cycle.

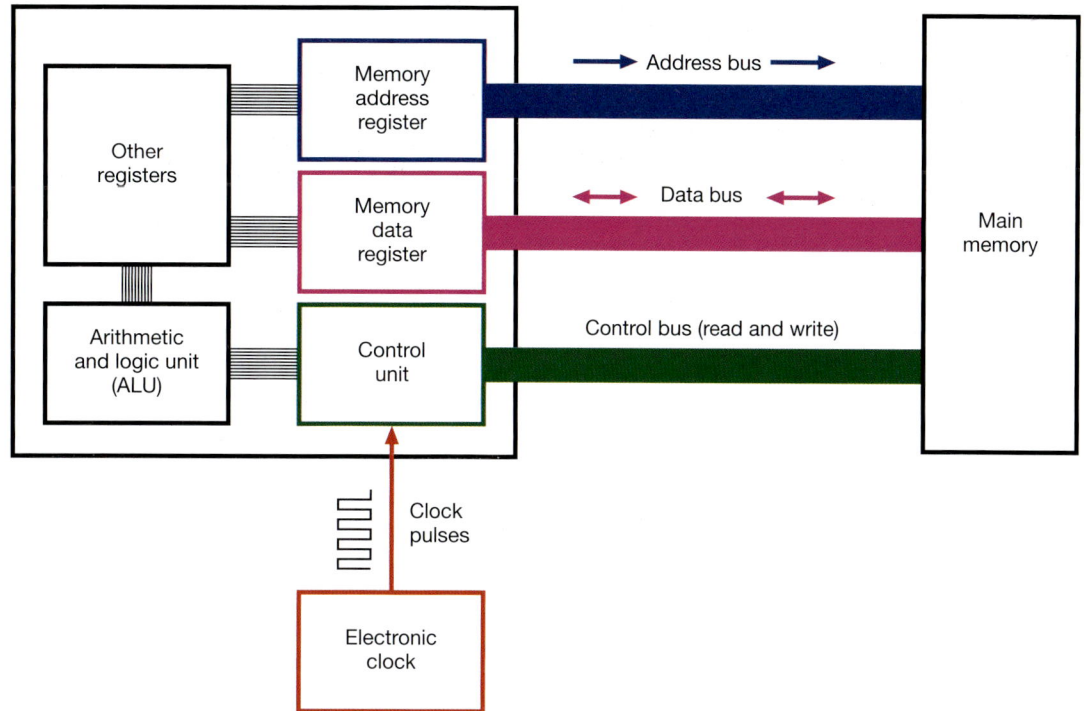

Figure 2.2 *Processor structure*

Buses

Three sets of wires called **buses** connect the processor to the memory and input/output devices. These are the **address bus**, the **data bus** and the **control bus**. Figure 2.3 shows how the buses are connected to these devices.

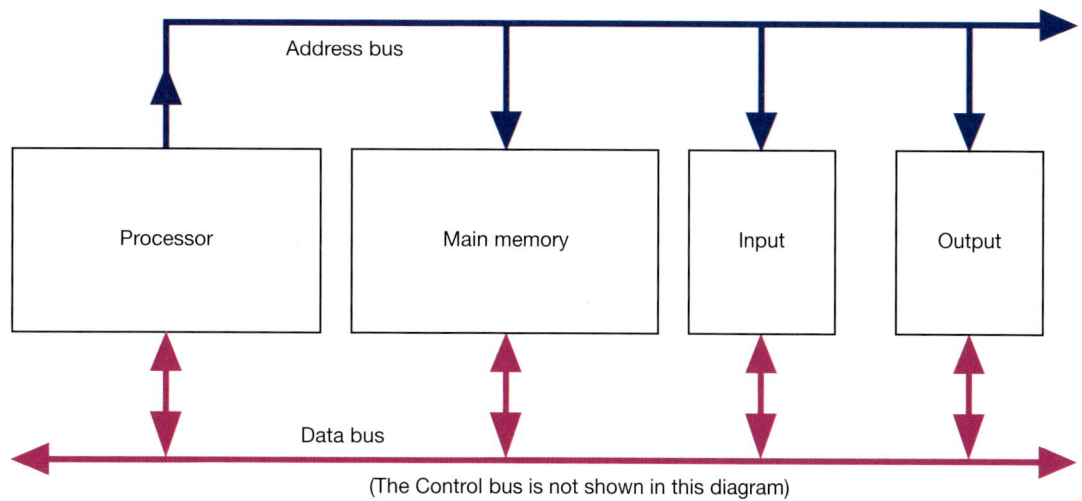

Figure 2.3 *Address bus and data bus connections*

Address Bus

The address bus carries the address information from the processor to the main memory and any other devices attached to the bus. The address bus is *unidirectional* or one-way only. The number of wires in the address bus (the width of the bus) determines the number of storage locations which the processor can address. A typical microcomputer with 32 wires in the address bus is said to have a 32-bit address bus. Each of the wires in the bus can be switched on (set to 1 in binary) or off (set to 0 in binary). A 32-bit address bus can therefore address a series of memory locations starting from address:

0000 0000 0000 0000 0000 0000 0000 0000 (decimal 0)

up to and including address:

1111 1111 1111 1111 1111 1111 1111 1111 (decimal $2^{32}-1$)

making a total of 2^{32} addresses.

Every time a bit is added to the width of the address bus, the address range doubles. Increasing the width of the address bus, for instance, from 32 bits to 64 bits, will increase the total number of memory locations which the processor can address from 2^{32} in decimal, to 2^{64} in decimal.

Data bus

The data bus carries data to and from the processor, main memory and any other devices attached to the data bus. The data bus is therefore *bi-directional* or two-way. The number of wires in the data bus determines the quantity of data which the bus can carry. A typical microcomputer with a 32-bit data bus can carry 32 bits of data or instructions at a time. Increasing the number of wires in the data bus will increase the quantity of data which the bus can carry. This is one method of increasing the performance of a computer system.

Control bus

The control bus is made up of a number of separate wires or lines, each with its own function. These include the **read**, **write**, **clock**, **interrupt**, **non-maskable interrupt** and **reset**.

Read and write
See *The fetch-execute cycle* later in the chapter.

Clock
The clock line carries a series of clock pulses at a constant rate. These pulses are used to keep the processor and its related components in step with one another. The **clock rate** is the frequency at which the clock generates pulses. Frequency is measured in hertz, and a computer's clock rate is measured in either *Megahertz* or *Gigahertz*. (1 *Gigahertz* = 1000 *Megahertz*). Increasing the clock rate will increase the speed at which the computer operates. This is another method of increasing the performance of a computer system. See figure 2.2.

Interrupt and non-maskable interrupt
An interrupt is a signal to the processor, typically from an input or output (peripheral) device. The interrupt system allows peripheral devices to communicate with the processor. An interrupt causes a break in the execution

of the processor's current program. When an interrupt occurs, the processor saves a copy of what it is doing at that moment, runs a program to deal with the interrupt, and then reloads its original task and continues what it was doing before the interrupt occurred.

Software can be used to make the processor ignore or mask the interrupt signal from a peripheral. For example, if the programmer wanted to ignore the fact that a printer which was being used was out of paper, then she could write some code which would mask the interrupt sent by the printer to the processor so that her main program would not cause the computer to 'hang', waiting for paper to be added to the printer.

A non-maskable interrupt behaves in the same way as an interrupt, except that the processor cannot mask, or ignore, the interrupt.

Reset

The reset line on the processor is used to return the processor and indeed, the whole computer system to its initial state, as if it had just been switched on. The main use of the reset line is to recover from a system crash, for instance when the computer has 'frozen' and is not responding to any user commands. Many microcomputers have a small button somewhere on the case which can be used to activate the reset line.

Figure 2.4 *Reset*

The fetch-execute cycle

The processor of the computer is able to carry out a process only when it is given a set of instructions. A set of instructions which controls the operation of the processor is called a program. By changing the program which is stored or held in the computer's main memory, a computer can carry out a completely different process. This is known as the *stored program concept*.

Each program instruction is stored in a separate storage location in the computer's main memory. In order for the processor to carry out a process, it must be supplied with instructions from the memory, one at a time, in the correct order.

This method of operating a computer was first described by *John Von Neumann (1903-57)*, and nearly all modern computers are based on this *Von Neumann architecture*.

The fetch-execute cycle is the name given to the way in which the processor takes in an instruction from memory (**fetch**) and carries out that instruction (**execute**).

The fetch-execute cycle consists of two parts or phases. The fetch phase is where the instruction is copied into the control unit of the processor and decoded (See *Memory read operation,* below). The execute phase follows next, in which the instruction is carried out. It is sometimes useful to think of it as the fetch-decode-execute cycle.

Reading from and writing to memory

The fetch part of the fetch-execute cycle involves taking in an instruction. This is a memory **read** operation. The execute part of the cycle, in which the instruction is carried out, may involve either another read operation or a memory **write** operation. Looking back at figure 2.2 will help you to understand this process.

Memory Read Operation
The steps involved are:

1. The processor sets up the address bus with the required memory address. It does this by placing a value in the Memory Address Register.

2. The control unit of the processor activates the read line on the control bus.

3. The contents of the particular storage location in memory are released onto the data bus and are copied into the processor's Memory Data Register. If it is an instruction, it is decoded and executed (carried out).

Memory Write Operation
The steps involved are:

1. The processor sets up the address bus with the required memory address. It does this by placing a value in the Memory Address Register.

2. The processor sets up the data bus with the value to be written to memory. It does this by placing the value in the Memory Data Register.

3. The control unit of the processor activates the write line on the control bus.

4. The contents of the Memory Data Register are transferred to the required storage location in the computer's memory.

Summary of the fetch-execute cycle
*   The processor sets up the address bus with the required address.
*   The processor activates the read line.
*   The instruction is transferred from memory to processor by using the data bus (fetch).
*   The instruction is decoded.
*   The instruction is executed.

The concept of addressability

The place where each item is stored in a computer's memory is important because the computer has to be able to find any given item of data. An item is stored in memory in a *storage location*.

Each storage location has its own unique **address** in the computer's main memory. The method a computer uses to identify storage locations is called its **addressability**.

The number of storage locations in the computer's memory that a processor can identify depends on the number of bits in the address or the number of wires in (the *bus width* of) the address bus. A *one-bit address* only has two values, 0 and 1, so a one-bit address could only identify two storage locations, one at address 0 and one at address 1. With a *two-bit address* you could identify four locations (00, 01, 10 and 11). A *three-bit address* could identify eight locations, (000, 001, 010, 011, 100, 101, 110, 111) and so on.

Here are some more examples:

Table 2.1 *The relationship between the number of bits in the address and the number of storage locations*

Number of bits in address (width of address bus)	Number of storage locations that can be identified
1	2
2	4
3	8
4	16
5	32
10	1024
16	65536
20	1048576
30	1073741824

Each storage location in a computer's memory can hold a single unit of storage, which is called a *word*. A *word* is the number of bits that the processor can process *in a single operation*.

Calculating the addressable memory in a computer system

The quantity of memory which may be addressed, can be calculated using the formula:

Total addressable memory = Number of storage locations × size of each storage location

The number of storage locations depends upon the width of the address bus, so that a 16 bit address bus would allow the processor to address 2^{16} or 65,536 storage locations.

The size of each storage location depends upon the width of the data bus or *word* size. An eight-bit data bus means that each storage location can hold one byte, because there are 8 bits in a byte.

Let's look at an example calculation.

Suppose that the address bus of a computer system is 32 bits and the data bus is 16 bits.

The number of storage locations = 2^{32} because the address bus is 32 bits wide.

The size of each storage location = 2 bytes because the data bus is 16 bits wide.

The total addressable memory will therefore be $2^{32} \times 2$ bytes, or 2^{33} bytes.

Depending upon the question that you are asked, you may be required to change the answer from bytes into Megabytes or Gigabytes. Remember that 2^{10} bytes is 1 Kilobyte, 2^{20} bytes is one Megabyte, and 2^{30} bytes is one Gigabyte. So, taking the example above:

2^{33} bytes = $2^{30} \times 2^3$ = $2^3 \times 1$ Gigabyte = 8 Gigabytes

Elements of computer memory

The elements of computer memory are **registers**, **cache**, **main memory** and **backing storage**.

These elements of memory, their **function** and **speed of access** are described below.

Registers

The registers are a group of *storage locations in the processor* which are used **to hold data being processed**, **instructions being executed** and **addresses to be accessed**. Since registers are memory locations on the processor chip itself, then their speed of access may be regarded as being immediate, or around 1 nanosecond. One nanosecond is 10^{-9} seconds.

Cache

Cache memory is a relatively small amount of memory, for instance, 1 or 2 Megabytes, which is used as a temporary store for often used instructions. Cache memory may be referred to as Level 1 or Level 2, which indicates its relative proximity to the processor. Level 1 cache is usually built in to the processor chip, and connected to the processors registers by a bus which may be 128 or 256 bits wide. Level 2 cache may also be on the chip or very close to it. Cache memory which is built into the microprocessor chip is called internal, and that outside the chip, external. Whatever the location of cache memory, it is much faster for the processor to access data held in cache memory than in main memory. The function of cache memory is explained in figure 2.5. The speed of access to Level 1 cache memory is around 5 nanoseconds, and around 15 nanoseconds for Level 2 cache.

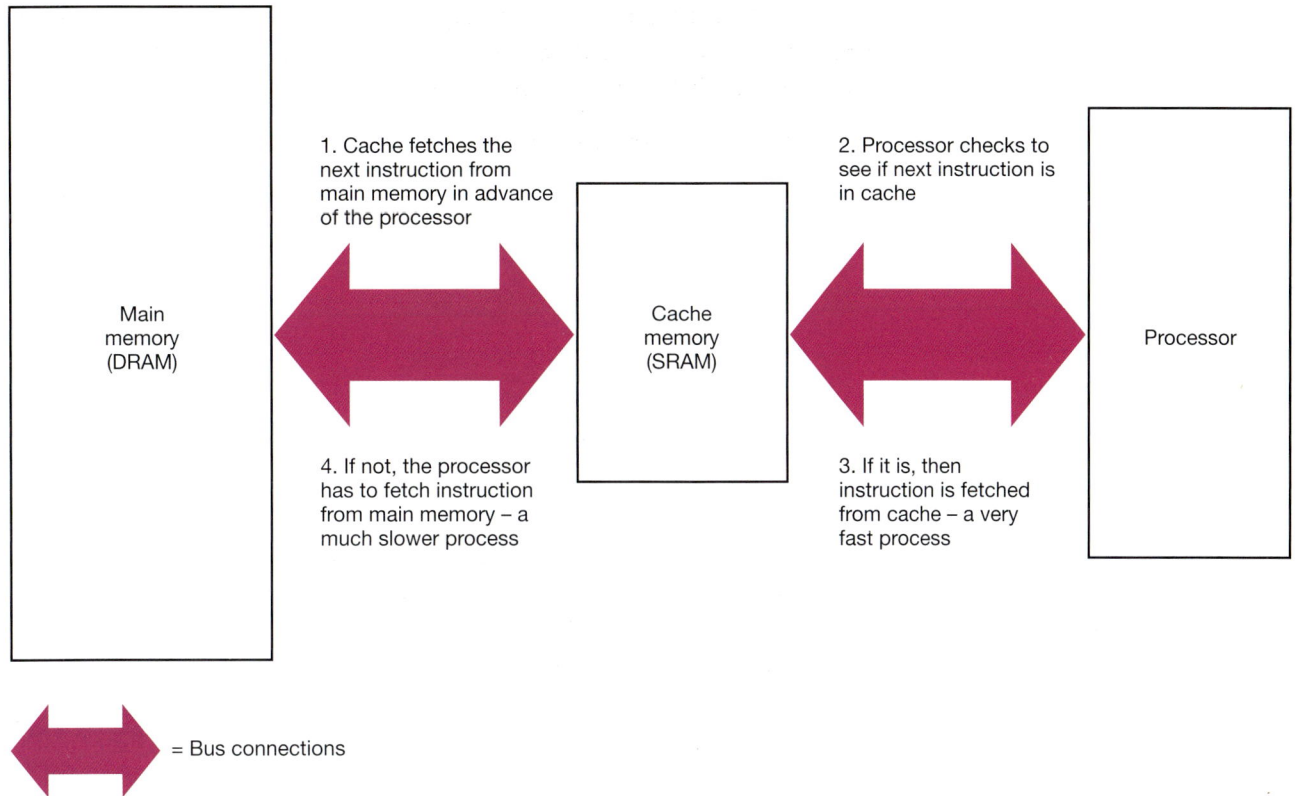

Main
memory
(DRAM)

1. Cache fetches the
next instruction from
main memory in advance
of the processor

Cache
memory
(SRAM)

2. Processor checks to
see if next instruction is
in cache

Processor

4. If not, the processor
has to fetch instruction
from main memory – a
much slower process

3. If it is, then
instruction is fetched
from cache – a very
fast process

= Bus connections

Figure 2.5 *The function of cache memory*

Main Memory

Main memory of a computer is a general term for any type of computer memory other than backing storage. Main memory consists of a number of storage locations, each of which is identified by a unique **address**. The ability of the processor to identify each storage location is called its **addressability**. Each storage location can hold a quantity of data called a **word**. A word is the number of bits that can be processed by the processor in a single operation. This is the same as the number of wires in (the width of) the computer's data bus. The width of the computer's data bus and hence the **word length** is usually larger than a byte, and may consist of 16, 24, 32 or as many as 64 bits.

Types of main memory

Main memory consists of two types, **Random Access Memory** (RAM) and **Read Only Memory** (ROM).

Random Access Memory

Random Access Memory is a type of computer memory which holds its data as long as the computer is switched on. When the computer is switched off, any data held in RAM is lost. RAM is volatile memory. Data held in RAM can be read or written to by the processor in any order. RAM is therefore a direct access medium.

The purpose of random access memory is to hold the computer's programs and data while they are being processed. In most microcomputers, random access memory is also used to hold the operating system program.

Types of Random Access Memory

- **Dynamic Random Access Memory** (DRAM) is a type of RAM chip which needs to have its contents constantly refreshed (about 1000 times a second) or any data contained in it will be lost. Typical access time for DRAM is around 50 nanoseconds. (1 nanosecond = 10^{-9} seconds).

Figure 2.6 *DRAM*

- **Static Random Access Memory** (SRAM) is a type of RAM chip that doesn't need to be constantly refreshed. It will retain its contents as long as power is applied to the chip. Static RAM has a much faster access speed (around 10 nanoseconds) than Dynamic RAM, and so is used in the processor's **cache** memory. One other use for static RAM is to hold the computer's date and time settings. It is able to do this when the computer is switched off, because it is powered by a small battery.

The majority of a computer's main memory is normally made up of dynamic RAM since it is much less expensive to produce than static RAM. Figure 2.7 shows the memory installed in one of the computers which I am using to write this book.

Memory Slot	Size	Type	Speed	Status
DIMM1/J4001	1 GB	DDR SDRAM	PC3200U-30330	OK
DIMM0/J4000	Empty	Empty	Empty	Empty

DIMM1/J4001:

Size: 1 GB
Type: DDR SDRAM
Speed: PC3200U-30330
Status: OK

Figure 2.7 *Built-in memory*

Other uses of Random Access Memory

- **Video Random Access Memory** (VRAM) is designed to hold the data which is to be displayed on the computer screen or monitor. The amount of VRAM in the computer is directly related to the number of colours and the available resolution. VRAM is sometimes contained in a separate **graphics** card, which can be added to the computer system. VRAM is measured in Megabytes – a graphics card may contain 256 Megabytes or more of VRAM. In addition to memory expansion, graphics cards may provide functions such as acceleration, anti-aliasing and 3 dimensional graphics, which are particularly useful for graphic design and games applications.

Read Only Memory

- Read Only Memory is a type of computer memory which holds its data permanently. When the computer is switched off, any data held in ROM is preserved. ROM is permanent memory. Data held in ROM can be read by the processor in any order. ROM is therefore another type of direct access medium.

Figure 2.8 *ROM*

The purpose of read only memory is to hold both programs and data permanently. The contents of ROM are fixed when the computer is manufactured. In many microcomputers, read only memory is used to hold part of the operating system program, the bootstrap loader, which is used to help start up the computer. ROM has an access time of around 50 nanoseconds.

Some types of Read Only Memory

- Programmable Read Only Memory (PROM) is empty of data when manufactured, and may be permanently programmed by the user.
- Erasable Programmable Read Only Memory (EPROM) can be programmed, erased and reprogrammed. A typical EPROM chip package has a small window on top, which allows the chip to be erased by shining ultraviolet light on it. After the chip has been reprogrammed, the window is covered to prevent its new contents from being erased.
- Flash ROM has the advantage that it may be reprogrammed while it is still inside the computer. Flash ROM is now a very popular backing storage medium. Flash ROM is used in USB Flash Drives and Memory cards for use in devices such as digital cameras.

Other uses of Read Only Memory

In some small computers and in particular games machines, software is stored on ROM cartridges. This method of distributing software is popular with manufacturers, because it prevents the software from being easily copied.

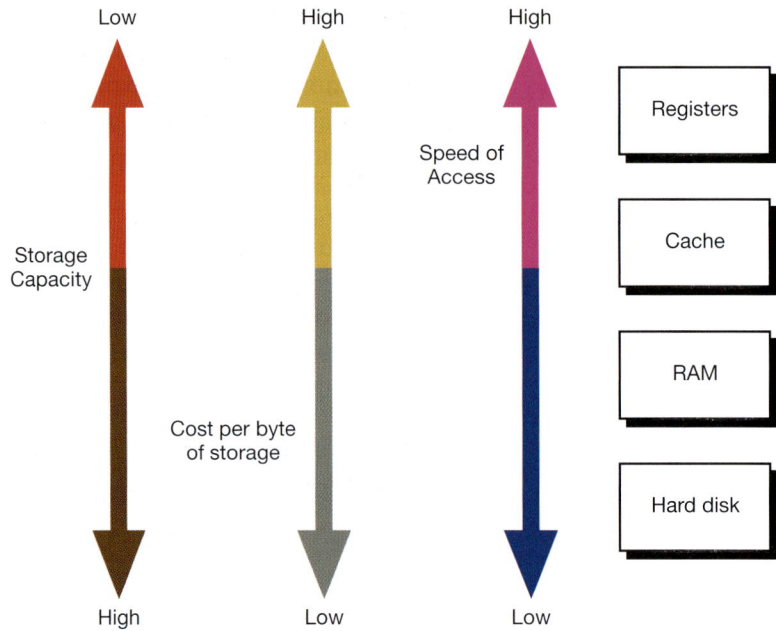

Figure 2.9 *Comparing types of memory*

Backing Storage

Backing storage functions as permanent storage for programs and data in a computer system. Backing storage is also called *secondary memory*. Backing storage is required because data, which is held in main or *primary memory*, is lost when the computer is switched off. Magnetic disks, magnetic tape, optical disks and USB flash ROM are all examples of *backing storage media*. The hardware which uses, or holds the media is known as the *backing storage device*.

The speed of access to backing storage depends upon the type of backing storage device and media in use. All disks give direct or random access to data, while tape is a sequential access medium. At the time of writing, the fastest backing storage device is the hard disk drive, with an access time measured in milliseconds (10^{-3} seconds). A typical hard disk drive has an access time of between 5 and 10 milliseconds.

Figure 2.10 *Backing storage (hard disk drive)*

A special case

Virtual memory is a way of using fast backing storage as a temporary location for programs and data. Virtual memory is useful in situations where a computer has insufficient RAM to hold a complete program and its associated data.

Virtual memory sets aside part of the computer's backing storage device (like a hard disk) as a temporary storage area. Data and programs are swapped between RAM and the backing storage device as the processor requires them for processing.

Virtual memory is a cheap way of being able to run large programs (or many programs) on a computer, but there is a price to pay for this convenience. The processor can access RAM in terms of nanoseconds, but it takes milliseconds to access a backing storage device such as a hard disk. This means that using virtual memory is much slower than using RAM.

How many times slower is virtual memory than RAM?

Table 2.2 *Elements of computer memory compared*

Element of computer memory	Function	Speed of access (relative)	nano-seconds
Registers	Hold data being processed, instructions being executed and addresses to be accessed	immediate	1
Cache – SRAM	Holds frequently accessed instructions	very fast	Level 1 = 5 Level 2 = 15
Main memory – DRAM	Holds programs and data when the computer is switched on	fast	50
Main memory – ROM	Holds programs when the computer is switched off	fast	50 to 100
Backing storage – hard disk, including virtual memory	Holds programs and data when computer is switched off	slow	1,000,000
Backing storage – optical disk	Holds programs and data when computer is switched off	slow	More than 1,000,000

Measures of performance

In order to tell how fast a computer system can process data, it is necessary to measure its performance. A number of different measures of computer performance have been developed. The measures of computer performance which we will look at in this unit are: **clock speed**, **MIPS**, **FLOPS**, and **application based tests**.

Clock speed

The computer's clock signal is carried by one of the lines on the control bus. (See figure 2.2) The clock generates a series of clock pulses at a constant rate. The clock rate is the frequency at which the clock generates pulses. Frequency is measured in *hertz*, and a computer's clock rate is measured in either *Megahertz* or *Gigahertz*. (1 *Gigahertz* = 1000 *Megahertz*). Everything that the processor does is kept precisely in time with the clock. The fetch-execute cycle described earlier in this chapter is a good example of how this works.

Example

Suppose a processor's clock rate is 1000 *Megahertz*. This means that the clock is generating pulses one thousand million times a second. One single pulse is called a **clock cycle**. Fetching a single instruction from the computer's memory takes a length of time measured in clock cycles, say 10 clock cycles, for instance. So our example processor will be able to fetch *one* hundred million of these instructions in one second. If the clock rate was increased to 2000 Megahertz, then the processor would be able to fetch *two* hundred million of the same instructions in one second.

This example shows just how significant the effect of increasing the clock rate can have on a computer's overall performance.

You should note that in fact, different instructions will take different numbers of clock cycles to fetch.

At the time of writing this book, typical microcomputers had a clock rate of over 3 *Gigahertz*. It should be noted, however, that a microcomputer's clock rate is always quoted as that of the processor. In fact, a microcomputer's buses may have separate clocks, each working at a much slower rate than the processor's clock. A typical microcomputer's data bus, for example, might have a clock rate of 800 *Megahertz*. This difference between the clock rates of the processor and the bus can result in a processor '*bottleneck*' which can reduce a computer system's overall performance, because the data cannot be transferred as fast as the processor can process it.

The general principle of Chemistry that '*a reaction can only proceed as fast as the speed of its slowest step*' also applies to computers. Regardless of how fast the processor may be able to process instructions, if, say, the memory access speed is slow, then that will limit the computer system's overall performance. The slowest component in any system, therefore, may be regarded as the '*limiting factor*'.

MIPS

MIPS stands for **Millions of Instructions Per Second** and is a measure of performance based on the average number of machine code instructions executed. Like clock speed, MIPS is only a useful measure of computer performance if in all other respects the rest of the test conditions remain the same.

FLOPS

FLOPS stands for **Floating Point Operations Per Second** and is a measure of the arithmetical calculating speed of a computer system. One *MegaFLOP* is a million FLOPs and one *GigaFLOP* is a billion FLOPs. One definition of a *Supercomputer* is that it can operate at speeds of at least one GigaFLOP.

Application-based tests

No matter which one of these measurements is used, it does not really mean much to the ordinary user. While it may impress some people to be able to say that their latest processor is 20 times faster than a *Pentium I 100 Megahertz* or whatever, it is of more importance to the user how fast applications run, and this depends on the performance of the whole computer system, not just one particular component.

A **benchmark** is a standard set of computer tasks designed to allow a computer's performance to be measured. These tasks may be used to compare different software or hardware. Typical tasks may involve timing how long it takes to reformat a 100 page word-processed document, how many pages can be printed per minute, or how long it takes to save a 1000 record database to disk. Figure 2.11 shows a screen shot of one type of benchmark application for a microcomputer, *Speedometer*™, which produces an overall test score for the particular system under examination.

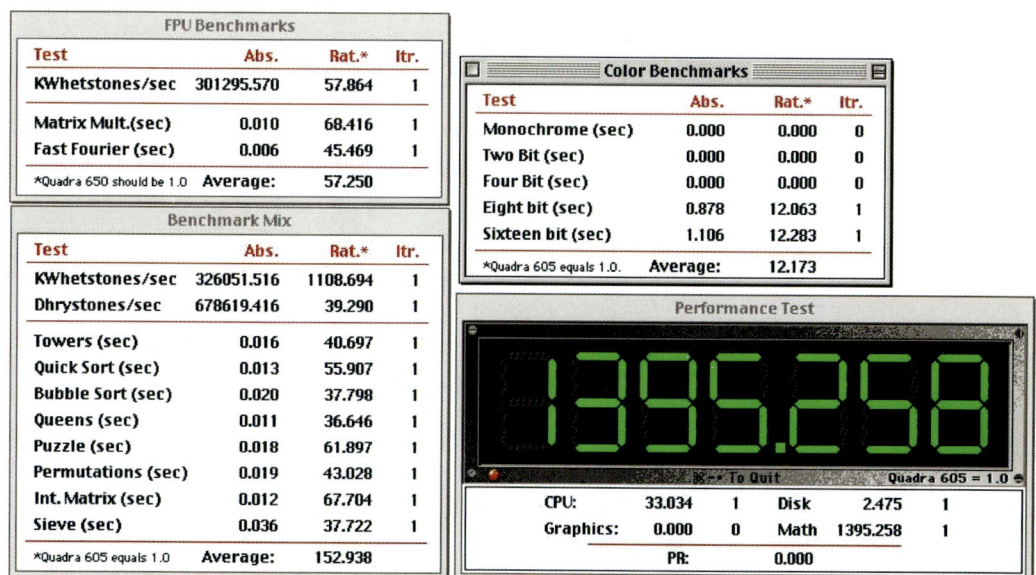

FPU Benchmarks

Test	Abs.	Rat.*	Itr.
KWhetstones/sec	301295.570	57.864	1
Matrix Mult.(sec)	0.010	68.416	1
Fast Fourier (sec)	0.006	45.469	1
*Quadra 650 should be 1.0	**Average:**	57.250	

Benchmark Mix

Test	Abs.	Rat.*	Itr.
KWhetstones/sec	326051.516	1108.694	1
Dhrystones/sec	678619.416	39.290	1
Towers (sec)	0.016	40.697	1
Quick Sort (sec)	0.013	55.907	1
Bubble Sort (sec)	0.020	37.798	1
Queens (sec)	0.011	36.646	1
Puzzle (sec)	0.018	61.897	1
Permutations (sec)	0.019	43.028	1
Int. Matrix (sec)	0.012	67.704	1
Sieve (sec)	0.036	37.722	1
*Quadra 605 equals 1.0	**Average:**	152.938	

Color Benchmarks

Test	Abs.	Rat.*	Itr.
Monochrome (sec)	0.000	0.000	0
Two Bit (sec)	0.000	0.000	0
Four Bit (sec)	0.000	0.000	0
Eight bit (sec)	0.878	12.063	1
Sixteen bit (sec)	1.106	12.283	1
*Quadra 605 equals 1.0.	**Average:**	12.173	

Performance Test

```
1395.258
```

To Quit   Quadra 605 = 1.0

CPU:	33.034	1	Disk	2.475	1
Graphics:	0.000	0	Math	1395.258	1
	PR:	0.000			

Figure 2.11 *Speedometer*

SPEC CPU2000 – The Standard Performance Evaluation Corporation (SPEC) is one example of an organisation which produces standard benchmarks. Their CPU2000 suite of benchmarks is designed to reveal details of a whole machine's performance that cannot be learned simply by knowing a processor's clock speed. If performance depended only on Megahertz, there would be no performance difference between two identical processors, and a faster processor would always win.

Many computer magazines in their comparative reviews of computer systems, use so-called *real world* tests which involve timing the performance of certain applications carrying out demanding tasks which occupy a great deal of processor time. The *SYSmark2000* test devised by the publisher *VNU* involves 12 applications including: *Photoshop*™ and games such as *Quake*™.

Even taking all this into account, a modern computer system is very much over-specified for common tasks like surfing the web or word processing. Extreme specifications and top of the range performance are only important for demanding users such as graphics or video professionals.

Factors affecting system performance

Many different factors can affect the performance of a computer system. The factors which we will look at include: **data bus width, use of cache memory** and **rate of data transfer to and from peripherals**.

Data bus width

The width of the data bus determines the quantity of data which the bus can carry at any one time. A microcomputer with a 32 bit data bus can carry 32 bits of data or instructions at a time. This means it has a **word length** of 32 bits.

Increasing the data bus width will increase the quantity of data which the bus can carry at any one time. Doubling the width, assuming that all other factors remain the same, will, in theory, double the quantity of data which may be transferred between the processor and the memory. This will have a significant effect on the performance of the computer system.

Large data bus widths are used to speed up data transfer between the processor's internal registers. The buses inside a processor may be 256 bits wide. Large buses are also used to communicate with cache memory. If the normal data bus width of a microcomputer is 64 bits, then the bus which connects the Level 2 cache to the processor may be 128 bits wide.

The use of cache memory

Significant improvements in system performance may be gained by **the use of cache memory**. It is much faster for the processor to access data and instructions held in cache memory than in main memory.

There are two reasons for this:

(a) The internal (Level 1) cache is on the processor chip and can benefit from the increased width of the processor bus. The Level 2 cache is connected to the processor by its own bus (on some systems this is called the 'backside' bus) which is also wider than the normal data (or 'frontside') bus which connects the processor to the main memory.

(b) The cache memory is made up from fast static RAM rather than slower dynamic RAM.

The rate of data transfer to and from peripherals

The rate of data transfer to and from peripherals can have a major effect on systems performance. The rate of data transfer is controlled by the type of interface used to connect the peripheral to the processor. Common interfaces in use on microcomputers include USB (Universal Serial Bus) and IEEE 1394 (*Firewire* or *iLink*).

Older computers and some devices like keyboards and mice use the USB 1 interface. USB 1 has a maximum data transfer rate of 12 Megabits/second. Current computers use USB 2, which has a data transfer rate of 480 Megabits/second.

Firewire currently has two versions, *Firewire 400* and *Firewire 800*, which have transmission speeds of 400 and 800 Megabits/second respectively.

If you compare a device like a scanner, using a USB 1 interface, with a new model bearing a USB 2 interface, you will notice a significant increase in the performance of the USB 2 scanner when connected to a computer system which has a USB 2 interface.

It is important to remember that, as we discussed earlier in this chapter, a reaction is only as fast as the speed of its slowest step. Connecting a USB 2 scanner to an older computer with a USB 1 interface will not improve performance.

Are there any other factors which affect system performance?

Increasing clock speed

This is another way of increasing the performance of a computer system. We discussed increasing clock speed earlier in this chapter on page 36.

Adding more main memory

One way of increasing a computer system's performance is by adding more main memory (RAM). This additional memory will have the benefit of allowing larger programs and more data to be held in immediate access store rather than on backing storage. This will increase the computer's performance because it is much faster to access data from RAM than from a hard disk, which is the case when using *virtual memory*. See earlier in this chapter for more information on virtual memory.

Unfortunately computer manufacturers do not supply computers already fitted with the maximum amount of memory that the processor can address. The main reason for this is the cost of the memory chips. In a competitive market, a computer with a very large amount of memory would be much more expensive than its rivals. Another reason is that the application packages in common use don't require the maximum possible amount of memory to be able to run. A third reason is that some memory locations which need to be addressed by the processor are in ROM rather than RAM and so a certain number of addresses need to be set aside for this.

It is always a good idea, however, to buy as much additional memory as you can reasonably afford, because when upgrading an application package or the computer's operating system program, you can be sure that the latest version will not require any less memory than your computer already has!

Increasing the Video Random Access Memory

Graphics performance may be improved by increasing the Video Random Access Memory (VRAM).

Adding more processors

Adding one or more processors to a computer system is an effective method of increasing performance. Some programs can take advantage of the presence of a second processor and this can have a significant effect in improving performance.

If you have enough processors, it is possible to link them together and produce a *supercomputer*. Figure 2.12 shows some of these machines. It is interesting to note that the top supercomputer in the picture is made up of 131072 *PowerPC 440* processors, each running at a clock speed of 0.7 *Gigahertz*. If you look at http://www.top500.org/ you can see the current list of supercomputers.

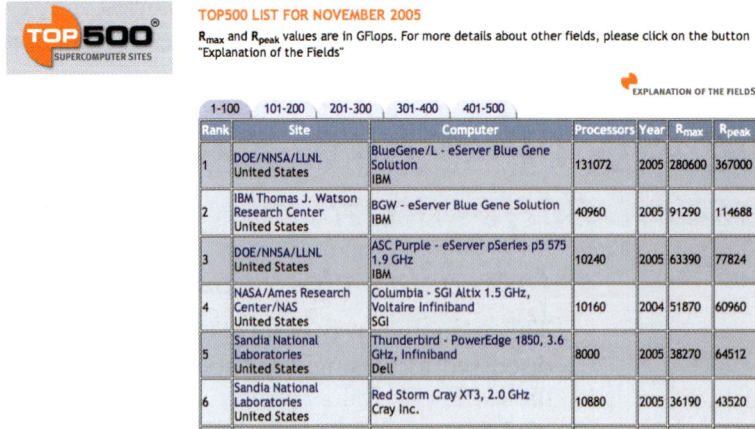

TOP500 LIST FOR NOVEMBER 2005
R_{max} and R_{peak} values are in GFlops. For more details about other fields, please click on the button "Explanation of the Fields"

EXPLANATION OF THE FIELDS

1-100	101-200	201-300	301-400	401-500					
Rank	Site		Computer		Processors	Year	R_{max}	R_{peak}	
1	DOE/NNSA/LLNL United States		BlueGene/L - eServer Blue Gene Solution IBM		131072	2005	280600	367000	
2	IBM Thomas J. Watson Research Center United States		BGW - eServer Blue Gene Solution IBM		40960	2005	91290	114688	
3	DOE/NNSA/LLNL United States		ASC Purple - eServer pSeries p5 575 1.9 GHz IBM		10240	2005	63390	77824	
4	NASA/Ames Research Center/NAS United States		Columbia - SGI Altix 1.5 GHz, Voltaire Infiniband SGI		10160	2004	51870	60960	
5	Sandia National Laboratories United States		Thunderbird - PowerEdge 1850, 3.6 GHz, Infiniband Dell		8000	2005	38270	64512	
6	Sandia National Laboratories United States		Red Storm Cray XT3, 2.0 GHz Cray Inc.		10880	2005	36190	43520	

Figure 2.12 *Supercomputers*

Address bus width

Every time a bit is added to the width of the address bus, the address range doubles. Increasing the width of the address bus, for instance, from 32 bits to 40 bits, will increase the total number of memory locations which the processor can address from 2^{32} to 2^{40}. *Increasing address bus width has NO effect on performance.*

Table 2.3 *Computer system performance summary*

Tactic	Effect on computer system performance
Increase clock speed	increase
Increase data bus width	increase
Increase cache memory	increase
Increase width of address bus	none
Increase number of processors	increase
Increase RAM	slight increase in performance
Increase VRAM	increase graphics performance
Increase rate of data transfer to and from peripherals	increase

Figure 2.13 *Computer performance*

Current trends in computer hardware

The current trends in computer hardware which we will look at in this section are: **increasing clock speeds**, **increasing memory** and **backing storage capacity**.

Increasing clock speeds

It is relatively easy to obtain an increase in computer performance by increasing the clock speed of a processor. However, manufacturers have found that this increase cannot go on indefinitely. Technical problems are being experienced with heat dissipation and increased power consumption, among other difficulties. The faster a processor runs in terms of clock speed, the more heat it produces and the more energy it consumes. Some processors on current desktop computers are now liquid-cooled, using equipment like a miniature refrigerator.

One alternative method of increasing performance which does not involve increasing the clock speed, is to use two or more processors in a single computer. Some computer manufacturers are using two separate processor chips or two processor 'cores' on a single chip, in order to maintain the progress of increasing processing capability. You can take a look inside a dual core processor chip in figure 2.14.

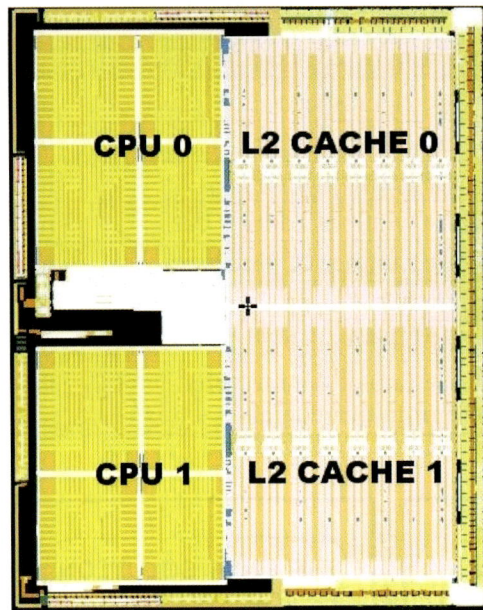

Figure 2.14 *A dual core processor chip*

The IBM/Sony/Toshiba Cell chip, announced in 2005, has eight 'processing centres' on a single chip. You can read more about this chip in the article below.

```
Tuesday 17th May 2005

Sony unwraps PlayStation 3

Sony has finally taken the wraps off the next generation of its
PlayStation gaming platform. PS3 was unveiled in Las Vegas ready
for its first public performance at the Electronic Entertainment
Expo (E3), the world's largest interactive entertainment
exhibition held in Los Angeles.

PS3 is built around a 3.2GHz Cell processor - jointly developed
by IBM, Sony and Toshiba, with a total system performance rated
at 2.18 teraflops - with 256MB of 3.2GHz RAM. It has a graphics
processor(RSX) co-developed by Nvidia and Sony backed by 256MB
GDDR VRAM.

The enhanced processing and graphics power should enable a new
level of gaming realism, with landscapes and virtual worlds
rendered in real time.

As well as DVD-R/W and CD-R/W it supports the Blu-ray high-
definition storage standard, with discs capable of holding up to
54GB. Blu-ray also provides high-levels of copy protection.

There will also be a 2.5in hard drive attachment, a Memory Stick
Duo, SD slots, Bluetooth support with up to seven wireless
controllers and six USB system ports.

'Multicore' chips

The Cell processor is comprised of several computing engines, or
cores. A core based on IBM's Power architecture controls eight
'synergistic' processing centres. In all, they can simultaneously
carry out 10 instruction sequences, compared with two for
current Intel chips.
```

Increasing memory

One trend in computer hardware which has not slowed, is the continual requirement for increased main memory onboard computer systems. Current desktop computers have between 512 Megabytes and one Gigabyte of RAM. A few years ago 32 Megabytes was sufficient. The reason for this trend is that there is an increased requirement for multiprogramming and an increase in the memory required to hold the computer's operating system.

Memory requirements for individual applications have also risen. It is not unusual for the technical documentation of a program to state that 256 Megabytes of 'free' RAM is required. 'Free' RAM refers to what is left available to applications after the operating system has been loaded.

Increasing backing storage capacity

Increasing backing storage capacity is another trend which will continue for a long time to come. It is so easy to save work on a computer system that everything is saved. The increase in the use of digital still cameras, digital video cameras and MP3 players has also contributed to the increase in backing storage capacity. See figure 2.15.

A typical digital photograph, even if stored as a compressed JPEG file, can take up between 1 and 2 *Megabytes* of storage space, depending upon the degree of compression used and the number of *Megapixels* in the camera's sensor.

Digital video in compressed DV format takes up a backing storage space of 13 Gigabytes per hour.

A typical desktop computer may have a hard disk capacity of between 50 and 500 Gigabytes. One problem, which many users choose to ignore, is the requirement for an effective backup strategy of such large quantities of data. At the time of writing, a single-sided, double layered DVD-R disk was capable of holding 8.5 Gigabytes of data.

Figure 2.15 *iPod*

Questions

1. A microcomputer's processor has three main parts. Name each of these three parts and describe their function.

2. What is a bus in a microcomputer?

3. A microcomputer has three buses. Name each of these buses and describe their function.

4. Which bus can be described as:
   a. unidirectional?
   b. bi-directional?
   c. a collection of single lines ?
   d. With respect to a bus, what is meant by the term width?
   e. State one effect of increasing the:
      i. unidirectional bus width?
      ii. bi-directional bus width?

5. What is meant by the terms:
   a. address?
   b. addressability?
   c. storage location?
   d. word?

6. What is:
   a. the clock?
   b. the clock speed (rate)?
   c. a clock cycle?
   d. an interrupt?
   e. a non-maskable interrupt?

7. What steps does the processor take when a peripheral device sends an interrupt?

8. What is the purpose of the reset button on a microcomputer?

9. In the fetch-execute cycle, what happens during execute?

10. List the steps involved in a:
    a. memory read operation
    b. memory write operation.

11. State a formula that may be used to calculate the addressable memory in a computer system.

12. How many Terabytes of memory would a 40 bit address bus be able to address, if the system word length was:
    a. 8 bits?
    b. 16 bits?
    c. 32 bits?

13. a. Name the four elements of computer memory.
    b. Write the names of these elements in order of speed of access – fastest first.

14. Two types of main memory are RAM and ROM.
    a. What do the terms RAM and ROM mean?
    b. State one difference between RAM and ROM.

15. Two types of RAM are Static RAM (SRAM) and Dynamic RAM (DRAM).
    a. State two advantages SRAM has over DRAM.
    b. If SRAM has advantages over DRAM, why is the majority of a computer's main memory made up of DRAM?

16. What is:
    a. cache memory?
    b. VRAM?

17. Why are computer games programs often sold stored in ROM cartridges?

18. Which type of ROM may be used as a backing storage medium?

19. State four measures of performance.

20. State three factors which affect systems performance.

21. Explain what effect adding a single wire to the:
    a. address bus
    b. data bus
    will have on system performance.

22. The data bus on a microcomputer has a clock rate of 800 Megahertz. The clock rate of the processor is 3.5 Gigahertz. What is the likely effect of the bus speed on the performance of the microcomputer?

23. Give one reason why adding more:
    a. main memory
    b. cache memory
    can improve system performance.

24. If the addition of more main memory can improve the performance of a computer system, why do manufacturers not supply computer systems with the maximum possible main memory already installed?

25. Mary has a 2.3 *Gigahertz PowerPC G5* Power Macintosh and Sarah has a 3.2 Gigahertz *Pentium* Dell PC. Sarah says her computer is faster than Mary's because it has a higher clock rate.
    a. Who do you think is correct? Give a reason for your choice.
    b. What type of test could be done to help decide who is correct?

26. State three current trends in computer hardware.

• Key points •

- The processor of a computer includes the arithmetic and logic unit, control unit and registers.
- The control unit controls all the other parts of the processor and makes sure that the program instructions of the computer are carried out in the correct order.
- The arithmetic and logic unit carries out the calculations and performs the logical operations.
- The registers are a group of storage locations in the processor which are used to hold data being processed, instructions being executed and addresses to be accessed.
- Wires called buses connect the processor to the memory and input/output devices of the computer.
- The address bus carries the address information from the processor to the main memory and any other devices attached to the bus.
- The address bus is unidirectional.
- The data bus carries data to and from the processor, main memory and any other devices attached to the data bus.
- The data bus is bi-directional.
- The control bus is made up of the read, write, clock, interrupt, non-maskable interrupt and reset lines.
- The clock line carries a series of clock pulses at a constant rate in order to keep the processor and its related components in step with one another.
- An interrupt is a signal to the processor from a peripheral device.
- A maskable interrupt may be ignored by the processor.
- The reset line on the processor is used to return the processor its initial state.
- A computer operates by fetching and executing instructions from a stored program.
- The fetch-execute cycle is the name given to the way in which the processor takes in an instruction from memory (fetch) and carries

out that instruction (execute).
- The steps involved in a memory read operation are:
  - The processor sets up the address bus with the required memory address. It does this by placing a value in the Memory Address Register.
  - The control unit of the processor activates the read line on the control bus.
  - The contents of the particular storage location in memory are released onto the data bus and are copied into the processor's Memory Data Register. If it is an instruction, it is decoded and executed (carried out).
- The steps involved in a memory write operation are:
  - The processor sets up the address bus with the required memory address. It does this by placing a value in the Memory Address Register.
  - The processor sets up the data bus with the value to be written to memory. It does this by placing the value in the Memory Data Register.
  - The control unit of the processor activates the write line on the control bus.
  - The contents of the Memory Data Register are transferred to the required storage location in the computer's memory.
- Summary of the fetch-execute cycle:
  - The processor sets up the address bus with the required address.
  - The processor activates the read line.
  - The instruction is transferred from memory to processor by using the data bus (fetch).
  - The instruction is decoded.
  - The instruction is executed.
- The place where each item is stored in a computer's memory is important because the computer has to be able to find any given item of data.
- An item is stored in memory in a storage location.

- Each storage location has its own unique address in the computer's main memory.
- The method a computer uses to identify storage locations is called its addressability.
- The number of storage locations in the computer's memory that a processor can identify depends on the number of bits in the address or the number of wires in the address bus.
- The quantity of memory which may be addressed, can be calculated using the formula: Total addressable memory = Number of storage locations x size of each storage location.
- The elements of computer memory are registers, cache, main memory and backing storage.
- Cache holds frequently accessed instructions.
- Main memory consists of a number of storage locations, each with a unique address.
- The ability of the processor to identify each storage location is called its addressability.
- Each storage location can hold a quantity of data called a word.
- A word is the number of bits that can be processed by the processor in a single operation.

- Main memory consists of Random Access Memory (RAM) and Read Only Memory (ROM).
- Random Access Memory holds its data as long as the computer is switched on.
- DRAM needs to have its contents constantly refreshed, SRAM does not require to be refreshed.
- SRAM is more expensive than DRAM.
- SRAM is faster to access than DRAM.
- Backing storage functions as permanent storage for programs and data in a computer system.
- The measures of computer performance are: clock speed, MIPS, FLOPS, and application-based tests.
- The factors which can affect the performance of a computer system are: data bus width, use of cache memory and rate of data transfer to and from peripherals.
- Adding more main memory and adding more processors can also increase the performance of a computer system.
- Current trends in computer hardware are: increasing clock speeds, increasing memory and backing storage capacity.

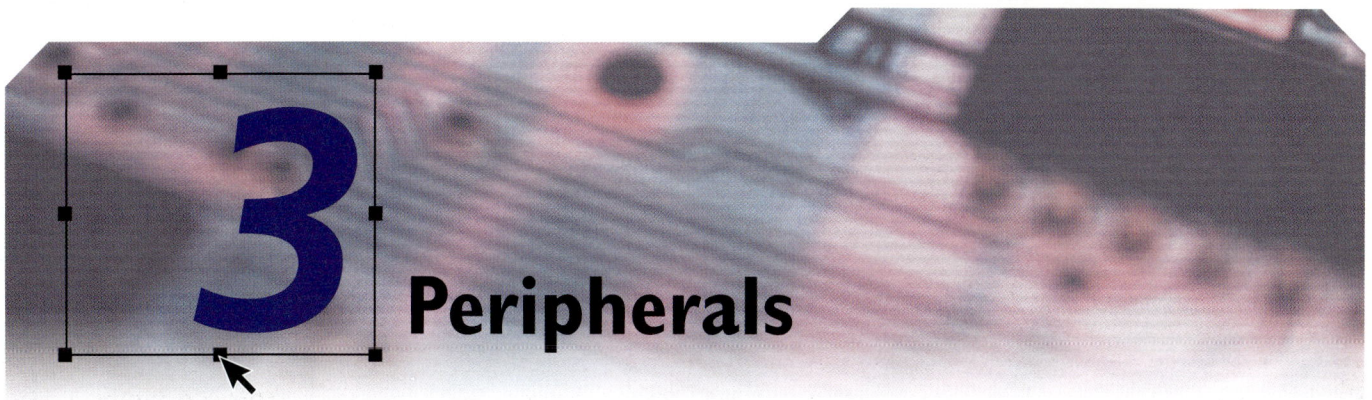

3 Peripherals

Interfaces

An **interface** is the hardware and associated software needed to allow communication between the processor and its peripheral devices and to compensate for any differences in their operating characteristics. Such differences may include speed and voltage levels used.

Functions of an interface

The functions of an interface include **buffering**, **data format conversion**, **voltage conversion**, **protocol conversion** and the **handling of status signals**.

Buffering or temporary data storage

Buffering in an interface involves holding data temporarily while it is in transit between the processor and the peripheral. The data is held in an area of RAM within the interface called a **buffer**. One example of buffering is the temporary storage of characters entered at a keyboard. You can read more detail about buffers and another method of temporary data storage later in this chapter.

Data format conversion

Data format conversion involves changing the data received from the peripheral into a form that the processor can deal with and vice versa. One example of data format conversion is changing the flow of data from **serial to parallel** and vice versa. See figure 3.1.

Serial and parallel data transmission

- Data transmission is the passing of data from one device to another. This may be between parts of a computer system or between computers in a network. A **serial interface** uses serial data transmission. A **parallel interface** uses parallel data transmission.
- **Serial data transmission** sends the bits for each character in the data one after another along the same data line. This means that serial data transmission only requires two wires, one for the data and one for the ground, or return line, although in practice, more may be provided. These additional wires may be used to transmit status information, like ready and busy or done signals. Serial data transmission is relatively slow, but is more efficient over longer distances, for instance on a network.
- **Parallel data transmission** sends each bit which makes up a character or instruction simultaneously along separate data lines. This means that parallel data transmission of an eight-bit byte requires at least nine wires, eight for the data and one for the ground, or return line. Parallel data transmission is fast, but only suitable for short distances, for instance, between a processor and its peripheral devices or within the processor itself.

Conversion of Serial to Parallel

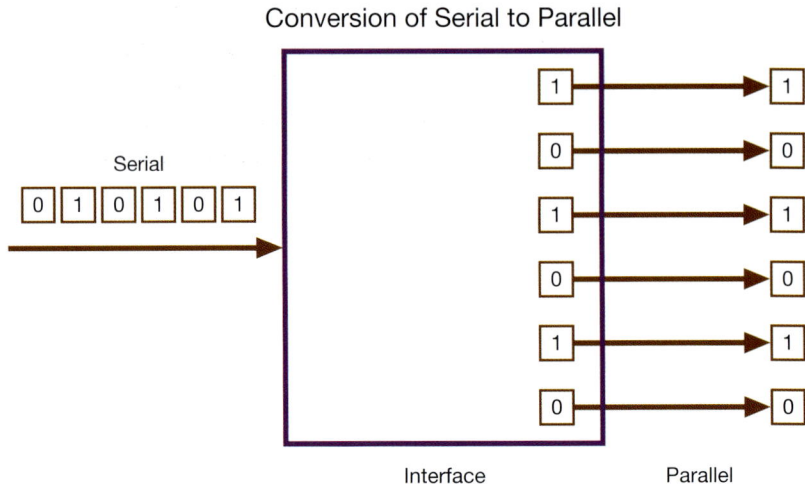

Figure 3.1 *Serial to parallel data format conversion*

Analogue to digital conversion
Another example of data format conversion is changing **analogue signals to digital** signals.

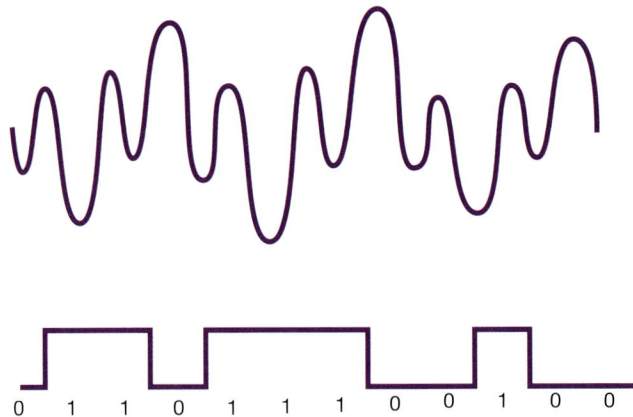

Figure 3.2 *Analogue and digital signals*

- **Analogue signals**. Many electrical signals, like the output from a microphone, are **analogue** signals. Sound and light are analogue. Analogue signals can vary continuously between two limits. If you could see an analogue signal it would look roughly like the shape a skipping rope makes when you hold the ends and shake it up and down (something like figure 3.2).
- **Digital signals**. Computers can only work with **digital** signals, which have only two values – on or off. A digital signal therefore consists of a series of 'ons' and 'offs'. An 'on' signal is represented by a 1 and an 'off' by a 0. Figure 3.2 shows what a digital signal would look like if you could see it.
- **Analogue to Digital (A to D) and Digital to Analogue (D to A) converters**. A computer is connected to another device (a printer, a disk drive, a robot or another peripheral), by an **interface**. This interface has to be able to change the digital signals from the computer to an analogue signal that the other device can understand. This is done by a **digital to analogue**

converter. Signals can be changed in the other direction by an **analogue to digital converter**. Digital to analogue and analogue to digital conversion is shown in figure 3.3. An analogue to digital converter samples the incoming analogue signal at regular intervals, changes the continuously varying voltage to binary numbers, and sends the resulting bits to the processor.

Examples

An audio CD player contains a Digital to Analogue Converter to change the digital data on the CD into analogue data, music, so that we can hear it.

A scanner converts an image from a photograph or drawing into digital form that a computer can process. This is an example of Analogue to Digital conversion.

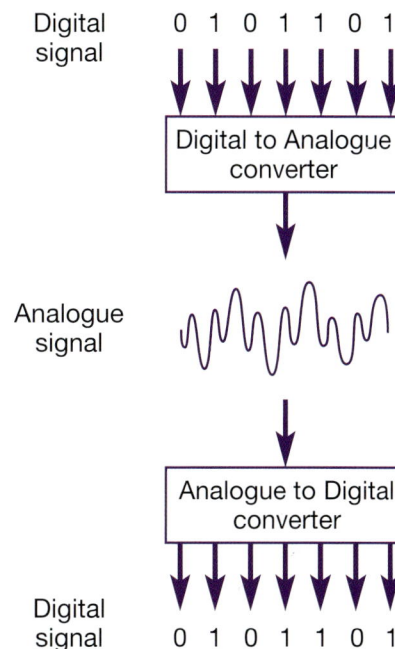

Digital signal   0 1 0 1 1 0 1

```
┌─────────────────────┐
│ Digital to Analogue │
│     converter       │
└─────────────────────┘
```

Analogue signal

```
┌─────────────────────┐
│ Analogue to Digital │
│     converter       │
└─────────────────────┘
```

Digital signal   0 1 0 1 1 0 1

Figure 3.3 *Digital to Analogue and Analogue to Digital conversion*

Voltage conversion

Voltage conversion is required when a peripheral operates using a different voltage from that used by the processor and its associated components on the *motherboard* of the computer. This voltage is usually around 5 volts. Some types of keyboard use a higher voltage, and this must be changed to 5 volts by the keyboard interface.

Protocol conversion

A **protocol** is a standard that enables the connection, communication, and data transfer between computers or between a computer system and a peripheral. Protocol conversion means ensuring that the protocols used by the peripheral can be understood by the computer it is attached to and vice versa.

Example

Parity is an example of a protocol used during data transmission. Parity is used to check for errors. One bit in every byte of data is reserved as the parity bit. Two methods are used: odd *parity* and *even parity*.

In odd parity, the parity bit is altered (to either 1 or 0) to make the total number of 1s in the byte odd. In even parity, the parity bit is altered to make the total number of 1s in the byte even.

When the data is checked, then an error will be detected if the parity bit is incorrect – for instance:

Even parity *0111 1000 – parity bit set to 0 to make the total number of 1s even*

Odd parity *1101 0101 – parity bit set to 1 to make the total number of 1s odd*

Protocol conversion would be required for successful communication between two devices which used different parities.

Handling of status signals

The purpose of status information is to show whether or not a peripheral device is ready to communicate, that is, to receive or to send data. This information is used to inform the user, for instance, of a problem requiring attention. Status information on a printer will show if the printer is busy or ready to receive data, has a paper jam, or is out of either ink or paper. Some printers also display additional information about their status on a small LCD panel. Figure 3.4 shows a typical printer status display.

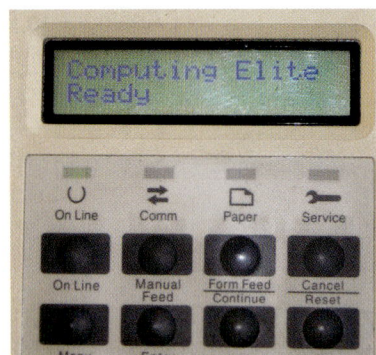

Figure 3.4 *Printer status display*

Example

Here is a working example of the operation of an interface between the processor and a printer:

(i)   The processor checks the interface to see if the printer is ready

(ii)   The interface returns a printer ready signal to the processor (status signal)

(iii) REPEAT

(iv)   The processor sends data to the interface until the interface returns a buffer full signal

Peripherals

3

(v)   The interface sends data from its buffer to the printer
(vi)   The data is removed from the buffer as it is printed by the printer
(vii) The interface returns a buffer empty signal to the processor
(viii) UNTIL print job complete

International standards

A number of international standards have been developed for interfaces. Here are some common examples:

RS 232 – Recommended Standard (Serial)
SCSI (Small Computer Systems Interface) (Parallel)
IDE (Integrated Drive Electronics)
SATA (Serial Advanced Technology Attachment) – Data transfer speed of 1.5 Gbps
Centronics (Parallel)
USB 1 & 2 (Universal Serial Bus) – Data transfer speeds of 1.5 Mbps, 12 Mbps and 480 Mbps
IEEE (Institute of Electrical and Electronic Engineers) 1394 (Apple – *Firewire 400 & 800*, Sony – *iLINK*) – Data transfer speeds of 400 Mbps and 800 Mbps (Serial)
MIDI (Musical Instrument Digital Interface)
PCI (Peripheral Component Interconnect)
PCMCIA (Personal Computer Memory Card International Association)

Figure 3.5 *Some common interfaces*

The use of interface standards by a computer manufacturer means that their computers will be able to connect to peripherals using the same standards. The use of interface standards by a peripheral manufacturer means that their peripherals will connect to a computer which uses the same standards. For example, at the time of writing this book, every new computer was equipped with at least one USB 2 socket. This means that any existing peripheral using either USB 1 or USB 2 will be able to connect to any new computer.

Unit 1 Computer Systems | 51

The use and advantages of buffers and spooling

Buffers

A **buffer** is an area of memory used for the transfer of data between a computer and a peripheral. A buffer provides temporary storage of data. Using a buffer provides a link between a device and the processor and helps compensate for any differences in their working speeds or data organisation.

Example

A **printer buffer** is an area of RAM, usually in the printer, which is used for the temporary storage of print jobs. A laser printer, for example, may have a buffer size of 64 Megabytes. This means that the printer could hold up to 64 Megabytes of data while printing. A printer is a relatively slow peripheral, compared to the speed at which the processor can send data, so the processor, and hence the user, normally has to wait for the print job to complete. A buffer is able to receive the data at a much higher speed than the printer can print, thereby freeing the computer from the print job.

Suppose a user was printing a document of 25 Megabytes in size, then a printer with a 64 Megabyte buffer could easily hold the complete document. This would free the computer immediately so that the user could go on working. If the printer had no buffer at all, then the user would have to wait for the printer to print the complete job before she could resume working.

Spooler

A **spooler** is a program which is used to address the same problems as a printer buffer. A spooler uses fast backing storage such as a hard disk for the temporary storage of print jobs. The data is held on disk and transferred to the printer gradually at a speed which the printer can accept. This is called *background printing*, because the user can continue with a completely different task, for example, word processing, in the *foreground*. Background printing makes use of the fact that the processor has idle periods, for instance, while it is waiting for the user to press a key. The processor can use this idle time to process the background task. However, if the processor becomes very busy in the foreground then its rate of processing the background task will slow or even stop until it becomes idle again.

One advantage of a printer spooler over a buffer is that a buffer is limited to a fixed size because it is RAM (typically Megabytes), but a spooler uses backing storage which has a much larger storage space (typically Gigabytes).

A spooler may be used in a local area network on a dedicated **printer server** computer with a large hard disk drive, or on an individual basis with each station on the network spooling the print jobs to the local hard disk drive on each machine.

You should note that in practice both buffers and spoolers are used together when printing.

Features, uses and advantages of solid-state storage devices including flash cards

A solid-state storage device contains no moving parts. Examples of solid-state storage devices include **flash cards** and **USB flash memory** (often called a *memory stick*). Both of these types of device contain the same type of backing storage medium, namely *flash ROM*. The effective difference between them is that they use different interfaces to connect to a computer system or another peripheral.

Flash cards

Flash cards are used mainly for data storage in cameras, although they can hold any type of program or data file.

There are a number of different standards for flash cards. These include:

- Compact Flash (CF)
- Secure Digital (SD)/Multimedia Card (MMC)
- Memory Stick/Pro
- XD–Picture Card

Each type of digital camera normally uses only one type of flash card. Some of these cards are shown in figure 3.6.

Figure 3.6 *Flash cards*

Specialised card readers have been developed which have 'slots' to fit all the different varieties of flash card. In addition, many printers and so-called 'all-in-one' devices (printer, scanner, photocopier) have slots into which flash cards may be placed. This allows photographs to be printed directly from the card, without a computer system having to be connected.

USB flash memory

There are two types of USB flash memory, according to the type of interface being used. They are USB 1 and USB 2. Most of these devices are now compatible with USB 2. USB 2 devices are also backwards compatible, that is they may be used on a computer system which has only a USB 1 interface. In this case the speed of access to the device will be USB 1, i.e. 12 Mbps.

USB flash memory comes in a variety of packages. Some of these are shown in figure 3.7.

Note the built in fingerprint scanner →

Figure 3.7 *USB flash memory*

Features and advantages of solid-state storage devices

Solid-state storage devices are *small*. Flash cards can fit inside cameras. USB flash memory can fit on key rings and in watches.

Solid-state storage devices are robust because they have no moving parts. This means that they are ideal for wearing because they are unaffected by vigorous movement. The music player shown in figure 3.8 and the watch and penknife shown in figure 3.7 all take advantage of this feature of solid-state storage devices.

Solid-state storage devices *use less power* than hard disk drives. This lower power requirement means that a music player which uses solid-state storage will play music for a longer time relative to a hard disk-based music player with the same battery capacity.

Solid-state storage devices are available in a range of capacities, from 16 Mb to 8 Gb (at the time of writing).

USB flash memory has now replaced floppy disks as a convenient, portable storage medium, which can fit into almost any modern computer system.

USB flash memory is used for security applications. One type has fingerprint recognition (See figure 3.7) and another type works with security software to prevent a computer system from starting up unless the USB flash memory is plugged in.

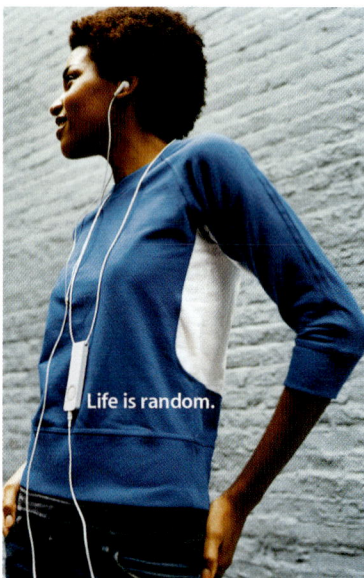

Figure 3.8 *iPod Shuffle*

Description of the development trends in backing storage devices

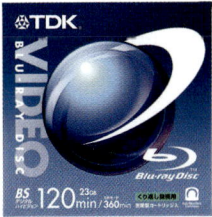

Figure 3.9 *A Blu-ray Disc*

Increased capacity

DVD

The DVD-Recordable format capacity was increased with the introduction of the dual layer DVD-R disk with a capacity of 8.4 Gb (Single layer DVD-R capacity is 4.7 Gb). Most computer systems now incorporate this dual layer drive.

Blu-ray

Blu-ray Disc (BD) is the name of a next-generation optical disc format. The format was developed to enable recording, rewriting and playback of high-definition video (HD). The format may become a standard for PC data storage and high-definition movies.

The following formats are part of the Blu-ray Disc specification:

BD-ROM – read-only format for software, games and movie distribution.

BD-R – recordable format for HDTV recording and PC data storage.

BD-RE – rewritable format for HDTV recording and PC data storage.

How much data can you fit on a Blu-ray Disc?

A single-layer disc can fit 23.3 GB, 25 GB or 27 GB.

A dual-layer disc can fit 46.6 GB, 50 GB or 54 GB.

Despite being the same physical size as a DVD, a blu-ray disk is able to hold much more. This increased storage capacity is possible because the laser beam in the drive is coloured blue (hence the name) and produces a narrower beam of light than a red laser on a DVD drive. Blue light has a shorter wavelength than red light.

The Blu-ray Disc format also includes support for multi-layer discs, which should allow the storage capacity to be increased to 100–200 GB (25 GB per layer) in the future simply by adding more layers to the discs.

Holographic storage

Holographic storage uses laser beams to encode and record data through the full depth of a recording medium rather than just on its surface. A single laser beam is split into a signal beam and a reference beam. A device called a spatial light modulator encodes the data onto the signal beam. The data is written onto the recording medium at the point where the two beams intersect.

Many different holograms may be written on the same recording medium by changing the reference beam angle, the wavelength of the laser or the position of the recording medium. The data is read by using the reference beam which projects the stored hologram onto a detector array.

Holographic storage allows very high data storage capacities (100 Gb/in^2) with data transfer rates of between 10 and 100 Mbps. One company claims 2 Gb on a postage stamp, 20 Gb on a credit card and 200 Gb on a disk.

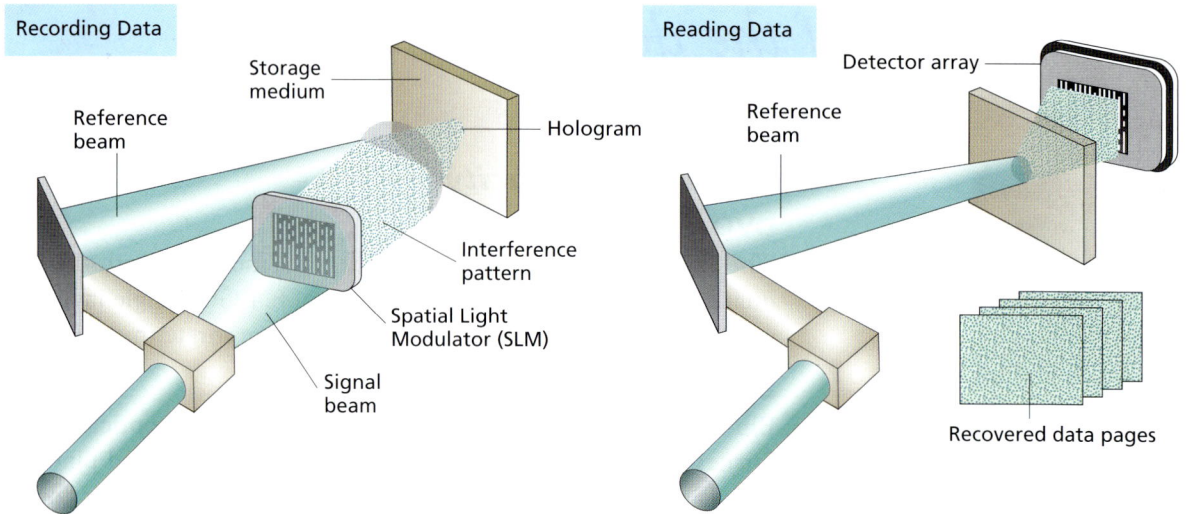

Figure 3.10 *Holographic Storage*

Increased read and write speeds

Faster interfaces are constantly being developed e.g. USB 2, *Firewire 800*, with speeds of 480 Mbps and 800 Mbps, respectively.

Reduced physical size

In 2004, Guinness World Records certified Toshiba's 0.85 inch diameter hard disk drive as the smallest hard disk drive in the world.

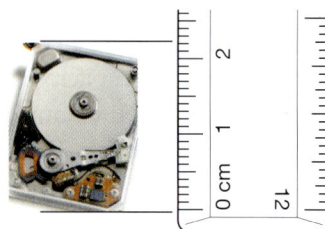

Figure 3.11 *Toshiba's 0.85 inch hard disk drive*

Lower cost per unit of storage

In 1995, a 100 Mb capacity hard disk drive cost £300. In 2005, a 100 Mb capacity ZIP disk cost £5, and a 512 Mb USB flash memory cost £25

Implications of development trends in storage devices

One implication of these development trends is that new peripherals and media may not work with old 'legacy' hardware. An older computer may not have a USB port, or if it does, it may not be USB 2, only USB 1. A DVD re-writer may not be able to read or write to new disk formats. Care must also be taken with archived data, to make sure that it is regularly copied to a current storage format so that it can always be accessed.

The year 2004 saw some electrical stores discontinuing the sale of VHS video recorders in favour of DVD. Digital video cameras, which record directly to DVD instead of tape, are now common.

3

Current trends towards increasing interface speeds and wireless communication between peripherals and CPU

New interfaces are continually being developed. One focus of development is to *increase the speed* at which the interface allows the peripheral and computer to communicate. Another aim is to allow *wireless communication between the peripherals and the CPU*.

Increasing interface speeds

Interface speed is measured in Megabits per second (Mbps). Be careful not to confuse Megabits and Megabytes, both of which may use the abbreviation Mb. Manufacturers normally use Megabits per second in their advertising because it allows them to print larger numbers on the advertisements.

One example of increasing interface speeds is the development of the *USB 2* and the *Firewire 800* interfaces. The *USB 2* interface improves upon the maximum 12 Mbps speed of the *USB 1* interface by 40 times to 480 Mbps. The *Firewire 800* interface provides 800 Mbps, double the speed of the *Firewire 400* interface.

Wireless communication between peripherals and the CPU

Current trends in wireless communication include the standards *WiFi* and *Bluetooth*.

Bluetooth and *WiFi* both use radio waves at the same frequency. Radio waves can pass through most materials and walls, and devices don't need to be pointing at one another, unlike *infrared* data transmission (TV remote control).

Bluetooth can make short-range links between personal devices, such as mobile phones and headsets, palmtop (PDA) and laptop (notebook) computers. *Bluetooth* is also used for wireless keyboards and mice.

Fig 3.12 *Bluetooth logo*

Figure 3.13 *Bluetooth wireless keyboard and mouse*

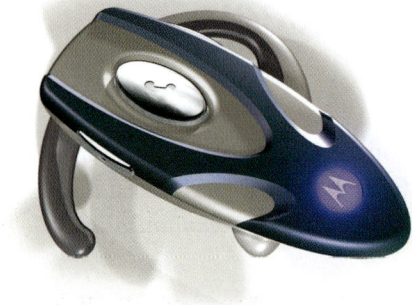

Figure 3.14 *Bluetooth wireless headset*

Figure 3.15 *This Bluetooth enabled printer allows users to print images directly from a mobile phone*

Figure 3.16 *WiFi logos*

Stand-alone *Bluetooth* devices have a range of 10 metres, and are able to transfer information at 1 Megabit per second (1 Mbps). The *Bluetooth* standard is also known as IEEE 802.15.1. Bluetooth allows devices to communicate even in areas with a great deal of electromagnetic interference because it continually changes the frequency at which data is transmitted and received This is called *frequency hopping*. It is expected that later versions of *Bluetooth* will be able to transmit data at a speed of 2 Mbps and for longer distances.

WiFi stands for the Wireless Fidelity Alliance. The main use for *WiFi* is in wireless local area networking (WLAN). *WiFi* devices have typical ranges from 12 to 50 metres and typical data transfer rates from 5 to 20 Mbps. Three current *WiFi* standards are IEEE 802.11a, 802.11b and 802.11g. IEEE 802.11b allows for maximum data transfer rates of up to 11 Mbps and 802.11a and 802.11g both allow up to 54 Mbps. Figure 3.17 shows a wireless router and switch which can be used to set up both a wired and a wireless local area network with broadband Internet access in a home or office.

Figure 3.17 *An 802.11g wireless router and switch*

Description of a suitable selection of hardware, including peripherals, to support typical tasks

Author's Note: The descriptions of hardware which follow have been deliberately expressed in general terms because the constant development of new hardware means that any detailed description will date very quickly. Costs are approximate figures and are current at the time of writing (2005). Note that all of the aspects of justification need not appear in every possible scenario.

The possession of a basic computer system consisting of processor, monitor, keyboard, mouse, and hard disk is assumed.

Production of a multimedia catalogue

A multimedia catalogue is a database of products or items which contains a variety of media, such as sound, graphics and video.

The following list of hardware and media would be appropriate to support this task:

Digital video camera
Digital still camera
Graphics tablet
Microphone – may be part of computer system
Sound card – may be part of computer system
Video capture card – may be part of computer system or may require to be purchased separately

Additional backing storage:
External hard disk
CD-R / DVD-R drive – most computer systems have these as standard
Blank CD-R and DVD-R media

Justification
Resolution – an expensive professional standard of video camera is not essential. A still camera of 2–3 megapixels resolution would be appropriate since enlargements of images are not required, they are only to be displayed on a screen.

Capacity – Digital video camera – minimum 5 minutes recording time. Digital still camera – a 256Mb flash memory card would hold over a hundred images at 3 megapixels (compressed as JPEG). Additional hard disk, around 200 Gigabytes.

Speed – DVD-Recordable drive – not critical, although a drive with a fast write speed would be useful if many copies were required

Cost – Digital still camera £100, Digital video camera £300, additional hard disk £200, Video capture card £100, Sound card £100, Graphics tablet £100, Blank media: CD-Recordable £15 per 100, DVD-Recordable £15 for 25

Compatibility – JPEG is a standard format for still images. Mini DV format is supported by a wide range of digital video cameras. IEEE 1394 (Firewire) is a standard interface for digital video cameras. USB is a standard interface for digital still cameras.

Setting up a LAN in a school

Local Area Networks are common in schools. In order to be connected to the network, each computer system must have a network interface card. Suitable cabling such as category 5 unshielded twisted pair (UTP) must be installed throughout the school in order to connect the computers together and create the network. Depending upon the topology chosen, switches or hubs may be required (See chapter 4). In addition, a suitable number of printers may be added. A fileserver is required to create a client-server network.

As an alternative to cabling the school, a wireless network may be set up. At least one wireless base station will be required, depending upon the physical extent of the network. Each computer will require a wireless network card in order to communicate with the base station.

Other servers, such as database or web, may be required depending upon the application(s) of the LAN. A network operating system is also required, although this section only deals with hardware. See chapter 5 for appropriate software.

Justification
Speed – A minimum of 100 Mbps for the transmission speed of the network, including hubs, switches, cabling and network interface cards. A server, if required, should use a gigabit network interface (1000 Mbps)

Cost – cabling £50 per 200 m, outlet boxes £5 each, patch leads £1 each, Server £2000, 40 port hub £100, 40 port switch £1000, wireless base station £100

Compatibility – Ethernet is a standard for local area networking, WiFi (IEEE 802.11) is a standard for wireless networking. The appropriate interface card will be required for all computers on the network.

Development of a school website

Very little additional hardware other than the basic computer system described above is required to create a school website. A digital still camera would be useful for photographs of school activities and events. A video camera would not be required since it is unlikely that the web pages would contain embedded videos or that video streaming would be required. It is assumed that the website is required only to be developed, and that it will be hosted by the school's ISP. Web server hardware is not specified in this answer. The essential requirement for creation of a school website is appropriate web page creation software, but this is not specified in this section. See chapter 5 for appropriate software.

Justification
Resolution – A digital still camera of 2–3 megapixels resolution would be appropriate since enlargements of images are not required, they are only to be displayed on a screen.

Capacity – Digital still camera – a 256 Mb flash memory card would hold over a hundred images at 3 megapixels (compressed as JPEG). Additional hard disk, around 200 Gigabytes.

Cost – Digital still camera £100

Compatibility – The developed website should be tested on a range of browsers running under a variety of operating systems to ensure the widest possible compatibility.

Questions

1. State five functions of an interface.
2. Name one function of an interface in use when using a:
   a. printer?
   b. keyboard?
3. What is a serial interface?
4. What is a parallel interface?
5. Which of the computer's buses:
   a. uses parallel data transmission?
   b. does not use parallel data transmission?
6. What is a protocol?
7. Give one example of a protocol.
8. Faulty data transmission can often result in devices sending sequences of bits like this: 0000 0000 0000 0000 0000 .... and so on. Which type of parity check could be used to detect faults such as these?
9. Name three standard interfaces.
10. Suggest why it is a good idea for interfaces to have international standards.
11. What is a buffer?
12. What is a spooler?
13. Describe a situation where it would be preferable to use a spooler rather than a buffer.
14. What can you say about the likely speed of operation of a spooler compared to a buffer in terms of accepting data from a user? Give a reason for your answer.
15. Some computer systems allow the user to switch off background printing. What effect would this have on the operation of the computer system?
16. Name one type of server which uses a spooler.
17. a. What is a solid-state storage device?
    b. What storage medium is used in solid state storage devices?
    c. What does the word 'solid' mean in this context?
    d. State one advantage of solid state storage devices over hard disk drives
18. Look at figure 3.18. What is the function of this device?
19. State one development trend in backing storage devices.
20. State one trend in interfaces.
21. State two methods of wireless communication between peripherals and the CPU.
22. State an item of hardware which would support the production of a:
    a. multimedia catalogue
    b. LAN in a school
    c. development of a school website.

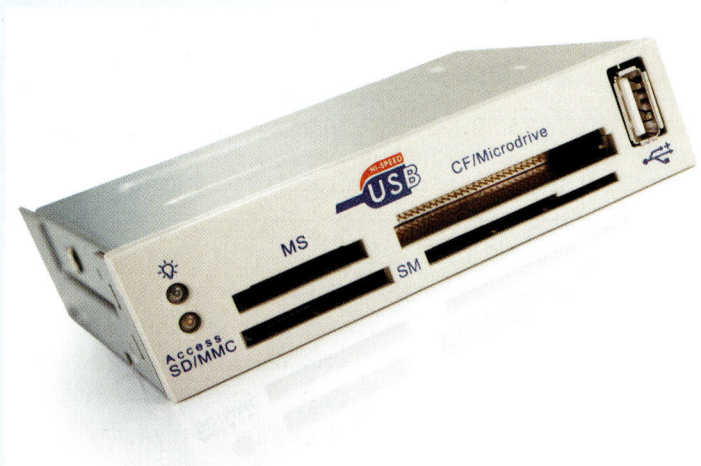

Figure 3.18 *for question 18*

• Key points •

- An interface is the hardware and associated software needed to allow communication between the processor and its peripheral devices and to compensate for any differences in their operating characteristics.
- The functions of an interface include buffering, data format conversion, voltage conversion, protocol conversion and the handling of status signals.
- Buffering involves holding data temporarily while it is in transit between the processor and the peripheral.
- Data format conversion involves changing the data received from the peripheral into a form that the processor can understand and vice versa.
- Serial data transmission sends the bits for each character in the data one after another along the same data line.
- Parallel data transmission sends each bit which makes up a character simultaneously along separate data lines.
- Voltage conversion is required when a peripheral operates using a different voltage from that used by the processor and its associated components on the motherboard of the computer.
- A protocol is a standard that enables the connection, communication, and data transfer between computers or between a computer system and a peripheral.
- Parity is an example of a protocol used during data transmission.
- The purpose of status information is to show whether or not a peripheral device is ready to communicate, that is, receive or to send data.
- Here is a working example of the operation of an interface between the processor and a printer:
  - The processor checks the interface to see if the printer is ready
  - The interface returns a printer ready signal to the processor (status signal)
  - REPEAT
  - The processor sends data to the interface until the interface returns a buffer full signal
  - The interface sends data from its buffer to the printer
  - The data is removed from the buffer as it is printed by the printer
  - The interface returns a buffer empty signal to the processor
  - UNTIL print job complete
- A number of international standards have been developed for interfaces.
- A buffer is an area of memory used for the transfer of the data between the computer and a peripheral.
- A buffer provides temporary storage of data and is an essential component of any interface.
- Using a buffer provides a link between devices and helps compensate for any differences in their working speeds or data organisation.
- A spooler is a program which is used to address the same problems as a printer buffer.
- A spooler uses fast backing storage such as a hard disk for the temporary storage of print jobs.
- A solid-state storage device contains no moving parts.
- Examples of solid-state storage devices include flash cards and USB flash memory.
- There are two types of USB flash memory, according to the type of interface being used, USB 1 and USB 2.
- Solid state storage devices are *small*.
- Solid state storage devices are *robust* because they have no moving parts.
- Solid state storage devices *use less power* than hard disk drives.
- The development trends in backing storage devices include:
  - Increased capacity
  - Increased read and write speeds
  - Reduced physical size
  - Lower cost per unit of storage.
- Two developments in interfaces are to:
  - increase the speed at which the interface allows the peripheral and computer to communicate
  - allow wireless communication between the peripherals and the CPU. For example using WiFi and Bluetooth.

4 Networking

What is a Network?

A **network** is two or more computers linked together in such a way that programs, data and messages may be exchanged between them. When a computer is not part of a network, it is called a **stand-alone computer**.

Local area networks

A **local area network (LAN)** covers a small area such as a room or a building and is usually owned by an individual, a single company or an organisation such as a school. The school or centre in which you are studying this unit on Computer Systems is likely to have a local area network.

Figure 4.1 *Desktop computers in a local area network*

Network interface cards

A **network interface card**, or NIC, is a small circuit board that is fitted inside a computer system to allow it to communicate with a computer network. A network interface card is shown in figure 4.2. The type of computer which is most likely to be connected to a local area network is a desktop computer, although many laptop computers also have network interface cards.

A network interface card also provides a computer with a unique network address. This number is known as the *Media Access Control address* or MAC address. Each MAC address is made up of 6 bytes (48 bits). This allows for 2^{48} different addresses. The most common type of local area network in current use is *Ethernet*, and the MAC address is also known as the *Ethernet address*.

In addition to a network interface card, some computers have a **wireless network interface** card which allows them to communicate with other

Figure 4.2 *A network interface card*

computers on a local area network from anywhere in the immediate vicinity of a *wireless base station. WiFi* is one current standard for wireless networking. We looked at *WiFi* in chapter 3. You can see a wireless network interface card in figure 4.3.

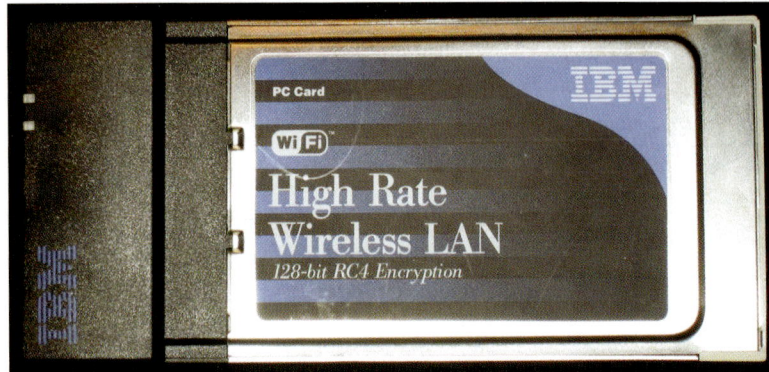

Figure 4.3 *A wireless network interface card*

Wireless hotspots

A **hotspot** is an area where wireless network signals may be received, and a computer may connect to the network. Usually hotspots are located in specific built-up areas close to offices and within public buildings and university campuses. These hotspots may be deliberately put in place for legitimate use, such as university students, or they may be accidentally created if a company's wireless local area network (*WLAN*) extends beyond the boundary of the building. Figure 4.4 shows a wireless hotspot in use on a train.

Figure 4.4 *A wireless hotspot on a train*

Advantages of local area networks over stand alone computers

- You can **share data** and programs between stations. If you don't have a network connection, you can only share files by copying them to a disk and carrying the disk from one computer to another. This is known as '*sneaker-net*'.

- Everyone on the network can **share peripherals** such as printers, which makes the system cheaper to set up than if every station had its own printer. This is called **resource sharing**.
- An electronic mailing service can be operated.

Peer-to-peer networks and client-server networks

Client-server network

A **client-server** network is a method of organisation in which **client workstations** make use of resources available on one or more **servers**. We will look at **file**, **print** and **web servers** later in this chapter.

Advantages of client-server networks:

- *Increased security over peer-to-peer – each user must log in to server.*
- *Different users can be given different levels of access to data.*
- *Resources are controlled through the server.*
- *Workgroup computing – many users can work on the same document simultaneously.*
- *Flexible use of stations – any user can log into the file server and can access their own data from any station.*
- *Backup is done centrally – the system administrator is responsible for making backup copies of all of the data on the file server.*

Disadvantages of client-server networks:

- *If the file server is not working then users cannot access their data.*
- *Client–server is more expensive than peer-to-peer – it is necessary to buy a server and server software.*

Peer-to-peer network

Every workstation on a **peer-to-peer** network has a similar status in the hierarchy, each having its own local storage devices for programs and data. One node on a peer to peer network may act as a file server, another as a printer server, but both of these nodes are also network nodes which are capable of being used as client workstations.

Advantages of peer-to-peer networks:

- *Each station on a peer to peer network has a similar status, with its own local storage devices.*
- *Cheaper than client/server – no need for file server or server software.*
- *Easier to set up current operating systems for peer-to-peer operations, for example, Windows XP.*

Disadvantages of peer-to-peer networks:

- *No central file storage – users must always use the same machine to access their data.*
- *Users must backup their own data.*
- *If one station is switched off, it may not be possible to access some resources.*
- *Peer-to-peer is less secure than client/server – users may not be required to login.*

Mainframe computer

A **mainframe** computer is a very large computer system, which can process a very large amount of data at high speed. It can occupy a whole room and may be connected to hundreds of user **terminals**. It is common to have many simultaneous users on a mainframe computer. This is why a mainframe is a **multi-user** or **multi-access** system. The users of a multi-access system each appear to have individual control of the computer at the same time, although only one program is actually being run at any one time. The mainframe computer also allows **multi-tasking** or **multi-programming** which allows several different tasks or applications to be processed at the same time.

A mainframe computer has a number of processors – it is a **multi-processor** machine. There is usually a vast amount of RAM, and many extra peripherals such as tape and disk drives.

A **dumb terminal** has no processor and no local storage devices. All that is required is a screen and a keyboard since all of the processing and storage will be done within the mainframe computer.

The computer operator is the person in charge of a mainframe computer. He or she will enter commands to control the running of various jobs from the operator's console, which resembles an ordinary user terminal.

Mainframe computer with terminals	Network of computers (client-server)
User terminals are 'dumb' – they do not have any processing power	Each network client machine has its own processor
All processing is done centrally in the mainframe, which is a multi-processor machine	Processing is done on the network clients
Multi-user	Single user

Figure 4.5 *A mainframe computer system occupies a whole room*

Supercomputers

A mainframe computer is not necessarily the fastest and most powerful type of computer. Instead, this term is reserved for the **Supercomputer**. Supercomputers are used for intensive mathematical calculations such as weather and climate forecasting, car design, aerospace engineering, molecular modelling or the production of high-resolution graphics such as digital animation in motion pictures.

A Supercomputer is likely to have many parallel processors in order to complete tasks quickly by processing data simultaneously as well as sequentially. Jobs need to be split into individual tasks in order to take advantage of parallel processing.

Figure 4.6 *Creating a supercomputer*

Some universities, research establishments and companies have created their own designs of supercomputer by linking together hundreds of processors, to provide a huge amount of processing power. Figure 4.7 shows a supercomputer which was created in this manner.

Figure 4.7 *XServe fileservers linked together to create a supercomputer*

Network topologies

Each computer on a network may be referred to as a *terminal*, *workstation* or **node**. Nodes in a local area network are relatively close together and can be connected by using wires, fibre optic cable or wireless technologies as the **transmission medium** or **communications channel**. The network **topology** is the way in which the nodes on a network are connected together. The network topologies we will look at in this unit are **bus**, **star**, **ring** and **mesh**. Bus, star and ring topologies are used in local area networks. Mesh topologies are more suited to wide area networks.

Bus topology

A network which uses a **bus** topology has each node connected to a main communications channel, the 'bus'. A bus network requires a device called a terminator at each end to catch stray signals and prevent them from interfering with other signals on the bus. If one of the nodes on a bus network fails, then it has no effect on the rest of the network. If the bus itself is faulty, then the network is unable to operate.

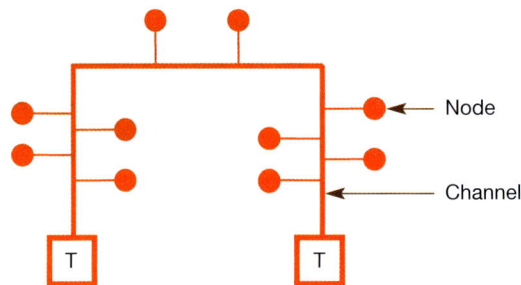

Figure 4.8 *A bus topology*

One advantage of a bus topology is that it is easy to add new stations onto the network, since new cables don't have to be laid, because all the stations connect directly to the same bus. Since all stations on a network using a bus topology use the same communications channel they may have to compete with each other in order to transmit and receive data.

Star topology

A network which uses a **star** topology has all of the peripheral nodes connected to a central node. If a peripheral node fails, it has no effect on the rest of the network. If the central node is faulty, then the network is unable to operate. If any one of the communications channels is broken, then this has the same effect on the network as a single peripheral node failure.

Each peripheral node may transmit or receive data simultaneously to and from the central node, and a great deal of network traffic may cause congestion at the central node. A star network is easy to expand.

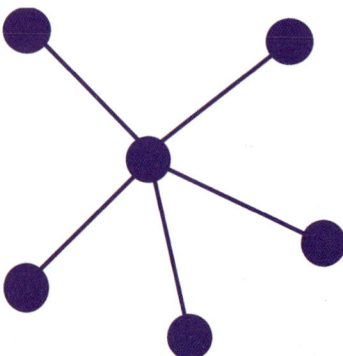

Figure 4.9 *A star topology*

Ring topology

A network which uses a **ring** topology sends signals around the network from node to node. If a node on a ring network is faulty, then there must be a mechanism for bypassing a failed node, so that the network can continue to operate. Like a bus network, if the communications channel fails, then the ring network cannot operate.

Mesh topology

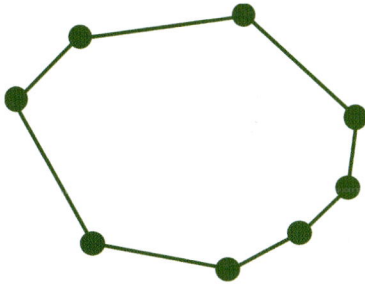

Figure 4.10 *A ring topology*

A network which uses a **mesh** topology has multiple direct connections between each node. If every node is directly connected to every other node it is known as a *fully connected* mesh. A fully connected mesh network provides the greatest possible protection against failure of a single communications channel since there are many alternative routes for the data to take. A node failure on a network using a mesh topology has no effect on the rest of the network. A mesh network is expensive to set up, since a great deal of wiring is required.

A wide area network such as the Internet is an example of a network which uses a mesh topology. The Defense Advanced Research Projects Agency Network or ARPANET in the USA was the predecessor of the Internet. ARPANET was designed as a distributed network using a mesh topology in order to minimise the effect of possible node failure during an enemy attack. Established in 1969, ARPANET served as a test bed for new networking technologies, linking many universities and research centres. The first two nodes that formed the ARPANET were UCLA and the Stanford Research Institute.

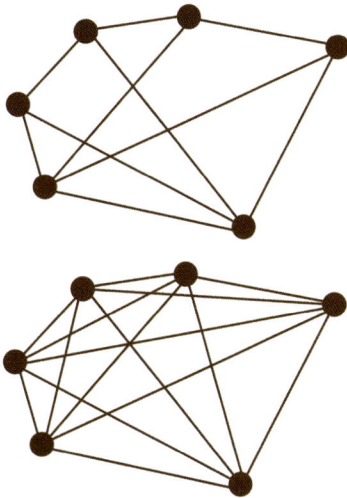

Figure 4.11 *Two mesh topologies*

The effect of network topology on system performance

Each topology has an effect on the performance of the network. A bus topology provides fast access but since stations on the network have to compete with each other in order to transmit and receive data, this can reduce the performance of the network. Access to the central node is very fast in a star topology but there may be congestion when all of the peripheral nodes are contacting the central node at the same time. This can reduce the speed of communication between the peripheral nodes. A mesh network is the best topology in terms of performance since a fully connected mesh has many communication channels for data to take.

Figure 4.12 *Ethernet*

The functions and uses of a hub, switch and router

Whatever type of transmission medium or topology is chosen for a network, there must be some means of connecting the workstations. Hubs, switches and routers are all devices which allow workstations to be connected and so create a network topology.

Hub

A **repeater** is a device which boosts or amplifies a signal on a cable. A repeater has two ports, or connections, one for the input signal, and one for the output. Figure 4.13 shows how a repeater works.

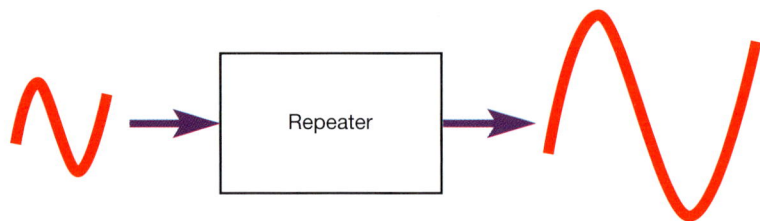

Figure 4.13 *How a repeater works*

A **hub** works in the same manner as a repeater, except that a hub has multiple ports, allowing more than one device to share the same wire. A hub may be thought of as a **multi-port repeater**. Figure 4.14 shows how a hub works.

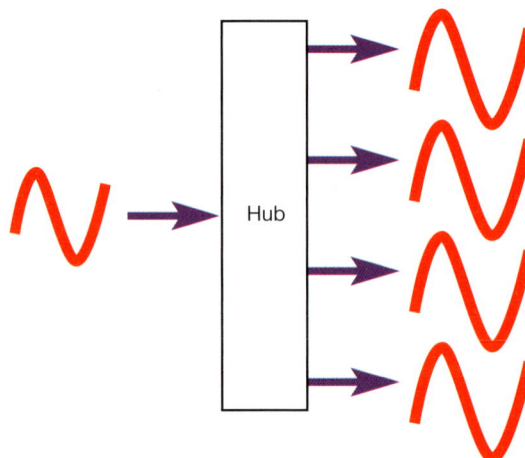

Figure 4.14 *How a hub works*

Each workstation which is connected to a hub may be up to 100 metres away. A hub is a shared device – only one station 'speaks' at a time. All connected stations hear the broadcast, even if it isn't meant for them. This places unnecessary traffic on the network, causing signal collisions which slow the network down. A hub is shown in figure 4.15.

Figure 4.15 *A four-port hub*

Switch

A **switch** operates like a 'smart' hub. A switch divides a network into separate *segments*, one segment for each connected machine. More than one machine can speak at once and only the intended recipients receive the data signal. Workstations which are connected via a switch benefit because there are no collisions between signals to reduce the speed of the network. Some switches are shown in figure 4.16.

Figure 4.16 *Switches*

Router

A **router** is a device which links two or more networks. The function of the router is to look at the destination addresses of the packets of data passing through it, and decide which route each packet should take. A router is shown in figure 4.17 and you can see how a router works in figure 4.18.

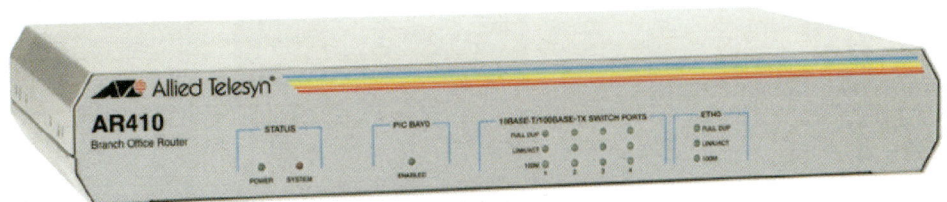

Figure 4.17 *A router*

Internet

Hub

Hub

Router

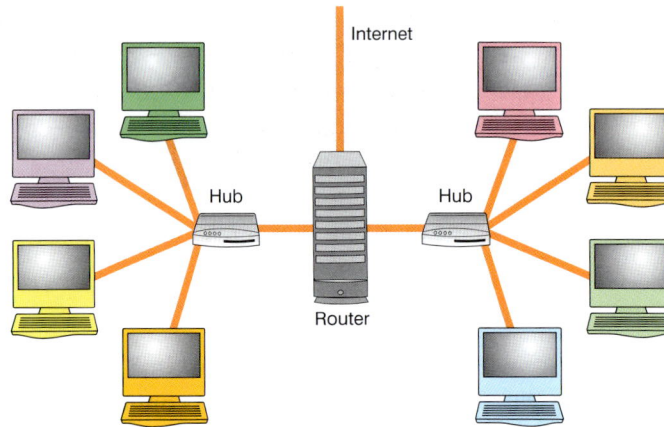

Figure 4.18 *A router determines the next network point to which data on a network should be forwarded*

File, print and web servers

A **client-server** network is a method of organisation in which **client** workstations make use of resources available on one or more **servers**.

File server

A **file server** provides central disk storage for user's programs and data on a network. A file server may be similar in appearance to a desktop computer, but usually has a greater amount of RAM and a much larger backing storage capacity. It is also likely to have a fast processor, or multiple processors, so that it can serve many users in as fast a time as possible. In addition, the components used to build a file server (like the hard disk drive) should be of a higher quality than an ordinary desktop computer, because the file server is designed to run constantly 24 hours a day, seven days a week. You can see two file servers in figure 4.19.

File server software is also required. The basic function of the file server software is to organise the storage of user data and handle the security of the network.

Figure 4.19 *Two file servers*

Before you can use a file server, you have to identify yourself to the file server – this is called logging on. To log on you must enter your user identity and then a password. When you have done this correctly the file server allows you access to the network – you are now on-line to the network and can load programs or look at your files. When you have finished using the network, you should log off, or go off-line. This means that the network will no longer accept any of your commands until you log on again.

A file server requires a faster connection to the network than an individual client station or node. For example, on an Ethernet network, with a communication speed of 100 Mbps for each client, a file server should have a typical connection speed of 1000 Mbps (Gigabit Ethernet).

Some form of backup device is essential for a file server, especially if the clients have no local storage. A Digital Audio Tape or DAT drive is often used for this. Other types of backing storage devices likely to be attached to a file server include RAID, or Redundant Array of Inexpensive Disks. A **RAID** is a set of hard disk units linked together and used as if they are a single backing storage device. By using two disks to hold the same data, a disk fault will be unlikely to have any effect on the operation of the whole system. This is known as *mirroring*. Furthermore, by writing some of the data to each of a number of disks, storage and retrieval of data can be speeded up.

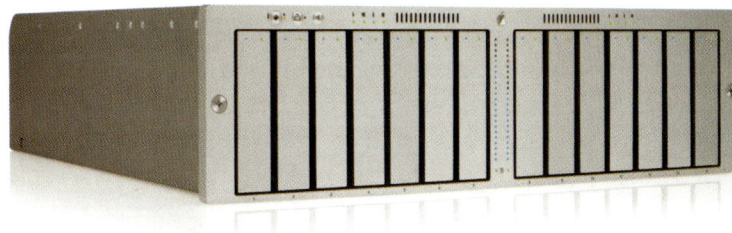

Figure 4.20 *XServe RAID*

Whatever type of backup hardware is used, backup software is also essential. This software is normally used to program a sequence of backups every day over a set period of a week or a month. A typical sequence for a school network, which is not used at weekends, is to backup the user data five times a week from Monday to Friday, using different media each day. Other types of backup strategy may involve copying the whole contents of the server hard disk to another hard disk drive. The advantage of having a complete copy is that it is faster to recover if the entire contents of the server hard disk is lost in a crash.

A fileserver which has to run 24/7 should be protected from power cuts by an *uninterruptible power supply* (UPS). The UPS contains a rechargeable battery which can provide enough power to run the server for a short period of time. If the mains power is not restored, then the UPS software can perform a controlled shutdown of the server, preventing any loss of data or hardware damage.

Figure 4.21 *An interruptible power supply*

Print server

A **print server** or **printer server** allows all of the client stations to use a printer controlled by it. A printer server may incorporate a **spooler program** to temporarily store data in transit to the printer on a fast backing storage device like a hard disk drive. It does not matter if the printer is busy, the print job is stored until the printer is ready to print. A printer server provides a queuing facility which allows users to receive their printouts in turn, or it may be programmed to give priority to particular users.

A network printer is designed to work quickly, so that users on the network will not have too long to wait for their printouts. Most network printers are large monochrome lasers, although colour laser printers are becoming more common. A network printer will have its own processor and a certain amount of RAM to act as a **buffer**. 64 or 128 Megabytes is a typical buffer size for a network printer. Many network printers are *Postscript*™ devices, that is, they contain an interpreter program for the *Postscript* or similar page description language.

Desktop computers on a network without a printer server usually spool data to their own local hard disk drive. This allows background printing. We looked at buffers and spoolers in the previous chapter.

Web server

A **web server** is a computer that provides World Wide Web services to a network. The term web server may also be used to refer only to the software. Any current computer can be turned into a Web server by installing web server software and connecting the machine to a network.

Every computer on the Internet that contains or 'hosts' a web site must have a Web server program. Two examples of Web servers are *Apache* and Microsoft's *Internet Information Server* (IIS). A Web server uses the World Wide Web's *Hypertext Transfer Protocol* (HTTP), to serve the files that form web pages as the clients request them.

Using a web server on a local area network means that you have the benefit of 'always on', fast access to the pages, with very little chance of downtime as compared to accessing the Internet. One other advantage of using a web server on a local area network is that it is easier to keep the stored data private to an organisation than if the web server was being accessed via a wide area network.

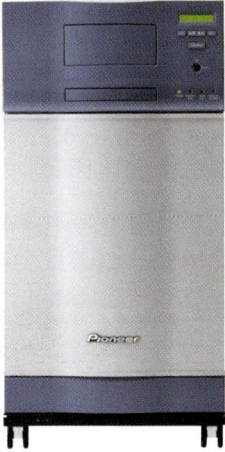

Figure 4.22 *CD-ROM jukebox server*

Other types of server

A **mail server** manages an electronic mailing system.

A **database server** manages a large database which may be accessed by client stations.

A **CD-ROM server** allows client stations to access data and programs from one or more CD-ROMs held within it. A CD-ROM *jukebox* can hold a number of CD-ROMs at once, and switch between them on request. Current jukeboxes can handle many different types of media such as CD-Recordable and DVD-Rewritable disks, and are used to make backups of data rather than just to access CD-ROMs. You can see a jukebox in figure 4.22.

Comparison of LANs, WANs, Intranet and Internetwork in terms of transmission media, bandwidth, geographical spread and functions

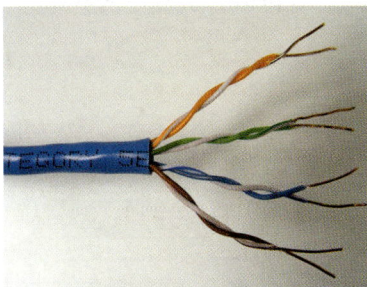

Figure 4.23 *Optical fibre and Category 5 Unshielded Twisted Pair (CAT5UTP) cables*

LAN

A Local Area Network (LAN) is confined to a limited geographical area, usually a room, department or a college campus.

The transmission media for a LAN is either cable or wireless (WLAN). One characteristic of the transmission media of a LAN is that it is owned by the organisation who owns the LAN. Cable is typically CAT(egory) 5 copper wire or optical fibre. See figure 4.23.

A LAN has a high bandwidth, for example 100–1000 Mbps. This bandwidth is available for both sending and receiving data.

The functions of a LAN include data sharing, peripheral sharing and email.

WAN

A **Wide Area Network** (WAN) is geographically widespread. The transmission media in a WAN may be any combination of copper cable, optical fibre, and wireless. The transmission media in a WAN are owned by many different organisations. A WAN has a low bandwidth compared to a LAN. A typical home computer may connect at 56 Kbps using a dialup modem, or 1–2 Mbps using ADSL Broadband. This bandwidth is normally download (receiving data) only. Sending (uploading) may be at a much slower rate, for example 250 Kbps for broadband. The bandwidth between ISPs on a WAN may be considerably higher (see figure 4.24), but a WAN may not be accessed at this bandwidth by a single user. The functions of a WAN are data sharing, email and video conferencing. WANs are not used for peripheral sharing.

Intranet

An **Intranet** is a private network belonging to a company or organization, for internal use only, although it may be geographically widespread. An Intranet uses normal Internet protocols, web browsers, HTML, and in general looks like a private version of the Internet.

Intranets may include connections through *gateway* computers to the Internet using *firewalls* for security. All Internet traffic is usually monitored by the organisation's security department, who can block web sites or specific content that they don't want employees to see.

The transmission media in an Intranet may be any combination of copper cable, optical fibre, and wireless. The transmission media in an Intranet may be owned by different organisations.

The bandwidth of an Intranet will be variable, depending upon the situation. Bandwidth will be high on a LAN which is part of an Intranet, but when data is being sent via the Internet, then bandwidth will be much lower.

The main purpose of an Intranet is to share company information and computing resources among employees. An Intranet can also be used for group work and for teleconferences.

Internetwork

An **Internetwork** is a collection of two or more Local Area Networks. The networks are connected by devices such as switches or routers in such a manner that all of the users and devices on the Internetwork can communicate. An Internetwork functions as a single network. The Internet is the largest example of an Internetwork.

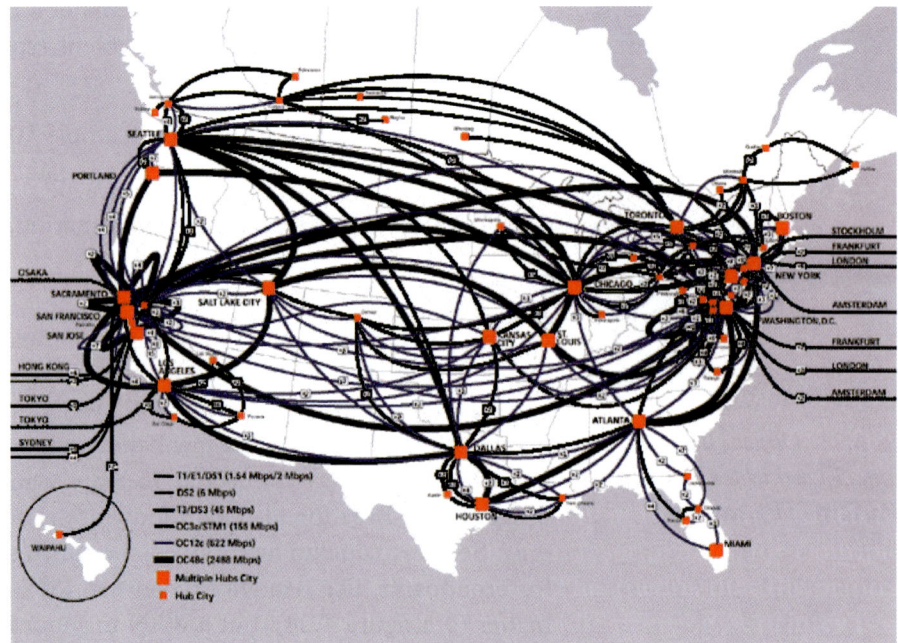

Figure 4.24 *An Internetwork in North America*

Bandwidth on an Internetwork will be variable, depending upon the situation. Bandwidth will be high on a LAN which is part of an Internetwork, but when data is being sent via the Internet, then bandwidth will be much lower. An Internetwork is shown in figure 4.24.

Figure 4.25 *It's guaranteed to take a lifetime to do anything ….*

LANs, WANs, Intranets and Internetworks are compared later on in this chapter in table 4.1.

Description and explanation of the trends towards higher bandwidth and wireless communications

Higher bandwidth

Bandwidth is a measure of the quantity of data which may be carried by a communications channel at any one time. A current Ethernet local area network has a bandwidth of 100 Mbps. A current fileserver may have a 1000 Mbps (*Gigabit*) bandwidth connection to a local area network. New desktop computers and laptops now have Gigabit network interface cards. To give some idea of what such bandwidth is capable of, consider the delivery of a DVD-quality, full-length Hollywood movie. At 1 Gbps it could take as few as 30 seconds to download, depending on network conditions, compared with several hours over a typical Internet broadband connection.

Basic home broadband using ADSL (Asymmetric Digital Subscriber Line) has a bandwidth of 512 Kbps, although 1 Mbps and 2 Mbps have now become standard. There are physical limits to current ADSL technology, mainly due to the distance between the subscriber and the local telephone exchange. The typical maximum distance for 512 Kbps ADSL is 5.5 km, falling to 3.5 km for 2 Mbps. Remember that the speeds quoted are for downloads only. Upload speed is considerably slower. Also, domestic ADSL is subject to a contention ratio – which means that each line is shared by a number of other users, for example 25 or 50.

Figure 4.26 *Warchalking*

Figure 4.27 *The Zigbee logo*

Wireless communications

More and more devices have wireless functions incorporated as standard. Most laptop computers are fitted with wireless network interface cards (see earlier in this chapter) in order to access networks without a physical connection. Areas within the range of wireless base stations (the *network cloud*[1]) are known as hotspots. 'Warchalking' symbols are used to identify hotspots where a wireless connection may be made.

WiFi

WiFi stands for the Wireless Fidelity Alliance. The main use for *WiFi* is in wireless local area networking (WLAN). *WiFi* devices have typical ranges from 12 to 50 metres and typical data transfer rates from 5 to 20 Mbps. Three current WiFi standards are IEEE 802.11a, 802.11b and 802.11g. IEEE 802.11b allows for maximum data transfer rates of up to 11 Mbps and 802.11a and 802.11g both allow up to 54 Mbps. IEEE 802.11b and IEEE 802.11g operate on a frequency of 2.4 Ghz and IEEE 802.11a operates on 5 Ghz.

Bluetooth

Many mobile phones have *Bluetooth*, which allows for short-range wireless communication between devices – up to 10 metres at the 2.4 GHz frequency. Bluetooth (IEEE 802.15.1) has a relatively low bandwidth (1 Mbps). In practice, Bluetooth is not much use for networking a wireless LAN. Bluetooth is cheap to manufacture. A Bluetooth phone can synchronise data wirelessly with, and also control some of the functions of, a computer fitted with Bluetooth.

Zigbee

Zigbee is a wireless standard which links consumer devices for control and entertainment purposes. Zigbee devices are low cost and have low power consumption. The Zigbee specification is a combination of HomeRF Lite and the IEEE 802.15.4 specification, operating in the 2.4 GHz band. It is capable of connecting 255 devices per network and supports data transmission rates of up to 250 Kbps at a range of up to 30 metres.

Ultra-Wideband (UWB)

UWB is a wireless radio technology originally developed for secure military communications. UWB technology has the capacity to handle the very high bandwidths required to transport multiple audio and video streams. This new technology operates at a level that most systems interpret as noise and, as a result, does not cause interference to other radios such as mobile phones or TV sets.

Most computer and consumer electronic devices require wires to record, play or exchange data. Using UWB, a digital video camera could play a video on a TV without using wires, or a mobile computer user could wirelessly connect to a digital projector in a conference room to deliver a presentation. UWB follows the IEEE 802.15.3 specification, with data rates of over 400 Mbps with a range of up to 10 metres in a Wireless Personal Area Network (WPAN), allowing for DVD quality video to be shared throughout the home.

---

[1] Network cloud: The term cloud is often used to refer to the connections on networks because of the complexity of routers, gateways, and other switching systems in networks and because of the number of connections that exist. A message sent through a network is like a plane flying through a cloud; it is visible only before and after it passes through a cloud.

Worldwide interoperability for Microwave Access (WiMAX)

WiMAX is a wireless technology that conforms to the IEEE 802.16 specification. WiMAX offers a bandwidth of up to 70 Mbps, slightly higher than WiFi. WiMAX's big advantage over WiFi is its increased range. WiFi has a range of 100 metres. WiMAX has a range of *50 kilometres*, and uses transmitters on masts (just like mobile phone masts). WiMAX makes it possible to overcome the distance limits of wired broadband access, especially for areas remote from telephone exchanges.

Technical reasons for the increasingly widespread use of networks

The technical reasons which we will look at are **advances in computer hardware** and **improved network related software**.

Advances in computer hardware

Advances in computer hardware include: **processors**, **main memory capacity**, **backing storage** and **data transfer rates**. Some of these advances are discussed in more detail elsewhere in this chapter and in chapter 2.

- **Processors** have become faster, and one trend is to increase the number of processors on a single chip or in one computer system in order to improve system performance.
- **Main memory capacity** has tended to increase as the cost of RAM chips continues to fall. This has allowed the development and implementation of larger, more complex **network operating system** software.
- **Backing storage** capacity has increased as the cost of hard disk storage falls and new types of storage media, such as Blu-ray, are introduced. Large capacity hard disk drives make it possible to store the data from many network users on one file server. Applications like video editing, which require a backing storage space of many gigabytes for a single movie, now use a technique called *Network Attached Storage* (NAS). NAS uses a large capacity hard disk drive which is connected directly to a local area network. NAS disks are sometimes called *Ethernet disks*.
- **Data transfer rates** are also increasing, for instance, 10 Mbps Ethernet is being replaced by 100 Mbps, which, in turn, will be replaced by 1000 Mbps (Gigabit Ethernet). This improvement in bandwidth allows larger files to be transferred in less time. It is now possible to edit and transfer large files such as video files efficiently across a local area network.

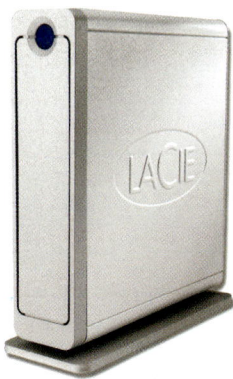

Figure 4.28 *An Ethernet disk*

Improved network related software

The software referred in this category includes **browsers** and **network operating systems**.

Browsers

Figure 4.30 shows two screenshots of browsers from 1993 (*Word Wide Web*, the first ever browser, written by Tim Berners-Lee) and 1997 (*NCSA Mosaic*). Compare these screenshots with the screenshot of a current browser in figure 4.31.

Figure 4.29 *A selection of browser logos*

Figure 4.30 *Screen shots of browsers from 1993 and 1997*

Figure 4.31 *Screen shot of a current browser (Mozilla Firefox)*

One notable difference in the development of browser software over the past few years has been the ability of modern browsers to have their functionality extended by the addition of various plug-ins. Plug-ins allow browsers to display different types of data other than plain HTML pages, such as animated graphic sequences and streamed video. Some examples of plug-ins are *Flash*, *Shockwave*, *RealPlayer*, *Acrobat*, *QuickTime* and *Cortona*.

Network operating systems

A **network operating system** controls all the devices on a network so that resources can be shared efficiently and files can be transferred. It handles the administration of all network functions. Network operating systems are usually in two parts *server* and *client/requester*. The requester makes disks, software, ports and other facilities available to the workstation from the server on request, such as print services and data sharing. Each service requested by a station is accessed via the client software.

Some operating systems, such as UNIX and the Mac OS, have networking functions built in. The term *network operating system* is usually reserved for software that enhances a basic operating system by adding networking features. Examples of Network Operating Systems are *Novell Netware*, *Artisoft's LANtastic*, *Microsoft LAN Manager*, *Windows NT*, *Windows 2003 Server* and *Mac OS X Server*.

The misuse of networks and the applicable Acts

The laws which apply to the misuse of networks include the **Copyright, Designs and Patents Act 1988**, the **Computer Misuse Act 1990** and the **Data Protection Act 1998**. Since these Acts were passed, individuals may be prosecuted for carrying out certain activities relating to networks which are classified as illegal. Any conviction which is made is a result of the application of these Acts.

Copyright, Designs and Patents Act

The Copyright, Designs and Patents Act covers **breaches of copyright**, such as illegal copying of software, music and movies.

Copyright

Some of the information on the Internet is free to use but much of it is not.

Suppose you are looking for information for a school project and find a graphic of a laser printer, which you download and save to disk. You then use an application package to paste the image of the printer into your report, print it, and hand it in. This type of use of the graphic would be classified as personal study and there should be no financial or legal implications of using the image in this way.

Let's compare the previous example with another one. Imagine you are writing a Computing textbook, and you download and save the same graphic of the laser printer for use in your new book. It would be illegal to use the image in the book, which is a commercial publication, without first seeking the permission of, and perhaps paying a fee to, the copyright owner.

Commercial software is not free and should be paid for. There are considerable restrictions upon its use. When you purchase commercial software you are only allowed to use it on one computer system and are not allowed to make copies of it, or distribute it in any way.

If you wish to use a piece of software on more than one computer system, you should purchase one of the following:

- A sufficient number of single copies to match the number of computer systems required, or
- A limited licence for the specific number of machines required, or
- A site licence, which allows you to use the software on all computer systems at a single location, such as a school.

Piracy

Computer networks with broadband connections make it easier for software and movies to be stolen from their legitimate copyright owners. A variety of compressed file formats, such as MP3 and AAC, can reduce the time it takes to download a single musical track to seconds. These downloads may be legal, for example in the case of the *iTunes Music Store*, but many are from illegal sources.

The size of a typical movie file makes it a substantial download, even with a broadband connection, and may take many hours. To reduce excessive downloading, many Internet Service Providers (ISPs) have introduced a monthly limit. A figure of between 15 and 30 Gigabytes is a typical 'cap'.

Many people justify their actions in buying pirated copies of movies by referring to the profits made by film companies. What these individuals may not realise is that the profits from piracy are going straight into the pockets of organised criminals and could be used to fund other criminal acts such as the distribution of drugs.

Computer Misuse Act

The **Computer Misuse Act** covers **hacking** and **planting viruses**. The Computer Misuse Act makes it a criminal offence to gain unauthorised access to a computer system, to hack, or to write and distribute viruses, which can damage data on a computer. Both of these types of crime are now widespread because so many computers may be accessed through networks such as the Internet. Viruses are discussed in more detail in the next chapter.

Hacking

In the computer security community, a *black hat* is a skilled hacker who uses his or her ability to pursue their interest illegally. They are often economically motivated, or may be representing a political cause. Sometimes, however, it is pure curiosity. The term comes from old Western movies (viewed in black and white), where heroes typically wore white or light-coloured hats and outfits, and the villains wore black outfits with black hats.

Organisations have been set up to combat the activities of black hats. One such organisation is Honeynet (www.honeynet.org). Honeynet constructs its own networks especially in order to trap black hats. Each Honeynet contains one or more honeypots. A honeypot is a system which is deliberately left open to attract the activities of black hats, in the same way as bears are attracted to honey. Once a black hat has entered the Honeynet, then the hacking techniques that they use can be monitored in order to provide information to combat their activities.

The Honeynet
P R O J E C T

Figure 4.32 *Honeynet*

Data Protection Act

The Data Protection Act covers how information may be held and for what purposes. The Data Protection Act places limits on the storage and use of personal information. Many individuals and companies need to store information about us in order to provide goods and services such as healthcare. Computers make it easy to store this information, and should make companies more efficient in their service provision. While we may not like to give out personal information, most people agree that it is necessary in some cases. You may well resent a '*cold caller*' knowing your telephone number, but perhaps not be so upset if a doctor's computer held the statement '*allergic to penicillin*'.

Users of *Google's* email system, *Gmail*, should not be surprised if the character of the on-screen advertisements which appear when they are using the service, gradually changes to reflect the types of search that they have been carrying out and the pages they have browsed. This harvesting and use of personal information is valuable to companies and they argue that targeted advertising is of benefit to the individuals concerned.

The use of networks makes it easy to pass information between organisations, and this means that it is possible to build up a more or less complete picture of an individual when a series of separate data items is gathered together and combined in a database.

Identity theft is one activity that has been made easier for criminals because of the use of networks. According to the UK Fraud Prevention Agency, CIFAS, the recorded cases of identity fraud have increased from 20,000 in 1999 to 101,000 in 2003.

Spyware is a type of computer program which can record the user's keystrokes, like passwords and forward them to another computer.

Phishing is an attempt to trick someone into giving away personal information using the Internet by pretending to be a well-known company. A typical phishing technique involves emailing people and pretending to be a bank, and asking the recipients to enter their bank details. According to the *International Anti-Phishing Working Group*, phishers are able to convince up to 5% of their targets to give them personal information. Remember that legitimate companies do not need to ask for your personal information, because they already have it.

http://www.itsafe.gov.uk/

ITsafe is a government service, launched on 23 February 2005, to provide both home users and small businesses with proven, plain English advice on protecting computers, mobile phones and other devices from malicious attack.

Questions

1. What is a network?
2. What is a stand-alone computer?
3. What is a local area network?
4. What is a network interface card?
5. What is the purpose of a network interface card?
6. What is a MAC address?
7. How many different MAC addresses can there be?
8. What is a WLAN?
9. Name one wireless standard for networking.
10. What device is needed on a computer for wireless networking?
11. What device is needed in a building or room where wireless networking is to be used?
12. What is a hotspot?
13. State one place where you would expect to find a hotspot
    a. deliberate
    b. accidental.
14. What is a client-server network?
15. What is a peer-to-peer network?
16. State two advantages of client-server networks as compared to peer-to-peer.
17. State two disadvantages of client-server networks as compared to peer-to-peer.
18. What is a wide area network?
19. What is a mainframe computer?
20. What is a dumb terminal?
21. Compare a mainframe computer and terminals with a network of computers.
22. What is a supercomputer?
23. What is a network topology?
24. What is a communications channel?
25. State one type of transmission medium.
26. Draw a labelled diagram of a bus topology.
27. What is the purpose of a terminator on a bus network?
28. Why is mesh an unsuitable topology for a LAN?
29. Compare a star topology and a ring topology, with respect to node and channel failure.
30. What is a repeater?
31. What is a hub?
32. What is a switch?
33. State one advantage of a switch over a hub.
34. What is a router?
35. State three types of server.
36. What is RAID?
37. What is mirroring?
38. What is a UPS?
39. a. Which type of server requires a user to log on to use its services?
    b. State the function of this type of server.
40. What is a spooler?
41. Which type of server normally uses a spooler?
42. State two ways a print queue may be managed.
43. What use is a jukebox on a network?
44. Which type of network is likely to have the highest bandwidth?
45. What is UTP?
46. Why are WANs not used for sharing peripherals?
47. What is an Intranet?
48. What is the main purpose of an Intranet?
49. What is an Internetwork?
50. State two trends in networking.
51. What is ADSL?
52. What limits does ADSL have?
53. What is a network cloud?
54. What is the purpose of warchalking?
55. What is WiFi?
56. Describe one example of WiFi.
57. What is Bluetooth?
58. State one advantage that WiFi has over Bluetooth.
59. State two technical reasons for the increasingly widespread use of networks.
60. Explain one advance in computer hardware related to the increasingly widespread use of networks.
61. Name two types of network related software.
62. Which laws apply to the misuse of networks?
63. State one breach of copyright which may take place on a network.
64. What is hacking?
65. In relation to hacking, what is a:
    a. black hat?
    b. honeypot?
66. What is spyware?
67. What is phishing?

• Key points •

- A network is two or more computers linked together in such a way that programs, data and messages may be exchanged between them.
- A local area network (LAN) covers a small area such as a room or a building.
- A network interface card is a small circuit board that is fitted inside a computer system to allow it to communicate with a computer network.
- Some computers have a wireless network interface card.
- A *hotspot* is an area where wireless network signals may be received, and a computer may connect to the network.
- Advantages of Local Area Networks over stand alone computers.
  - You can share data and programs between stations.
  - Everyone on the network can share peripherals.
  - An electronic mailing service can be operated.
- A wide area network (WAN) covers a larger geographical area.
- A client-server network is a method of organisation in which client workstations make use of resources available on one or more servers.
- Advantages of client-server networks:
  - Increased security over peer-to-peer – each user must log in to the server.
  - Different users can be given different levels of access to data.
  - Resources are controlled through the server.
  - Workgroup computing – many users can work on the same document simultaneously.
  - Flexible use of stations – any user can log into the file server and can access their own data from any station.
  - Backup is done centrally – the system administrator is responsible for making backup copies of all of the data on the file server.

- Disadvantages of client-server networks:
  - If the file server is not working then users cannot access their data.
  - Client–server is more expensive than peer-to-peer – it is necessary to buy a server and server software.
- Every workstation on a peer-to-peer network has a similar status in the hierarchy, each having its own local storage devices for programs and data.
- Advantages of peer-to-peer networks:
  - Each station on a peer to peer network has a similar status, with its own local storage devices.
  - Cheaper than client/server – no need for file server or server software.
  - Easier to set up current operating systems for peer-to-peer operations.
- Disadvantages of peer-to-peer networks:
  - No central file storage – users must always use the same machine to access their data.
  - Users must backup their own data.
  - If one station is switched off, it may not be possible to access some resources.
  - Peer-to-peer is less secure than client/server – users may not be required to login.
- A mainframe computer is a large computer system, which can process a huge amount of data at high speed.
- A mainframe computer can occupy a whole room and may be connected to hundreds of user terminals.
- A dumb terminal has no processor and no local storage devices.
- It is common to have many simultaneous users on a mainframe computer – a mainframe is a multi-user or multi-access system.
- Each computer on a network may be referred to as a *terminal*, *workstation* or node.
- Nodes in a local area network are relatively close together and can be connected by using wires, fibre optic cable or wireless technologies as the transmission medium or communications channel.

- The network topology is the way in which the nodes on a network are connected together, for example, bus, star, ring and mesh.
- Topology Summary – each topology has an effect on the performance of the network.

Failure	Bus	Star	Ring	Mesh
Node	No effect on rest of network	Network down if central node down – otherwise no effect on rest of network	Failed node can be bypassed to maintain integrity of ring	No effect on rest of network
Channel	Network down	No effect on rest of network	Network down	No effect on rest of network

- A repeater is a device which boosts or amplifies a signal on a cable.
- A hub is a multi-port repeater.
- A switch operates like a 'smart' hub, dividing a network into separate *segments*, one for each machine.
- Workstations connected via a switch benefit because there are no collisions between signals to reduce the speed of the network.
- A router is a device which links two or more networks.
- A router looks at the destination addresses of the packets of data passing through it, and decides which route each packet should take.
- A file server provides central disk storage for user's programs and data on a network.
- A print server allows all of the client stations to use a printer controlled by it.
- A print server may incorporate a spooler program to temporarily store data in transit to the printer on a fast backing storage device like a hard disk drive.
- A web server is a computer that provides World Wide Web services to a network.
- A LAN is confined to a limited geographical area, usually a room, department or a college campus.
- A WAN is geographically widespread.
- An Intranet is a private network belonging to a company or organization, for internal use only, although it may be geographically widespread.
- An Internetwork is a collection of two or more Local Area Networks.

Table 4.1 *A comparison of LANs, WANs, Intranets and Internetworks*

Comparison of Networks	LAN	WAN	Intranet	Internetwork
Share data	✓	✓	✓	✓
Share peripherals	✓	✗	✗	✗
e-mail	✓	✓	✓	✓
Bandwidth	high	low	variable	variable
Media	cable/wireless owned by organisation	cable/wireless owned by others	cable/wireless parts owned by others	cable/wireless parts owned by others
Geographical spread	small	large	medium	large

- Bandwidth is a measure of the quantity of data which may be carried by a communications channel at any one time.

- Most laptop computers are fitted with wireless network interface cards in order to access networks without a physical connection.
- Three varieties of the 802.11 WiFi standard are in current use. These are 802.11a, 802.11b and 802.11g.
- Bluetooth allows for short range wireless communication between devices – up to 10 metres.
- Zigbee is a wireless standard which links consumer devices for control and entertainment purposes.
- The technical reasons for the increasingly widespread use of networks are advances in computer hardware and improved network related software.
  - Advances in computer hardware includes processors, main memory capacity, backing storage and data transfer rates.
  - Improved network related software includes browsers and network operating systems.

- The laws which apply to the misuse of networks include the Copyright, Designs and Patents Act, the Computer Misuse Act and the Data Protection Act.
- The Copyright, Designs and Patents Act covers breaches of copyright, such as illegal copying of software, music and movies.
- The Computer Misuse Act covers hacking and planting viruses.
- The Computer Misuse Act makes it a criminal offence to gain unauthorised access to a computer system, to hack, or to write and distribute viruses, which can damage data on a computer.
- The Data Protection Act covers how information may be held and for what purposes.
- The Data Protection Act places limits on the storage and use of personal information.

5 Computer Software

What is an operating system?

The **operating system** is a program that controls the entire operation of the computer and any devices which are attached to it. Although it may not be obvious to the casual user of a computer, the operating system runs in a computer all the time from the moment it is switched on until the computer is switched off. The operating system program deals with the basic functions of the computer, such as detecting what has been typed in, displaying data on the screen and loading from and saving to backing storage.

The design of the operating system is often modular, allowing new features to be added easily and new hardware to be accommodated. Updating the operating system program is easy if the operating system is stored on disk. It is a different matter with a completely ROM-based operating system – if an update is required then the old ROM chips must be removed and new ones inserted. Another advantage of a disk-based operating system is that it is not always necessary to load the entire operating system on start-up – some parts of the operating system, such as a disk formatter, may be loaded only when required.

The function of a bootstrap loader

Starting up a computer which uses a ROM-based operating system is fast, because the speed of access to ROM is measured in *nanoseconds* as compared to *milliseconds* for a hard disk. A computer using a disk-based operating system has a small part of its operating system stored in ROM. This is called the **bootstrap loader**, and its function is to load the rest of the operating system from disk when the computer is switched on or restarted.

One disadvantage of a disk-based operating system is that it takes up a substantial amount of the computer's main memory once it is loaded. This means that less main memory is available to hold programs and data. The computer which I am using just now to write this sentence has a disk-based operating system and 256 *Megabytes* of main memory. Currently 55 *Megabytes* are in use to hold its operating system program.

A further disadvantage of a disk-based operating system is that it is vulnerable to corruption from other programs present in the computer's memory. This may be intentional and malicious in the case of a virus, or negligent, in the case of a program which had bugs in the code. In either case, the result is the same – if the operating system code is affected, the computer may crash or hang and will have to be restarted – any unsaved data will be lost.

What is a single user operating system?

A **single user operating system** is only capable of supporting one user at a time. A network operating system is designed to support multi-access operation.

The **main functions of a single user operating system** are:

- interpreting users commands
- file management
- memory management
- input/output management
- managing processes
- resource allocation

One way of describing the operating system program is to think of it as a series of layers or modules. Developing the operating system in this way means that software upgrades to a particular module become possible without the need to rewrite the complete operating system program.

Let's take a look at each of these layers, starting from the outer layer, which is closest to the user of the computer:

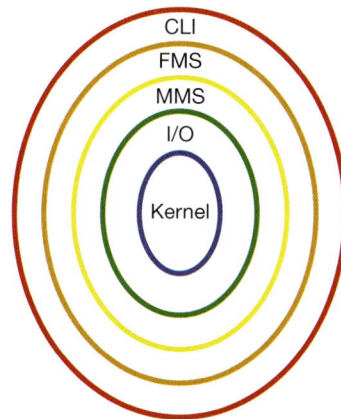

Figure 5.1 *One model of an operating system*

Interpreting users commands – the Command Language Interpreter

The **Command Language Interpreter** (CLI) is the outer layer or *shell* of the operating system program. This is the layer through which the user interacts in order to give instructions to the computer. The CLI may be **command-driven**, which means that the user must know and be able to enter typed commands into it. Alternatively, the CLI may be **menu-driven**, which means the user can choose commands from a list. Most computers in current use have a menu-driven CLI which is part of a **graphical user interface** or GUI. A pointing device like a mouse is used to select commands using a graphical user interface. The *Microsoft Windows*™ graphical user interface is the most widely used GUI.

Whatever type of CLI is in use on a computer system, its job is to **interpret** or *make sense of the* **commands** entered by the user and do its best to have them carried out. If the user makes a mistake and gives a wrong command, then the CLI should respond by giving an error message. A *user-friendly* system is one which will respond with helpful error messages and prompts to assist the user. Modern CLIs incorporate *context-sensitive* help systems, which tailor their response to suit the task which the user is trying to perform. If the user makes a mistake while trying to print a document, then a context-sensitive help system will first offer help on printing problems.

A user-friendly CLI will also warn the user when they are about to take any potentially destructive action which may remove data from the system, for instance, when deleting a file. *Windows*™ users will be familiar with the recycle bin and *Mac OS* users with the trash. In order to delete a file from the system, the file is first placed in the recycle bin. However, performing this action on its own does not actually delete the file – the user must then choose to empty the recycle bin, and at that point, they are asked to confirm the action before the file is really deleted.

It may be helpful to think of the CLI as a **process** which runs in the computer. Consider what happens in the situation where you are making a backup copy of a file to a removable storage medium. When you give the CLI the command to copy, the action which the CLI takes is to pass the copy command to the next layer of the operating system. While this is happening, the CLI process is temporarily suspended or *blocked*, and the CLI can no longer accept any commands until the copy is complete. When the copy is complete, the CLI process is resumed and you can give the next instruction. This is an example of how the operating system **manages processes**.

The type of CLI which is available to the user can influence their performance when using a computer system in the sense that it is faster for an experienced user to type commands using the keyboard than it is to choose from a menu using a mouse. The designers of menu-driven operating systems have taken account of this by providing keyboard equivalents for often-used menu choices. *Windows*™ users will be familiar with *CONTROL-Q* for Quit and Macintosh users with *COMMAND-C* for Copy.

File management

The **File Management System** (FMS) is concerned with the efficient use of the computer's backing storage devices and media. The FMS is also known as the Disk Operating System (DOS).

In addition to storing the files on disk, the FMS also uses part of the disk storage space to hold the details of where the files are stored. This information is held in the disk catalog, which normally occupies the outer tracks of the disk surface. The user's view of the catalog is a neat, ordered list, which may be alphabetical or sorted by date. By itself, this is not enough information to allow the operating system to locate the file, so the catalog also holds details of the precise physical address on the disk where the file can be found. This information is needed by the **Input/Output management system** in order to find and load the file when instructed to do so by the FMS.

The FMS organises files in a *hierarchical filing system*, which stores files in separate directories and sub-directories. Storing files like this is helpful to the user, because it is easy to use particular directories in order to keep related files together. It has the additional benefit that two files or sub-directories may have the same name if they are stored in separate directories. Look at figure 5.2, which shows a diagram of a hierarchical filing system. Tracing a path from the main or root directory, that is, by giving its pathname may uniquely identify each file or sub-directory.

Book 5.Chapter 1.Figures.Fig 1.2 is an example of a complete pathname for a file.

What is the pathname for the Visual Basic sub-directory in figure 5.2?

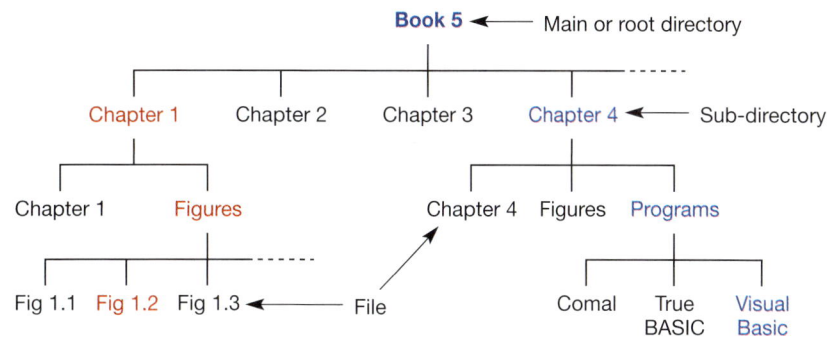

Figure 5.2 *A hierarchical filing system*

Memory management

The Memory Management System (MMS) controls where programs and data are placed in main memory. The MMS keeps track of the total amount of main memory available, and which programs and data are currently loaded. The MMS allocates space in memory for programs and data. Sometimes this is not possible, perhaps because the size of a file means that there is insufficient free or unused memory. If this happens, the MMS sends an error message to the CLI, which informs the user. The user can then decide what action to take. For example, quitting another program which is already loaded, to free additional memory.

Many computers have MMSs which allow more than one program to be loaded into memory at the same time. This is a form of **multi-tasking,** although in fact the processor is actually running only one program at any one time. The MMS allows the user to switch between any of the programs in memory at will.

One other task performed by the MMS is to ensure that any user programs do not interfere with the area of main memory which is used by the operating system. If this does happen, then the computer could crash, and you would lose any unsaved data. This is an important area of development for designers of current operating systems, who are incorporating features such as *memory protection* to reduce the likelihood of situations like this from occurring. Crashing is more likely to occur in a computer using a disk-based operating system rather than a ROM-based operating system – can you explain why?

Often when an individual program crashes or 'hangs', the computer is still operational. Modern operating systems also allow the user to recover from this situation without the computer system having to be switched off or restarted by pressing the reset button. The 'force quit' feature allows the user to remove a 'hung' program from the computer's memory, and allow them to continue working. This is a very useful feature, since it reduces the likelihood of damage to other parts of the computer, such as the hard disk drive. Can you explain why suddenly switching the computer off could damage the hard disk drive?

Input/Output management (I/O system)

The **Input/Output management system** is also known as the BIOS or Basic Input/Output System. The computer hardware manufacturer supplies the I/O management system, because it needs to be tailored to suit the particular hardware in use. The I/O system communicates directly with the peripherals and handles the transfer of data between the peripherals and the processor. Some computers have their BIOS stored in flash ROM for ease of updating. We looked at flash ROM in chapters 2 and 3.

Process management – the kernel

The kernel is the part of the operating system responsible for **managing processes** and handling any interrupts. Interrupts are signals used by peripherals to communicate with the processor. You can read more about interrupts in chapter 2. The temporary suspension or blocking of the CLI, which we looked at earlier, is an example of how the operating system manages a process. On a single user system the operating system has only two processes to deal with, the user application and the operating system itself. The operating system has a great deal more process management to do in a multi-user environment such as a network operating system.

Resource allocation

Any **process** which is taking place in a computer system requires resources to be made available to it. A user program is an example of a process. This process requires a number of resources, for example, an area of the computer's memory, access to data in a device interface buffer, one or more files, and some part of the processor's time.

Resource allocation is the way of managing which of these resources is available for use at any one time by a process. Efficient resource allocation ensures that the processor is kept constantly busy, by maintaining a queue of processes that are always ready for the processor. The *scheduler* (which itself is a process) makes the decisions as to which process from the queue is given the processor's time.

Example

Here is a simplified explanation of one method that may be used by a scheduler.

A process may be in any one of several different states:

- *Running* – a process which has the processor's time
- *Ready* or *Free* – a process which could run if it had the processor's time
- *Blocked* – a process which cannot run because it is waiting for a resource which has been allocated to another process
- *Terminated* – a process which has finished.

A process which makes a request to use a printer, or is waiting for the user to click a mouse button, becomes blocked. A process which has just completed saving data to disk becomes ready.

When the current process becomes blocked, or terminates, then the scheduler is able to allocate to the processor a process which is free, until that process terminates or is blocked.

A computer with a single processor can only run one process at any given moment, regardless of how many processes are actually loaded at once. A computer with only one processor may *appear to the user* to be running two or more processes at the same time. However, what is actually happening is that the processor divides its time between each process, using a method called *time slicing*. Each process is given a *slice* of the processor's time, and the processor swaps processes in and out at very high speed so that it appears to be doing many tasks at once. If you could stop the processor at any single moment, you would only see one task being processed.

In addition, a process may be given a priority, for example, high or low. High priority processes may be given extra time slices, or be processed ahead of low priority processes in a queue.

A computer with multiple processors can run multiple processes simultaneously. How many simultaneous processes may be run depends upon the exact number of processors available. Remember from chapter 2 that a single silicon chip may have more than one physical processor, or 'core'.

Programs which can take full advantage of the presence of two or more processors in a computer system need to be specially written to do this. These programs allow the creation of processes which may be run simultaneously and are independent of one another so that no blocking can take place between processes. *Adobe Photoshop* is an example of a program which can be run in this manner on a dual processor machine.

Working in concert

Loading a file from backing storage involves the I/O management system and all the other layers of the operating system in a neatly choreographed sequence of operations which are too many to list here in detail. It's a bit like the idea of driving a car without appreciating what happens under the bonnet. Here is a simplified version:

Suppose the file that you wish to load is called *myfile*, and that it is stored on disk.

1. You issue the command to the CLI, OPEN, either by entering the instruction or by choosing from a menu.
2. The kernel suspends the current CLI process, and passes the request to the FMS.
3. The FMS requests the I/O system to read the disk's catalog track, and loads a list of the filenames.
4. The CLI allows the user to choose the filename from a list in a menu.
5. The FMS passes the physical location of the file to the I/O system.
6. The I/O system loads the file from disk and hands over to the MMS.
7. The MMS places the file in main memory.
8. The kernel allows the CLI process to resume, and you again have control of the computer.

Suggest how the above sequence of events might change if:

a. There was insufficient space in the computer's main memory to hold the file?
b. The application which created the file was not already present in main memory?

Utility programs

A **utility program** is a type of systems software designed to perform an everyday task, for example, transferring data from one backing storage device to another, or editing the contents of a disk directly using a disk editor. Some utilities are provided as part of the operating system program itself, such as a program to format a disk. Other utilities are separate programs.

Description of Utility Programs

Virus checker

Virus checking software is an essential utility. A virus is a rogue program written with the deliberate intention of causing damage to a computer system, perhaps by deleting data from backing storage or displaying foolish messages. What is special about a virus is that it can copy itself from one computer system to another, either by being carried on a removable disk, or through a network via email. Most viruses are specific to a computer's operating system, and many thousands of viruses have been written to infect the Windows operating system. The writing and distribution of viruses is a criminal offence under the **Computer Misuse Act** (1990).

Virus checking software should be able to detect a virus infection and remove it from a computer system. When copying a file from a disk or downloading a file from the Internet, the virus checking software should also check that the file does not contain a virus.

New viruses are constantly being written, so most companies which produce virus checking software allow the user to download updates to the software from the Internet. This ensures that the virus checking software is always up to date. An anti-virus program is shown in figure 5.3.

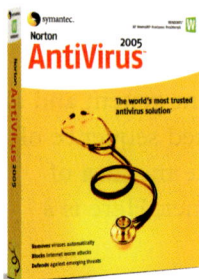

Figure 5.3 *Symantec Norton AntiVirus*

Disc editor

A **disc editor** allows the user to edit data directly on the surface of a disk, by-passing the normal loading and saving features of the operating system. This a very powerful feature, but must be used with caution, since you run the risk of completely destroying all your data if you do not know what you are doing.

However, most disc editor programs incorporate automatic *disk repair* functions, which will repair a damaged disk and recover any data.

A disk repair program is essential for all serious computer users. Regardless of how many backups you keep, there is always going to be one occasion when a message like 'This disk is unreadable – would you like to initialise it' appears. If this happens to you, and you have not kept a backup copy of your files, then possibly the only way to recover your valuable data is to use a disk repair program.

Disk repair programs repair any mistakes, usually in the disk catalog, which prevent you from accessing your files. If you had the foresight to install the disk repair program on your computer before the disk error took place, then you would have had a much better chance of recovering your files, because most disk repair programs save their own duplicate copy of the disk catalog, which can speed up the recovery process.

Some developments in this area are designed to reduce the chances of disk damage and data loss:

Disk journaling is a type of filing system which writes changes to a special area set aside on a disk, called a *journal*, before writing them to the main filing system. This reduces the chance of data being lost, because the File Management System can use the journaling information to help restore the disk catalog to the last known good state in the event of a crash. One disadvantage of journaling is that it takes slightly longer to write a file to disk because more data is being written.

Smart disk is a monitoring and self-analysis feature built in to many new hard disks which can report the condition of the hard disk and gives notice of when, or if, it is likely to fail.

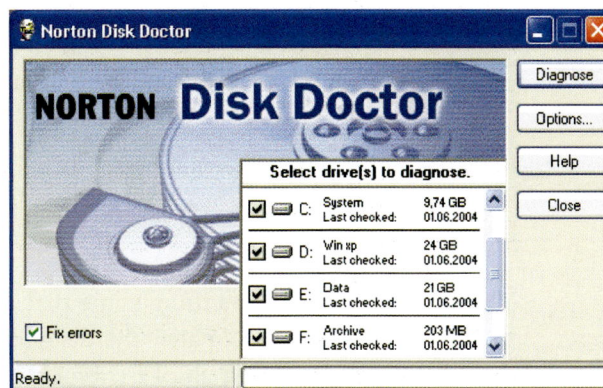

Figure 5.4 *A disk repair program*

Defragmenter

Filing systems try to save files in adjacent blocks on a disk, but as files are saved and deleted through time, it is not always possible. Eventually not enough disk space remains to save files in this manner and parts of files on disk become scattered across the surface of the disk. One effect of this is to increase the amount of time taken for file access.

A **defragmenter** program allows you to **defragment** your disk. This is a useful feature, because it gathers all the free space on the disk together and reunites scattered file fragments. This process may result in an improvement in the performance of the disk, especially if it is nearly full. A typical hard disk, for example 100 *Gigabytes* capacity, may take many hours to defragment, depending upon how much data is on the disk, how fragmented it is to begin with, the speed of the hard disk and the overall performance of the computer system. Figure 5.5 shows a diagram of a very small part of a disk before and after defragmentation.

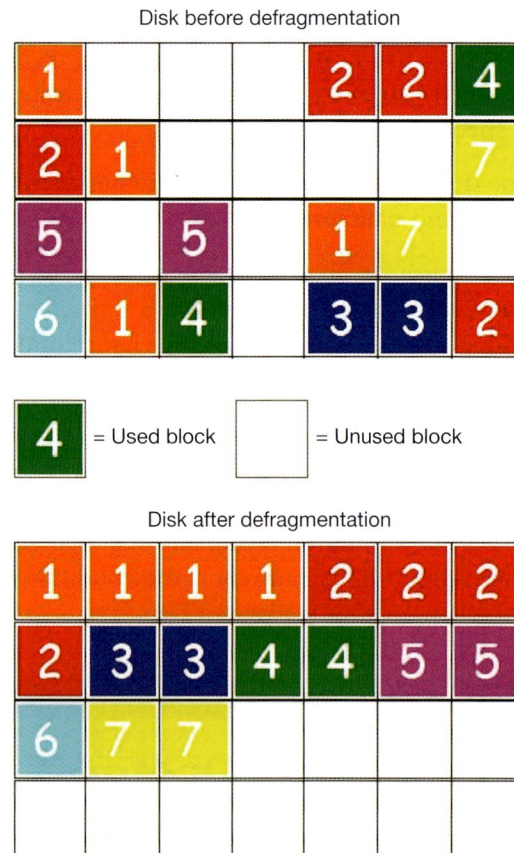

Figure 5.5 *A diagram of the disk defragmentation process*

The reason why defragmenting some disks may help to improve their performance is that the smaller the distance the read-write head on the disk drive has to move to find all of the blocks of a file, the faster the file will load. If the blocks of each file are immediately adjacent to one another, then the speed of loading a file will improve compared to loading the same file if each block was scattered across the surface of the disk.

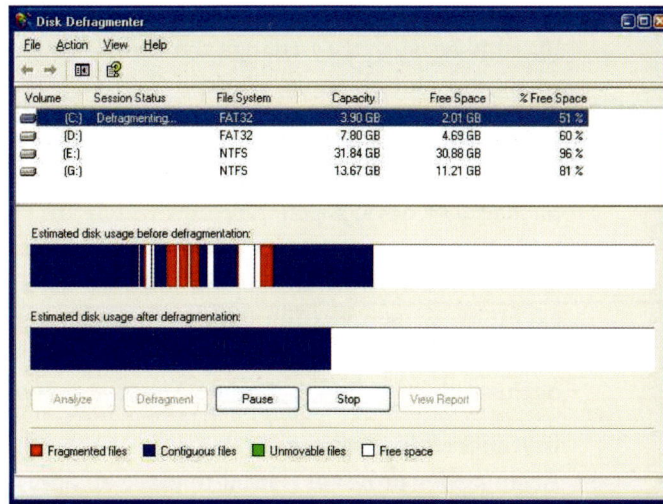

Figure 5.6 *Defragmenting a disk using the disk defragmenter program built in to Windows XP*

Other types of utility software

Backup

If you **backup** your files regularly, then you shouldn't need to worry too much about disk recovery programs. Backup software can help to automate the process of making regular backups. Backup software allows you to select the type of backup media, for example removable disk or tape. Other choices include the frequency of backup, for instance daily or weekly, and the scheduled time for the backup to take place, such as overnight.

Backup software may also allow you to *synchronise* files between two devices or media. Synchronising files means that where the same files exist on separate media, except that one of the files has a more recent modification date, then the newer copy will replace the older file. This same technique is used when a palmtop computer is linked to a desktop or laptop computer.

Emulators

An **emulator** is a program that allows one computer (the host) to behave as if it were a completely different type of computer. An emulator allows software to be used on a type of computer other than the type it was designed for.

A computer running an emulator is normally much slower than the computer it is trying to emulate because of the extra processing involved. It is therefore advisable to use a machine with a fast processor and lots of RAM to get the best performance from emulator programs.

One example of an emulator is *Virtual PC*, which allows Apple Macintosh computers to emulate a PC by running the *Windows*™ operating system. One additional benefit of this particular set-up is that the PC software runs in a screen window on the Macintosh desktop. This makes it easy to transfer data between application packages running on both systems.

Converters, compressors and expanders

Converters. All applications save the files that they create in a unique format. It is often impossible to take a file created by one application package and simply load it into another package. Data converters can help to solve problems like this because they change the format of a data file from one application type to another, for example, *Graphic Converter*.

Compressors/Expanders. Data compression allows the size of a data file to be reduced. Data compression is commonly used in situations where application packages or devices generate files which are very large, for example graphics and video data, to save backing storage space. Another use for data compression is to reduce network traffic and improve the speed of data transmission, for example, by compressing a file before sending it via the Internet. On receipt, an expander program may be used to restore the file to its original size. Examples of this type of software include *Stuffit* and *WinZip*.

Installers/Uninstallers

An **installer** program is used to place an application package or an operating system on a computer's hard disk. Current application packages may take up hundreds of *Megabytes* of backing storage space. For this reason, many installer programs provide the user with the option of a full installation, a custom installation or a minimal installation. This allows the user to choose the most suitable option for their particular system. Installer programs often provide a helpful interface to the user. This is called a **wizard** and it guides the user through the various choices they may have to make during the installation process.

An **uninstaller** program is used to remove an application package from a computer system. Because of the complexity of current software, uninstalling a program involves more than just deleting a file or a directory. The installation process may have added new fonts to the system, for example. A good uninstall program will remove all traces of a particular piece of software from a computer system.

Printer drivers

Printers can produce many different printing styles, such as <u>underline</u>, **bold**, *italic*, and different typefaces, such as TIMES, HELVETICA, COURIER, BOOKMAN.

Before a printer can produce these effects, it must have the correct code sent to it from the computer. The code required for any given effect is different depending on the type of printer that is in use. For example, one code may produce **bold** print on a BROTHER laser printer and the same code may produce *italic* print on an EPSON ink jet printer.

To overcome this problem, **printer driver** programs have been developed. A printer driver takes the codes used in the document, and translates them into the appropriate code for the type of printer in use. If the user has access to a monochrome laser printer via the office network, and a stand-alone colour ink jet printer attached to their own computer, then all they need do is to select the correct printer driver.

When you buy a new printer, it is usually accompanied by a CD-ROM containing the printer driver and any associated files such as additional typefaces. The printer driver program must be installed before the printer can be used. If the printer has to be used on a peer-to-peer network, then each of the individual stations on the network must have the printer driver installed. Once installed, then the user must select the correct printer driver for the printer they require.

Email and web filters

An **email filter** is a piece of software that monitors emails which are sent on a network. The **Regulation of Investigatory Powers Act (2000)** is a law which, among other provisions, gives employers the right to monitor messages sent by employees on the company computers. In a school email system, emails containing unsuitable language may be filtered out. Most email programs allow the user to set up a filter to automatically delete unsolicited email messages. It is inadvisable to open any email which is sent to your mailbox unless you are certain of its origin, because email is one of the principal ways in which viruses are transmitted.

A **web filter** monitors the URLs and the content of web pages being accessed by a user, and may be set up to prevent access to unsuitable material. Some web browsers can also be set up to provide web filtering.

On a school network, it is particularly important to monitor pupil access. One method is for the system administrator to set up lists of allowed and denied web sites. Some filtering software will lock or prevent the user from accessing the Internet if they have more than a set number of violations involving sites on the denied list.

System administrators must strike a careful balance in their choices if they are not to make the system frustrating to use. One example of how strict web filters can be was brought home to a pupil who was prevented from viewing the bottom half of a shoe shop's web page because it contained a graphic of a ladies sandal.

Figure 5.7

File formats

Whenever an application package is used to create and save a file to backing storage on an *Apple Macintosh* computer, some additional information is saved within the file besides its normal data. This additional information is called the **resource fork**. The resource fork contains type and creator information, which is used by the operating system of the computer to identify the application which created the file in the first place.

Files saved on a computer running the *Windows* operating system do not have any additional information saved in order to identify their creator application. Instead, a file on a PC is recognised by its file name extension. File name extensions follow the file name and usually consist of three letters, for instance .TXT, .JPG, .DOC, .TIF, .GIF

Whichever system is used, when the user wishes to load the file again, then all they need do is issue the command, and the operating system will automatically load the file and the application program which created it.

All application packages have their own particular file type. Software manufacturers, however, have always recognised that users can increase their productivity and reduce their workload if it is possible to save files and data in such a way as to ease the transfer of data between different packages. For these reasons, various **standard file formats** have been developed and adopted. In the same manner as standard interfaces allow interconnection between devices from different manufacturers, so it is with software. If two application packages are capable of saving or loading files in a standard file format, then it is easy to transfer data between them.

As an example, the word processing package I am using has 88 different file formats for saving its files. Just like programming language translators, this word processing package possesses translators for different file formats.

Each type of application software has its own set of **standard file formats**. Here are some examples of standard file formats:

GIF (Graphics Interchange Format)

GIF is a format for storing bit-map colour graphics images as files. The data in these files is compressed making them faster to load and transfer via the Internet. GIF images are limited to 256 colours. GIF is designed to handle images such as logos or line drawings which contain large blocks of the same colour or repeating patterns. The GIF standard also allows *interlaced* images, which means that a low quality version of the image can be displayed whilst the rest of the data is still being transmitted. You may have noticed this effect while waiting for a web page to appear on screen. Simple animations can also be stored and transmitted in GIF format. GIF supports transparency, which means that each pixel in the image may be fully transparent (to let the web page underneath show through) or fully opaque. GIF uses lossless compression, which means that no detail in the original image is lost when it is compressed.

JPEG

The **Joint Photographic Experts Group** has defined standards for still picture compression, and this format is called JPEG. JPEG is designed for either full colour or greyscale images of natural scenes. JPEG uses 24 bits per pixel to store RGB colour images, allowing 16.7 million possible colours to be represented. JPEG works well on photographs, but not so well on line drawings, lettering or logos. JPEG handles only still images, MPEG is used for motion pictures. JPEG files are compressed to save backing storage space, anywhere between 2 : 1 and 30 : 1. JPEG uses lossy compression, which means that some detail is lost from the image. However, the amount of compression used may be changed, allowing a trade-off between file size and image quality.

TIFF (Tag(ged) Image File Format)

TIFF is a format used for high resolution bitmapped images, although TIFF files may be any resolution. TIFF files are large, and are not used on web pages, unlike JPEG or GIF, because of the time taken to download them. TIFF is an uncompressed file format. TIFF is widely used in applications such as *Photoshop*, Desktop Publishing and scanning. TIFF files are used when a high quality image is required, for example when printing a photograph for publication in a book or a magazine. Every photographic image in this book was supplied to the publisher in TIFF.

Description of a suitable selection of software to support typical tasks

Author's Note: A description of hardware associated with these tasks may be found in chapter 3

Production of a multimedia catalogue

A multimedia catalogue is a database of products or items, which contains a variety of media, such as sound, graphics and video.

The following software would be appropriate to support this task.

Multimedia authoring software, or a database which allows the inclusion of different multimedia elements, would be appropriate to create the catalogue itself. Multimedia authoring software ranges from easy to learn packages like *Hyperstudio*, to major applications like *Macromedia Director*.

There is not enough space in this chapter to explain all of the features of an application like *Macromedia Director*. A visit to www.macromedia.com will provide more information. Similarly, www.hyperstudio.com contains information about that application.

A database which allowed multimedia elements to be included may fulfil the requirements of the task, but the degree of interaction available to the user would be limited to the sorting and searching available within the database application itself. An authoring package enables the designer to use its built-in scripting language to create a stand-alone application with virtually any feature included.

Additional software may be required to edit the individual media elements before they are incorporated into the catalogue. Video editing, sound and graphics editing software, together with a word processing package or a text editor may be required.

Figure 5.8 *Hyperstudio and Macromedia Director*

After the catalogue has been created, then software would be required to transfer the multimedia catalogue to an appropriate distribution medium, such as CD or DVD. Most computer systems which have CD or DVD writers built in, have the appropriate writing software as a part of the operating system. Alternatively, the catalogue may be published as a series of web pages.

Setting up a LAN in a school

The following software would be appropriate to support this task.

Any modern operating system should be capable of peer-to-peer networking. If a client-server network is to be set up, then file server software is required. Typical server software includes: *Microsoft Windows Server* and *Mac OS X Server*. The choice of server software is governed by the type of hardware used for the file server, but both of the examples given here are capable of acting as a server for *PC* and *Macintosh* clients.

In a school with a number of different platforms, it is common to see both types of server being used. If the server was being set up in a single school department, then it is more likely that the computers in the department all share the same platform and the choice of server hardware and software would be matched to that platform.

If other types of server were required, such as database servers, then specific software would also be needed. *Microsoft SQL Server* is one such application, and database packages like *FileMaker Pro* are available in both single user versions and server versions.

Development of a school website

The following software would be appropriate to support this task.

The essential requirement for creation of a school website is appropriate web page creation software. Virtually any software which can create web pages is capable of allowing the creation of a website. However, specialist web creation software may contain a wider range of operations, such as WYSIWYG page editing.

Once again, the packages available range from relatively straightforward applications, like *Microsoft FrontPage*, to packages like *Dreamweaver*. The choice depends upon the degree of complexity of the task to be carried out and the expertise of the website designer. The departmental part of the school website may contain features like on-line multiple choice tests with customised *Flash* or *Shockwave* animation. A more sophisticated piece of software would make it easier for the designer to create this type of feature, compared to a simple set of web pages with no interactivity.

Additional software may be required to edit the individual media elements before they are incorporated into the website. A bit-mapped graphics package, such as a photo editing application would be useful to prepare images before they are incorporated into the web pages. A word processing package may be used to edit text or set up tables.

One other item of software which is important in the development of a website is a browser. A browser would be used at the development stage to view the web pages as they were being created. A range of different browsers would be useful to test the appearance and function of the website which should be designed to operate ideally in all browsers and on all platforms. The simpler the web site, the easier it is to be sure that it will operate successfully on another browser or platform.

Description and exemplification of software compatibility issues

Software which runs on a particular computer system is said to be **compatible** with that system. There are a number of **issues which affect software compatibility**. Software compatibility issues include: **memory requirements**, **storage requirements** and **OS compatibility**.

Memory requirements

RAM is used to hold the programs and data in a computer system while they are being processed. As operating systems and programs become more complex, the demands for more RAM increase. The **technical guide**[2] for an application specifies the amount of RAM required by the application. Sometimes the requirements are expressed in terms of *free RAM*. This refers to the amount of RAM which is unused or unoccupied after the operating system has been loaded. If there is insufficient free RAM then the program cannot be loaded and therefore cannot run.

If insufficient RAM is available to hold a complete program, then part of the program may be stored on disk and swapped in and out of the RAM when required. This is called *virtual memory*. Using virtual memory slows down processing because it is around a thousand times slower to access data from disk than from RAM. The best method of solving this problem is to add more RAM. It is a good idea when purchasing a new computer, to include as much RAM as you can afford.

Storage requirements

The storage requirements refers to the amount of backing storage space which is required to hold the software after it has been installed. This is also specified in the technical guide for the software. Some application programs require hundreds of megabytes of backing storage space in order to install them on your computer system. Because of this, such programs usually offer a range of installation options – a full or *complete installation, customised* or a *minimal installation*. The minimal installation is useful if your computer system has a limited amount of free backing storage space, or you do not need to use every feature of the application. The customised installation option allows the user to choose which parts of the software are installed. If the software is supplied on CD-ROM or DVD-ROM, then anything less than a full installation may

---

[2] A technical guide explains how to install the software on to a computer system. It lists the type of computer systems(s) upon which the software will run, and the installation requirements. Installation requirements include the type and version of operating system, amount of free memory needed, amount of backing storage space required and type and clock speed of the processor. You can read more about the technical guide in chapter 6.

sometimes require the CD or DVD to be inserted into the computer each time the program is run.

A program called a *wizard* is often used to guide the user through the process of installing software. The wizard normally contains code which checks whether or not there is sufficient backing storage space before it will permit the installation to proceed.

Figure 5.9 *Operating systems logos*

OS compatibility

The three main types of operating system used on desktop and laptop computers are *Windows*, *Unix* and *Mac OS*. Software which is **OS compatible** is suitable for one type of operating system only, and will not run on any other. Recognising this, many software companies supply more than one version of their products, sometimes on the same installation CD-ROM or DVD-ROM. The wizard on the disk may be programmed to automatically recognise the type of computer, and automatically install the correct version.

Like any other software, operating systems are constantly under development, and new versions appear regularly. Some programs are only compatible with a particular version of the operating system, for instance, current software may

Figure 5.10 *Software Compatibility*

require some of the features of *Windows XP* in order to run and will not operate on a machine with an older version of the operating system such as *Windows 98*. The reverse applies in some cases. If you have a new computer, then it is possible that some of the existing applications from your old computer may not work.

Distinction between a virus, a worm and a Trojan horse

A **virus** is a program which can destroy or cause damage to data stored on a computer system. What is commonly known as **viruses** also includes **worms** and **Trojan horses**. What distinguishes a worm from a virus is that a worm can make copies of itself and spread between computers without having to be attached to a file, unlike a virus, which infects other *host* files and is distributed along with them. What distinguishes a Trojan horse from a virus is that a Trojan horse is disguised as another type of file, in some cases even pretending to be an anti-virus utility program. People group viruses, worms and Trojans together and call them *malicious software* or *malware*, because of the effects this type of software can have.

Note that other programs installed without the user's knowledge or consent also come into the category of malware. This includes *spyware*, which secretly gathers information and relays it to advertisers or other interested parties, *browser hijackers*, which redirect a browser's home page to another site, and *re-diallers*, which transfer dial-up users onto premium rate telephone lines.

Figure 5.11 *Worms*

Virus

A **virus** program must be run in order to infect a computer system. Viruses can attach themselves to other programs in order to ensure that this happens. A virus can cause an infected computer to do strange things, for instance, disabling the operation and booting up of a computer, perhaps by interfering with the disk catalogue.

Common symptoms of virus infection include:

- displaying unwanted messages
- unusual visual or sound effects
- loss of data from a storage medium
- computers restarting unexpectedly
- unwanted generation of emails.

Viruses can:

- corrupt or delete data
- disable the computer by changing the operating system
- cause silly messages to be displayed or sounds to be produced
- generate so many email messages that they cause email servers to crash or be shut down
- record every key pressed on the user's keyboard, and send the keystrokes, including your passwords, to the virus writer's computer

- use your computer to attack other computers by generating spam or overloading a company website with data. You may be held to be liable to others if this happens.

Viruses are spread through file downloads or infected storage media such as floppy disks. Suppose a spreadsheet program was infected with a virus. Each time the spreadsheet program runs, the virus runs, too, and it can reproduce by attaching to other programs. The first ever virus to infect other computers was called *Elk Cloner* and was written by Rich Skrenta in 1982. *Elk Cloner* infected the Apple operating system and was spread by floppy disk.

Worm

Worms operate differently to viruses. A **worm** can spread itself to other computers without needing to be transferred as part of a *host* program. In the Star Trek episode, *The Trouble with Tribbles*, these small furry creatures just kept replicating over and over again (if you perform an Internet search for 'tribbles' you will find images from this episode). Worms act much the same way. The first time a user may notice the presence of a worm is when the computer's memory unexpectedly fills up.

Worms generally come through email, but computers can also become infected by a Trojan horse containing a worm. This sends the worm out to everyone in the computer's email address book. In a large company or a school, hundreds of computers could be infected.

Example of an email worm

Mimail.I and *Mimail.J* are email worms which disguise themselves as an email from the Paypal on-line payment service and try to steal credit card information. This method of fraud is known as *phishing*. *Phishing* is an attempt to trick someone into giving away personal information using the Internet by pretending to be a well-known company.

Figure 5.12 *Phishing*

Trojan horses

The term **Trojan horse**, or just **Trojan**, is used to refer to a program that appears to be safe, but hidden inside is usually something harmful, like a worm or a virus. For instance, you may download a game or a picture, but once you run the file, the worm or virus gets to work. Sometimes Trojans will only provide a nuisance to the user by displaying a message, but usually a worm or virus hidden inside will cause damage to a computer system. A *backdoor Trojan* may be placed on your computer by a virus. Once in place, the person who sent the Trojan can take control of your computer over the Internet. One of the most common uses of backdoor Trojans is to make your computer into a source of spam email messages.

Figure 5.13 *The story of the wooden horse is thousands of years old. The story tells how Greek soldiers hid inside the horse and were able to capture the city of Troy.*

Example of malware

The '*I Love You*' virus is an example of all three types of '*malware*':

- It's a **Trojan horse** because it came disguised as a 'Love Letter' when it was carrying a harmful program.
- It's a **virus** because it infected files, turning them into new Trojan horses.
- It's a **worm** because it copied itself by sending itself out to everyone listed in the computer's email address book or Internet Relay Chat client software.

This type of attack is known as a *blended threat* because it uses a variety of techniques to increase the spread and the severity of the infection.

Figure 5.14 *The 'I Love You' virus*

Classification of viruses by type of file infected

Viruses may be classified by the *types of file which they infect*. Viruses may infect **files**, the **boot sector** on a disk, or a document which contains a **macro**.

File viruses

File viruses are so called because they attach themselves to files. They either replace or insert malicious code into the files. The types of files that are usually infected are those with the extensions .COM and .EXE.

Boot sector viruses

Every disk drive, both hard and floppy, contains a boot sector, whether or not the disk is bootable. The boot sector contains information about the format of the disk and a small program – the boot code. The boot code is a program which can be infected by a virus. By infecting this code, a boot sector virus can guarantee it gets run. Boot sector infections start when an infected disk is left in a PC's floppy drive and the machine is rebooted. When the viral boot code is read from the boot sector and executed, the virus infects the hard drive and remains resident in memory, lying in wait for uninfected boot sectors to become available, usually on other floppy disks. Boot sector virus infections have become less common now that software is distributed on CD-ROM, which is read-only.

Macro viruses

Programs like *Microsoft Word* and *Microsoft Excel* allow the user to create and embed **macros** in a document to automate a sequence of operations. A **macro virus** is a computer virus that infects a document and causes a malicious sequence of actions to be performed when the document is opened. A macro virus will also infect any new documents created by the same application. A macro virus can have a number of effects from putting up strange messages to destroying data. Macro viruses cannot affect documents created by applications which do not support macros.

One particularly harmful feature of macro viruses is that they can infect computers running different operating systems and platforms. For instance, a macro virus in a Microsoft Word document can infect users of *Microsoft Word* on *Apple Macintosh* computers as well as computers running the *Microsoft Windows* operating system.

Description of virus code actions

Viruses act differently according to how they are programmed. The **actions** that the program code in the virus may carry out when run include: **replication**, **camouflage**, **watching** and **delivery**.

Replication

A worm can make copies of itself. This is known as **replication**.

Camouflage

Viruses use a variety of methods to camouflage their existence. One method is to create false programming code mixed with good code. Each time the virus runs it changes the false code to avoid detection by an anti-virus program. Trojans attempt to avoid detection by appearing to be just another harmless program.

Watching

A virus can lie in wait or **watch** for a particular action or date before it is activated. The longer the time before activation, the greater the number of computer systems which will be potentially infected. A virus which watches for a date is called a *time bomb*, and a virus which waits for an action to take place is known as a *logic bomb*.

Delivery

The **delivery** of a virus is the method used by the virus in order to enter the computer system and cause the infection. Infected floppy disks used to be the most common method of delivery of viruses. Sharing infected floppy disks among computers would deliver a virus to each machine. Nowadays viruses are spread in seconds over computer networks, and in some cases, security flaws in the computer's operating system can allow viruses to infect your computer through the Internet connection, without you having to do anything. Email is now the main delivery method, along with file sharing and instant messaging. If you receive a message from an unknown address, DO NOT OPEN IT – DELETE IT IMMEDIATELY. This applies even more to messages which contain attachments. The act of clicking on the email to open it can allow a virus to enter your computer.

Description of anti-virus software detection techniques

Anti-virus software detection techniques include **use of checksum, searching for virus signature**, **heuristic detection** and **memory resident monitoring**.

Use of checksum

A **checksum** is a value calculated for a given set of data, and is normally used to check that data has been transmitted and received correctly. A calculation is done using the numbers in the original data. The answer to this calculation is the checksum. The checksum is transmitted along with the data, and the calculation is repeated after the data has been received, producing another checksum. Both checksums are compared to see if they match. If they do match, then the received data is correct. If they don't match, then an error has occurred, and the data will need to be transmitted again.

This same method may be applied to check for the presence of a virus. A checksum is performed on an uninfected program. Repeating the calculation on a suspect program allows the anti-virus software to test if the program has been changed, and if so, it will issue a warning that the program may be infected with a virus.

Searching for virus signature

Anti-virus programs can find viruses inside programs by scanning them for **virus signatures**. A **virus signature** is a characteristic pattern or sequence of bytes that is part of a virus. If a virus scanner finds such a pattern in a file, it notifies the user that the file is infected. The user can then delete or perhaps 'disinfect' the infected file. Some viruses employ techniques that make detection by means of signatures more difficult. These *polymorphic viruses* have the ability to modify their code on each infection, so that each infected file contains a different variant of the virus.

Heuristic detection

Heuristic detection is a method of finding viruses by using a *heuristic* or *rule of thumb* – what we would call having a general idea of what a virus looks like. Heuristic detection is a less precise method of virus detection than any of the others in this section. Heuristics allow rules to be set up to detect new viruses that have not been seen before – for example – if it looks like a virus, and behaves like a virus, then it probably *is* a virus. Many anti-virus programs allow the user to set the sensitivity of the heuristic rules, and these may also be turned off altogether.

Memory resident monitoring

Memory resident software loads into the computer when it is started up and stays in the computer's memory until it is shut down again. Anti-virus software does this in order to constantly check or **monitor** the computer for the presence of viruses. Memory resident monitoring can slow down the operation of the computer while checking for viruses.

Hoaxes

A hoax is not a virus; it is a report of a non-existent virus. Usually a hoax will carry a warning message and urge you to forward the warning to everyone in your email address book. If you do forward the message, then the resultant deluge of email can overload mail servers and cause them to crash. The effect of the hoax is real, but the person who started the hoax has not created a virus. Hoaxes cannot be detected or disabled by anti-virus software, because they are not viruses.

Example of a hoax virus warning

```
Dear all,

Please take this email seriously. I just received this
message,checked my C drive for it and found the virus.

Message to repair: I found out that I had this virus resident on
my hard drive and chances are that you have it too since you are
all in my address book. This virus lies dormant for 14 days and
then kills your hard drive. Here is how to stop it! If you've got
it, send this letter to everyone in your address book.

Remove it by following these steps:
```

1. Go to 'start', then to 'find or search' (depending on your computer.)
2. In the 'search for files or folders' type sulfnbk.exe – This is the virus.
3. In the 'look in' make sure you are searching drive 'C'.
4. Hit the 'search or find' button.
5. If this file shows up (it's an ugly blackish icon that will have the name sulfnbk.exe) – DO NOT OPEN IT!!
6. RIGHT click on the blackish icon – go down to 'delete' and left click it.
7. It will ask you if you want to send it to the recycle bin. Say yes.
8. Go to your desktop (where all the icons are) and double click on the Recycle Bin.
9. RIGHT click on the 'sulfnbk.exe' and delete again – or empty the bin.

The file *sulfnbk.exe* is actually a normal operating system file and is harmless.

Some virus statistics

The *Code Red* worm infected every vulnerable computer on the Internet within 14 hours; the *Slammer* worm did the same in 20 minutes. A virus spread by instant messaging could infect half a million computers in just 30 seconds.

Virus attacks increased from 1,334 reported attacks in 1993 to 137,529 in 2003.

Viruses cost businesses around the world $55 billion in 2003, up from $13 billion in 2001.

Questions

1. What is an operating system?
2. When does the operating system program run?
3. State one difference between a ROM-based operating system and a disk-based operating system (other than their storage media).
4. One model of an operating system describes it in terms of five layers.
   a. Name each layer and briefly describe its function.
   b. What part would each layer of the operating system play if the command was given to save a file to disk?
   c. Suppose that the operating system returned the message 'Unable to save this file'. Suggest one possible reason why such an error may have occurred.
   d. Which layer of the operating system reports error messages to the user?

5. If a disk-based operating system must be loaded into the computer's main memory before it can be used, how is this possible at start-up?
6. Name one item of utility software that you have used which is:
   a. built in to the operating system program that you use
   b. a separate piece of software from the operating system program.
7. If a system requirement typical application package states '*256 Megabytes of free RAM required for application*':
   a. Would this application work in a machine with 256 Megabytes of RAM in total?
   b. Why would additional RAM be required in this situation?

8. What is the function of a bootstrap loader?

9. Where is a bootstrap loader stored?

10. What is resource allocation?

11. Give an example of process management.

12. Draw a diagram of a hierarchical filing system, based on two sub-directories and five files of your own choice.

13. What is a utility program?

14. Describe the function of a:
    a. virus checker
    b. disk editor
    c. defragmenter.

15. a. Under what circumstances might you use a defragmenter?
    b. Draw a diagram of the defragmentation process.

16. Name three standard file formats for graphics files.

17. What does
    a. JPEG
    b. GIF
    c. TIFF
    stand for?

18. What is the maximum number of colours available in:
    a. JPEG?
    b. GIF?

19. a. What is software compatibility?
    b. What issues affect software compatibility?
    c. What advantage is it to a user buying a piece of software to be able to see the system requirements on the outside of the box?
    d. What would you expect to see listed in such a description?

20. An author wishes to send a graphics file to her publisher to be printed in a new book.
    a. Which graphics format should she choose?
    b. State one disadvantage of the graphics format you have chosen.
    c. The author would like a copy of the same graphic to be displayed on the publisher's web site. What graphics format should she choose?

    d. State one disadvantage of the file format you have chosen.
    e. Which graphics file format offers variable compression?
    f. Why is this an advantage?

21. A user attempts to install a piece of software only to find that it will not install and that the operating system displays a message to that effect.
    a. Suggest a reason why the software cannot be installed.
    b. The user tries to install another software package and is successful. However, once installed, the software will not run. Suggest a reason why the software will not run.
    c. The user decides to delete the newly installed software. State two operating system functions that are involved in the deletion and describe the role that each function plays.

22. What is a virus?

23. Name three types of virus.

24. What is a worm?

25. What is a Trojan horse?

26. State one difference between a:
    a. worm and a virus
    b. Trojan horse and a virus.

27. Name four virus code actions.

28. Describe the following anti-virus software detection techniques:
    a. use of checksum
    b. searching for virus signature
    c. heuristic detection
    d. memory resident monitoring.

29. a. What is a blended threat?
    b. Give one example of a virus which posed a blended threat when it was released.

30. What action should you take upon receiving an email from an unknown address?

• Key points •

- The operating system is a program that controls the entire operation of the computer and any devices which are attached to it.
- The bootstrap loader's function is to load the rest of the operating system from disk when the computer is switched on.
- A single user operating system is only capable of being used by one person at a time.
- The main functions of a single user operating system are:
  - interpreting users commands
  - file management
  - memory management
  - input/output management
  - managing processes
  - resource allocation.
- The Command Language Interpreter is the layer with which the user interacts in order to give instructions to the computer – it interprets user commands.
- The Memory Management System controls where programs and data are placed in main memory.
- The Memory Management System keeps track of the total amount of main memory available, and which programs and data are currently loaded.
- The File Management System is concerned with the efficient use of the computer's backing storage devices and media.
- The Input/Output management system communicates directly with the peripherals and handles the transfer of data between the peripherals and the processor.
- The kernel is the part of the operating system responsible for managing processes and handling any interrupts.
- Resource allocation is the way of managing which resource is available for use at any one time by a process.
- Efficient resource allocation ensures that the processor is kept constantly busy, by maintaining a queue of processes that are always ready for the processor.

- A utility program is a type of systems software designed to perform an everyday task, like formatting a disk.
- Examples of utility software include: virus checker, disc editor, defragmenter.
- Standard file formats have been developed to ease the transfer of data between different packages.
- Each type of application software has its own set of standard file formats.
- Some examples of standard file formats are GIF (Graphics Interchange Format), JPEG (Joint Photographic Experts Group) and TIFF (Tag Image File Format).
- Software which works on a particular computer system is said to be compatible.
- Issues which affect software compatibility include: memory requirements, storage requirements and OS compatibility.
- A virus is a program which can destroy or cause damage to data stored on a computer system.
- A virus infects other host files and is distributed along with them.
- A worm can make copies of itself and spread between computers without having to be attached to a file.
- A Trojan horse is disguised as another type of file.
- Viruses may be classified by the types of file which they infect.
- Viruses may infect files, the boot sector on a disk, or a document which contains a macro.
- Viruses act differently according to how they are programmed.
- The actions that the program code in the virus may carry out when run include: replication, camouflage, watching and delivery.
- Anti-virus software detection techniques include use of checksum, searching for virus signature, heuristic detection and memory resident monitoring.

Unit 2

Software Development

This chapter, and the three which follow, are part of the Software Development unit.

In this unit, the programming language or languages you will use, are known as your selected **software development environment**. The kind of software development environment you use will depend on what is available in your school or centre. The examples given in this chapter use a software development environment based mainly on high level languages such as COMAL, VISUAL BASIC and TRUE BASIC.

It should be noted that this book is not a programming manual. Your teacher or lecturer will provide support material tailored to your particular software development environment.

6 The Software Development Process

The **Software Development Process** may be divided into seven stages. These are:

1. Analysis
2. Design
3. Implementation
4. Testing
5. Documentation
6. Evaluation
7. Maintenance

In this chapter, we will consider each of these stages in turn. Instead of looking at each stage on its own, we will work through one or more software development problems and use them to exemplify each stage. You will be expected to know about and apply each of the stages of the software development process to any problem that you are given.

1. Analysis

Analysis first of all involves reading and understanding a problem. If you are set a problem in class, you should read the problem several times and think about it carefully. It often helps to write out the problem in your own words. Sometimes the problem contains parts which are not very clear, and you will have to make some assumptions about what you think is meant by these parts of the problem. Eventually you will get to the stage where you will be able to write down a precise **software specification**.

It is very important that the software specification is correct, since mistakes at this stage can be very costly to put right later on in the software development process. The software specification is a clear unambiguous statement of the problem and forms the basis of a legal contract.

Here is an example of what could happen if a software specification is not correct:

A farmer commissioned a software company to write a database program to store details of his herd of cattle. The maximum size was to be 1000 records. Cow number 1000 had a calf. The farmer entered the new calf's details into the program and the program crashed. Who was to blame? Was it the software company for not anticipating that the herd of cattle would increase in size or was it the farmer's fault for agreeing to the maximum size of 1000 records? In any case, if the program matched the software specification correctly, then the software company would still be entitled to be paid for their work.

Figure 6.1 *The software specification forms the basis of a legal contract between the client and the software company*

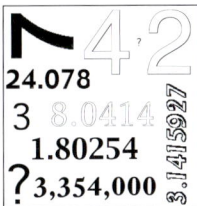

Figure 6.2 *Numbers*

Consider the following problem outline:

Average Problem

Write a program which calculates and displays the average of a set of numbers.

This could hardly be described as a precise software specification. If you, as a programmer, were given this task you would need to ask some questions before you could begin to design a solution.

Questions you may ask about the *Average Problem*:

How many numbers are in the set?
What is the maximum value of a number?
Are numbers to be whole numbers (integers) or numbers with a fractional part (real numbers)?
To how many significant figures should the average value be displayed?
How are numbers to be obtained as input to the program? (e.g. should the program ask the user to enter each number every time the program is run?)
Are any of the numbers entered to be stored after the program is complete?
What output device(s) are to be used? (i.e. display on screen or hard copy to printer)

If there is no one available to ask for clarification of a problem, then you should examine the problem carefully and write down some assumptions.

For the *Average Problem*, these assumptions might be:

The maximum amount of numbers is 10.
The minimum value of a number is 1.
The maximum value of a number is 100.

All the numbers are whole numbers, apart from the average, which has to be displayed correct to two decimal places.

Putting these assumptions together with the original Average Problem, would give a precise software specification, which would be of use to a programmer.

Hopefully any programming problem which you are given to solve will be much better specified than the original *Average Problem*.

The next step in problem analysis involves identifying the problem **inputs**, the **process**(es) and the problem **outputs**. To do this you would write down the three headings: Input, Process and Output and use the information given in the problem to complete a table like the one below.

Table 6.1 *Example table for the Average Problem:*

Input	Process	Output
A maximum of 10 numbers (integers), within a range of 0 to 100	Calculate the average (sum the numbers and divide the total by the amount of numbers)	Display the average value (a real number, correct to two decimal places)

Figure 6.3 *COBOL*

Analysis practice questions

Analyse the following problem outlines and produce a precise software specification by writing down any assumptions that need to be made and identifying the problem inputs, process(es) and outputs.

(a) Write a program which will ask the user for two numbers and give their sum (+), product (*) and quotient (/).

(b) Write a program which will take in a word of up to fifteen letters and display it on the screen backwards.

(c) Write a program which will only allow the user to enter words consisting of five letters and display them on the screen.

(d) Write a program which will calculate how fast a cyclist is travelling if you input their time taken to travel 100 metres.

(e) Write a program which will accept a temperature in degrees Celsius and output the temperature in either degrees Fahrenheit or degrees Kelvin as required by the user.
(Kelvin = Celsius + 273.15; deg F = 9/5 Celsius + 32)

(f) Write a program which will capitalise the first character of a word entered by the user.
(i.e. john → John)

(g) Write a program which will calculate the length of one side of a right angled triangle if the lengths of the other two sides is input (Pythagoras).

(h) Write a program which will change a pupil's percentage test mark into a letter grade (A–E).

(i) Write a program which will calculate the area of a triangle if you enter its base and height.
(area = 1/2 base × height)

(j) Write a program which will take in a message and display it on the centre of the screen.

Figure 6.4 *I don't know COBOL*

2. Design

Once you have a precise software specification, then you can begin to design your solution to the problem.

In a normal problem-solving situation, you should always ask this question:

Is writing a program the best way to solve this problem?
Can it be solved more easily in another way?

Take the *Average Problem* we discussed earlier. If the average is to be found for only ONE set of numbers, i.e. one-off, then it would probably be much more efficient to use a calculator and work out the average that way, rather than entering the numbers into a computer. However, if you have to work out many different averages for lots of sets of numbers, then it would be worthwhile using a computer software solution.

If you decide to use a computer to solve the problem, then you should begin by looking at the highest level of software you have available. For instance, would it be possible to solve this problem using a general purpose application package such as a spreadsheet or a database rather than by writing a program in a high level language?

How could you use a spreadsheet to solve the *Average Problem*?

(Answer : Create a new spreadsheet document; enter the set of numbers into a column or a row and enter the formula =AVERAGE(cell range) into an unused cell.)

However, in this unit on software development, you are concerned with producing a computer solution to a problem using some kind of programming language. Your approach to problem solving should therefore take account of this.

Program **design** is the process of planning the solution. The design of the program is very important for its success. Time spent at this stage is very worthwhile and can reduce the chance of errors appearing later on in the solution.

Example

This is nothing to do with programming but all to do with design!

Consider the many home improvement, do it yourself and gardening make over programs which appear on television. Their success appears magical as a team of 'experts' descends on a (usually unwitting) person's home, and completes the conversion in two or three days. Despite how casual it may appear, all of these transformations are planned out to the last detail. The 'experts' have all visited the homes weeks, if not months, in advance, and have gone away and drawn up detailed plans for the conversion. It is just the same with programming – the more time you spend thinking about and planning the design of the program – the less time you will spend wondering why your program does not work as it should!

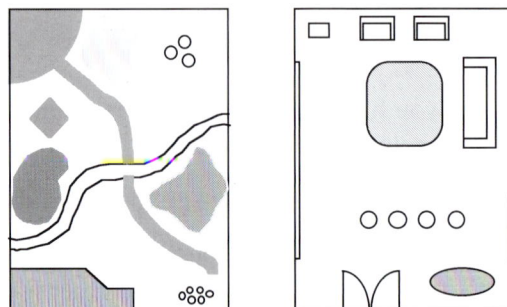

Figure 6.5 *Garden plans and room plans*

You can read more about different **design methodologies** and the **design notation** used to represent them later on in this chapter.

Note that it is not within the scope of this textbook (nor a 40 hour Higher Level Unit) to cover all the possible methods of program analysis and design which may be used as part of the software development process.

Design methodology

The design methodology is the approach that the programmer takes to the design of the solution. Design methodologies include **modular design**, **Jackson Structured Development** and **object-oriented design**. We will look only at modular design.

Modular design

Modular design is a method of organising a large computer program into self-contained parts called **modules**, which can be developed simultaneously by different programmers or programming teams. Modules are specially constructed so that they can be designed, coded and maintained independently of one another. Some modules may be linked to other modules and some may be separate programs. **Top-down design** and **bottom-up design** are both forms of modular design.

Top-down design. One method of designing the solution to a problem is called **top-down design**. Top-down design involves looking at the whole problem (**top**) and breaking it down into smaller, easier to solve, sub-problems. Each sub-problem may be further sub-divided into smaller and simpler sub-problems (modules). This process of breaking down sub-problems into yet smaller steps is called **stepwise refinement**. Eventually the stage is reached where each sub-problem can no longer be broken down and the refinement process comes to a halt. At this point each small step can be translated into a single line of program code.

Figure 6.6 *Breaking down a problem ...*

When stepwise refinement is complete, then you have created an **algorithm**, which is a sequence of instructions that can be used to solve a problem.

Bottom-up design. The bottom-up method of designing a solution to a problem begins with the lowest levels of detail and works upwards to the highest level of the idea. It seems strange to think that it is sensible to work towards something without really knowing what that something is before you begin! However, using a bottom-up design approach means writing *modules* or *procedures* first. This approach is sometimes called *prototyping*, where you construct a procedure separately before joining it together with the rest of a program.

Design notations

The way of representing the program design or algorithm is called the **design notation**. The programmer has a choice of design notations. Common **design notations** include drawing a **flow chart,** drawing a **structure diagram** or writing **pseudocode**. Some design notations use graphical objects such as icons to represent the design of a program.

Flow charts

A flow chart may be used to represent a program or a system. Flow charts use diagrams made up of differently shaped boxes connected with arrows to show each step in a program. One problem with this type of representation is that even the simplest program that has several conditions can quickly become unreadable. To get around this difficulty, systems flow charts were developed. A single box on a systems flowchart may represent many boxes on a program flow chart. A further problem with program flow charts is that it is difficult to represent multiple decisions such as may be used in a CASE statement in a high level language.

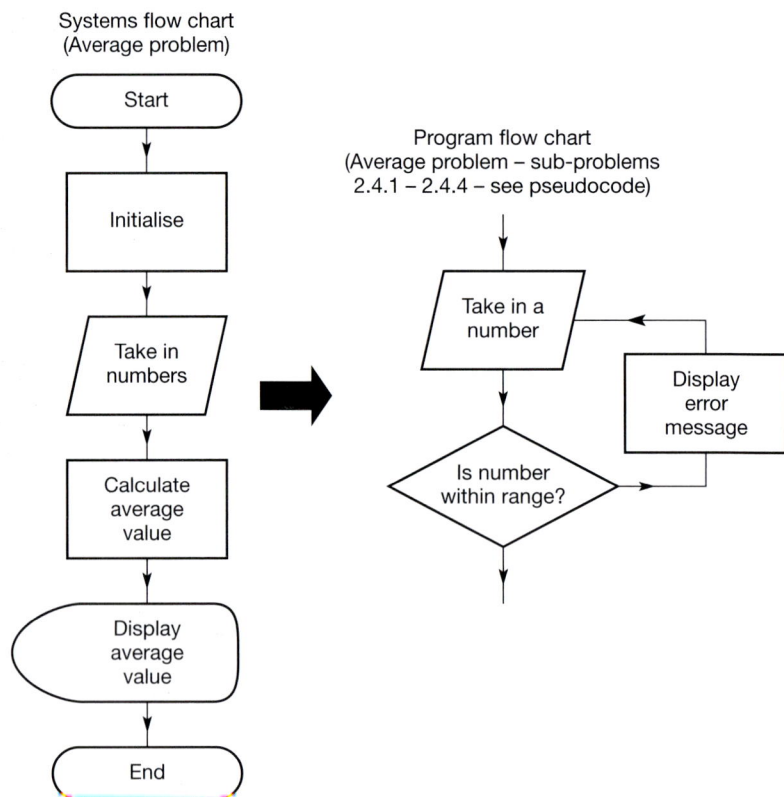

Figure 6.7 *Systems and program flow charts and how they may relate*

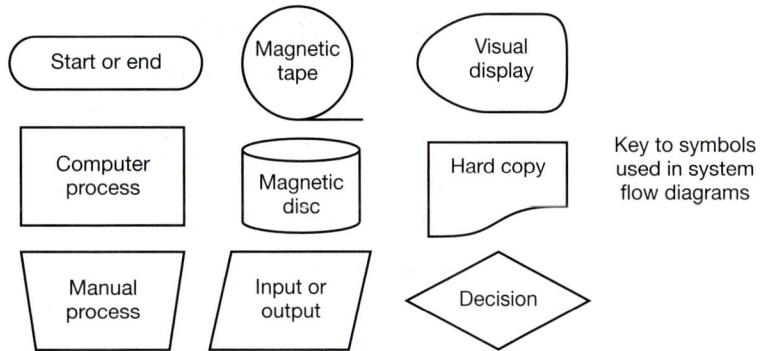

Figure 6.8 *Key to symbols used in flow charts*

Structure diagrams

Structure diagrams, like flow charts, use linked boxes to represent the different sub-problems within a program. The boxes in a structure diagram are organised to show the level or *hierarchy* of each sub-problem within the solution. In general, structure diagrams follow a left to right sequence.

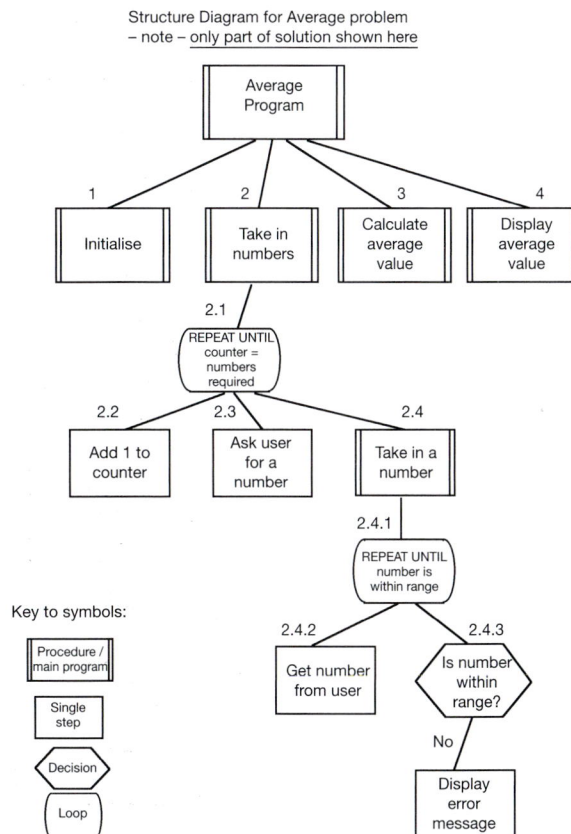

Figure 6.9 *Structure diagram*

Pseudocode

Pseudocode is the name given to the language used to define problems and sub-problems before they are changed into code in a high level computer language. Pseudocode uses ordinary English terms rather than the special keywords used in high level languages. Pseudocode is therefore language independent.

Here is some pseudocode showing *part of the design* of one possible solution to the *Average Problem*.

Algorithm:

1. initialise
2. take in numbers
3. calculate average value
4. display average value

Refine sub-problem 2:

2.1 loop REPEAT
2.2 add one to counter
2.3 ask user for a number
2.4 take in a number
2.5 UNTIL counter equals amount required

Refine sub-problem 2.4:

2.4.1 loop REPEAT
2.4.2 get number from user
2.4.3 IF number is out with range THEN display error message
2.4.4 UNTIL number is within range

Pseudocode is very useful when you are programming in languages like BASIC, COMAL or Pascal, because it fits in neatly with the structure of the code. The main steps in the algorithm relate directly to (in fact become) the main program, the refinements of each sub problem become the code in the procedures. (See chapter 8 for more examples of pseudocode.)

Short example of implementation

Suppose that your chosen software development environment is a high level programming language such as COMAL.

Let's look at how you might choose to implement part of the solution to the *Average Problem* in COMAL:

DESIGN (Pseudocode)	COMAL (actual program code)
	PROC take_in_numbers
2.1 loop REPEAT	*REPEAT*
2.2 add one to counter	*counter:= counter+1*
2.3 ask user for a number	*PRINT 'Please enter a number between 1 and 100'*
2.4 take in a number	*take_in_a_number*
2.5 UNTIL counter equals amount required	*UNTIL counter = amount_required*
	END PROC

Pseudocode is useful for representing the design of the types of problem that you are likely to face in this unit.

In a more complex professional programming situation, or in a much larger project, some of the alternative design notations such as structure diagrams or system flowcharts may be more appropriate.

Figure 6.10 *How do I delete?*

Data flow

Giving some indication of the **flow of data** between modules of your program is important. Some design notations allow data flow to be shown clearly. Pseudocode uses the terms *in:*, *out:* and *in-out:* to represent the flow of data used in sub-programs. You can find out more about data flow in chapter 8.

3. Implementation

When the design of your program is complete, you are ready to move on to the **implementation** stage of the software development process.

Implementation means changing your design into a set of instructions (or program) that the computer can understand. This usually means programming in a computer language.

One of the first things the programmer will do in the implementation stage, is to choose the particular computer language which she will use to write the program. The language she chooses will depend on various factors, for instance, which computer programming language (or languages) the programmer knows!

Some other points which should be taken into account are:

- The computer platform on which the software is expected to run – will the programmer have to write different versions of the software, or will it be possible to write one program which can be, for example, compiled to run on Intel and PowerPC microprocessors.
- The operating system in use – a program which works in Windows 98™ may not work in Windows XP™ or Windows 2000™.

In general a program which depends on having a particular processor, or makes use of a particular hardware feature, for example, a Sound blaster™ card, will not work well on a system without these features.

All of these features affect the **portability** of the software. You can read more about software portability later in this chapter.

The implementation stage of the software development process also includes the production of **internal documentation**. Internal documentation is so called because it is contained inside the program itself, as part of the language statements.

For example:

REM This is a REMark in the BASIC language

// This is an example of a comment statement in COMAL

{ PASCAL comments have curly brackets }

/ Allows comments in the C programming language */*

Internal documentation is sometimes called internal commentary because the programmer is *commenting* or *remarking* on what the code is doing at different stages throughout the program. You can put as many comment lines as you like in your program – they don't have any effect when the program is run.

Adding internal commentary to your programs can be a chore, especially if you are in a hurry to get the program finished and working. However, it is very useful if you, or someone else, has to look back at your program at any time in the future.

All of the programs which you will write in this unit should have internal commentary. At the very least, there should be several statements at the beginning of each program which tell the user the program name, the filename under which the program is stored, the author's name and the date when the program was written, like this:

{ Average program }
{ Saved as AVERAGE }
{ Written by Cecilia }
{ 3 March 2019 }

In general, the more detailed the internal commentary, the easier it will be to revisit your program at some time in the future (perhaps in order to update the program) and understand what each line of program code is actually doing.

In practice, you should also document each sub-program or module with a short statement to explain its purpose or function in your programs. This documentation should also include a list of the parameters required by each module.

We will look much more closely at program implementation in chapter 8. A short example of implementation is given on page 124.

Figure 6.11 *There's no risk*

4. Testing

To make sure that your program actually solves the problem it is supposed to (i.e. meets the software specification) you have to **test** it. Testing a program means that you have to run it to see whether or not it behaves as expected.

Testing should be both **systematic** and **comprehensive**. **Systematic testing** means that your testing should follow a plan and not just be haphazard. To properly carry out systematic testing it is necessary to develop a **test plan**.

A **test plan** should outline what you are trying to test and how you are going to do it – for example:

* What program (or module) is being tested
* What the program (or module) should do
* List suitable **test data** which can be input into the program
* Expected results or desired outcomes from the test data

Comprehensive testing means that you should test your programs as thoroughly and completely as you can. It would be ideal if it was possible to test *every* part of a program with all kinds of test data. This is called **exhaustive testing** and it is discussed in greater detail later on in this chapter. Unfortunately, exhaustive testing is not *always* possible, because that would mean testing every single line in the program and every possible program **pathway**. What is a program pathway?

Look at the following example of a program pathway:

> *<program line 1>*
> *<program line 2>*
> *<program line 3>*

This is a **sequence**, and it represents a single program pathway. However, it is usual for programs to have many different pathways. Which pathway is taken depends upon the result of **selection**, which is based on a **control** structure (such as IF ... THEN) together with at least one **condition**.

For instance:

> *IF number = target THEN*
>   *pathway 1*
> *ELSE*
>   *pathway 2*
> *END IF*

This represents two separate pathways, one for *number = target* and another for *number <> target*. This is fine for small programs but most programs have many possible pathways. See chapter 8 for more about sequence and selection.

Some people think that testing can *never* ensure that a program is totally correct, because it is impossible to test all the program pathways. However, any programs that you will be asked to write will be relatively short and should not have too many pathways for you to test, so you should be able to ensure that your programs are free from error!

Test data

To make sure that your program actually solves the problem it is supposed to (i.e. meets the software specification) you have to test it. One method of testing a program is to use a set of data, called **test data**. It would take far too long to test a program for all possible sets of test data, so you have to choose a representative set of data. If the program works correctly for the test data, then you can be reasonably certain that the program will work for other similar data. There are three different types of test data:

- Normal
- Extreme
- Exceptional

The best way to use test data is to calculate what the answer will be if your program works properly, BEFORE you run the program. Then, run the program with the test data. If the results from the program match the answers you got from your manual calculation, the program is probably correct.

Another way of testing a program is to get someone else to do it for you! By the time you've finished writing your program, you're usually so familiar with the program code you've written, that you can't see any mistakes. Someone else looking at it might be able to spot mistakes that you've missed.

Let's look at a problem which will help you to understand what is meant by *normal*, *extreme* and *exceptional* test data.

Remember the assumptions for the *Average Problem*.

The maximum amount of numbers is 10.
The maximum value of a number is 100.
All the numbers are whole numbers, apart from the average, which has to be displayed correct to two decimal places.

Suppose you have written a program which solves this problem, and you are getting ready to test your program. Here are some examples of test data:

Normal – the program should accept this data

	Expected Output
45,86,93,4,23,67,43	*Average = 51.57*
90,10,78,89,54,34,17,66,98	*Average = 59.56*

Normal data is data which is within the limits that your program should be able to deal with.

Extreme – the program should accept this data

	Expected Output
1,100,0	*Average = 33.67*
1,100	*Average = 50.50*
100,100	*Average = 100.00*
1,1	*Average = 1.00*
0,0	*Average = 0.00*
1	*Average = 1.00*
0	*Average = 0.00*

Extreme data is data which is at the ends of the acceptable range of data – on the limit(s) or boundaries of the problem. Extreme data may also be called **limit** or **boundary** data.

Exceptional – the program should reject this data

	Possible error message
–1	*Out of range, please enter a whole number between 0 and 100*
101	*Out of range, please enter a whole number between 0 and 100*
0.2	*Not a whole number, please enter a whole number between 0 and 100*
number	*Not a number, please enter a whole number between 0 and 100*

Exceptional data is data which is invalid. A well-written program should be able to detect any exceptional data, warn the user of the error, and give them another chance to enter the data. Sometimes it is possible to reduce the chance of error messages caused by invalid data appearing in your program. A well-written program should **validate** all user input. See chapter 9 for some examples of input validation.

Figure 6.12 *Testing, testing …*

Exhaustive testing

Suppose that you have written a program to solve the *Average Problem* and have tested it with the above test data. Your program passes all the tests and appears to work properly. Can you then say that you have *fully tested* your program? *No,* because you have not tested *all* the possible sets of numbers that the program is designed to handle.

How many different sets of numbers would you need to test?

Let's work it out:

Total range of numbers 0 to 100, a total of 101 numbers
Quantity of numbers, 1 to 10
That makes a total of 70,484,500,000,000,000,000 possible different sets of numbers!

You can see that even for a relatively simple (some would say trivial) problem, like the average problem, it is practically impossible to test all of the possible sets of numbers.

Suppose you decided to try and test all the possible sets of numbers, let's say it takes you one minute to run the program, enter the numbers, and record the output, that would be a total of 70,484,500,000,000,000,000 minutes.... that makes ..... hours .... years .... in fact, if you worked it all out (I did!) it would take you 134,102,930 million years to enter and test all the different sets of numbers you could possibly have with this program. Obviously it is unrealistic to expect anyone to try and carry out exhaustive testing. How could you speed up the testing process? (Answer – use a computer to test the program.)

Most commercial programs are so large and complicated that it is impossible to test them and be sure that you've got rid of all the errors.

Consider the following example:

On June 4, 1996, the maiden flight of the European Ariane 5 launcher crashed about 40 seconds after takeoff. Media reports indicated that the amount lost was half a billion dollars – uninsured. The subsequent enquiry concluded that the explosion was the result of a software error – possibly the costliest in history (at least in dollar terms, since earlier cases have caused loss of life).

One report on the incident recommended more software testing, but:

Testing can be used to show the presence of errors but never to prove their absence

and, the only fully 'realistic' test was to launch the rocket. However, the launch was not really intended as a $500 million test of the software!

Some software companies have exploited the need for exhaustive testing by producing special test software which will test applications and identify parts of the code which have not been tested. One such program is Rational software's *Rational PureCoverage for Windows NT™*, which is designed to test programs written in Visual C++, Visual Basic and Java. I wonder who tests the *PureCoverage* software......

However, it is possible to write programs that are correct if you follow the software development process carefully, paying particular attention to the analysis and design stages. Remember the iterative nature of the software development process described earlier in this chapter. You will certainly have to go through some stages of the software development process more than once before your program is correct.

Depending on the problem you've been asked to solve, you might be given a set of test data to use, or you might have to make up your own. If you have to make up your own test data, you should try to choose a set of test data which includes normal, extreme and exceptional data. If your program doesn't produce the results you expect, you'll have to check through each line of the code. Sometimes it is useful to put extra statements into your program which will print out the values of certain variables at different stages of the run. This is called printing a *snapshot of selected variables*. It can help you find out exactly where the program may be going wrong.

Field testing

Software companies whose programs are used on many types of computer system face a major challenge to ensure that their programs will work correctly under all circumstances. It is impossible for the software company to replicate all the different possible types of hardware set-up or operating system software that the user may have. In this case, the company is largely dependent on the user for error reporting – the user is in fact the program tester as well!

Field testing means allowing users (i.e. people other than the programmer who wrote the program) to test the program. When you are field testing a program you should keep a careful record of how the software behaves on your computer. If the program crashes, then the conditions which caused the crash should be noted, and the programmer informed, so that the error can be corrected.

In a field testing situation, a software company will send out different versions of a program for testing. The *alpha* test version is usually distributed within the company and is not released to outsiders. The *beta* test version is given to selected outsiders or is put on general release with users acknowledging the fact that they do not have a finished product. This beta test stage is also known as **acceptance testing**. Software companies often persuade a wide range of users to become *beta* testers by distributing free copies of software at this stage of its development. In some cases *beta* testers who do a good job of thoroughly testing the software may be given a free copy of the final version as a reward for their hard work.

Test reports may be produced at various points during the testing process. A test report summarises the results of testing. In commercial and professional programming situations, an **acceptance test report** often forms a contractual document within which acceptance of software is agreed between the programmer and the client for whom the software has been written.

Figure 6.13 *Acceptance testing*

Cost of faulty software

The cost of faulty software to some companies (in 1999):

- In medium to large companies, the average software error costs $140,000 (£85,000).
- It costs $20,000 (£12,000) per minute in unrecoverable lost income when the reservation system of a major airline goes down.
- A failure of a major credit card company's credit authorisation system loses revenue of $167,000 (£100,000) per *minute*.

'As software products get integrated and more organizations use networks for critical business operations, security vulnerabilities become serious threats. Microsoft has invested more than $100 million and is retraining more than 8500 programmers to improve the security of its products.' (The Economic Times, 2002)

Error reporting

Error reporting is the communication and explanation of errors in the software to the user. Most computers attempt to indicate the likely source of an error in a piece of software by producing **error messages**.

Debugging

Debugging is the process of finding and correcting the errors in your program. Program errors have been called 'bugs' since the early days of computing, because the failure of one of the first computers in 1945 was caused by a dead moth being caught in the electrical components. The first stage of debugging is to find the part of the program which is causing the error – the second stage is to fix it!

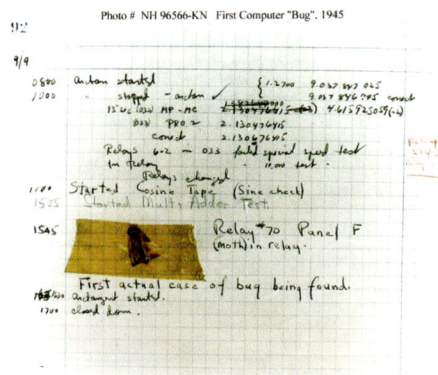

Figure 6.14 *The first ever computer bug*

Many different types of error can occur when you are programming.

Execution or run-time errors

Execution or run-time errors are errors which show up during program execution. **Overflow**, **rounding** and **truncation** are types of error which are caused by a limited amount of memory either in the computer (e.g. a fixed amount of space to store numbers) or decided by the programmer (e.g. a DIM statement). **Division by zero** is another typical run-time error.

- **Overflow** is a general term which describes what happens when something becomes too large to be processed accurately. For example, the result of a calculation may become too large to be stored in the space the computer has for numbers. The farmer and cattle problem at the beginning of this chapter is an example of an **overflow error**. An overflow error will normally cause a program to crash if it is allowed to occur. The error which caused the loss of the Ariane space rocket, described earlier in this chapter, was an example of an overflow error. The program tried to put a 64 bit number into a memory location capable of holding only 16 bits.

- **Rounding** happens when a number is reduced to a given number of decimal places, for instance 3.89 may be rounded up to 3.9. A **rounding error** is an error caused by rounding (+0.01) in this case.
- **Truncation** means shortening a number to a given number of decimal places. If the number 3.89 in the example above was truncated to one decimal place it would become 3.8. The truncation error would amount to −0.09 in this case.
- **Division by zero** may be caused by incorrect validation of an input variable or a result of a calculation. Division by zero will normally cause a program to crash if it is allowed to occur.

Compilation and syntax errors

A **compilation error** is an error which is detected during the process of compilation (or translation) of the program into the object code before it is run. Compilation errors are usually syntax errors.

- **Linking errors** may occur when a compiled program is linked to a subroutine or module library. For example, if the required module is not present in the library or if you have made a mistake in the parameter block.
- **Syntax errors** occur when the syntax, or rules of the programming language are broken.

A **statement syntax error** is misspelling a keyword, like typing *PRUNT* instead of *PRINT* or *WRITLEN* instead of *WRITELN*.

A **program** or **structure syntax error** happens when you have made a mistake in the structure of your program, such as incorrect use of a control structure. This type of syntax error may be detected by examining or **proof reading** a structured listing. (See figure 6.17)

Example of incorrect use of a control structure:

```
FOR counter := 1 to 10 DO
   For times:= 1 to 7 DO
      PRINT times,counter
   NEXT times
```

Can you spot the mistake?

If you are using a compiled language, you will find that it reports both types of syntax errors only when the program is compiled. An interpreted language usually reports **statement syntax errors** when the line containing the mistake is entered.

Logical errors

Logical errors are mistakes in the design of the program. Logical errors only show up when you run the program and you can spot them because the program does not do what it is supposed to do, for instance, it produces the wrong results.

Example of a logic error in part of a program written in the COMAL language:

```
counter := 0
REPEAT
   counter := counter+1
UNTIL counter = 0
```

Can you explain what will happen when this part of the program is run?

System errors

A **system error** occurs when the computer system (rather than just the program that you are working on) stops working properly. Windows™ users will no doubt be familiar with the so-called 'blue screen of death'.

Figure 6.15 *Debugging*

Detecting errors

Your chosen software development environment may have built in features to help the programmer check for bugs which cause errors. These may be part of a separate **debugger** program or may exist as a feature within the programming language. Using a **trace facility** and **hand testing** are two methods of detecting errors.

Trace facility

Many programming languages have a **trace** facility, which allows the programmer to follow the path through the program at the same time as it is being run.

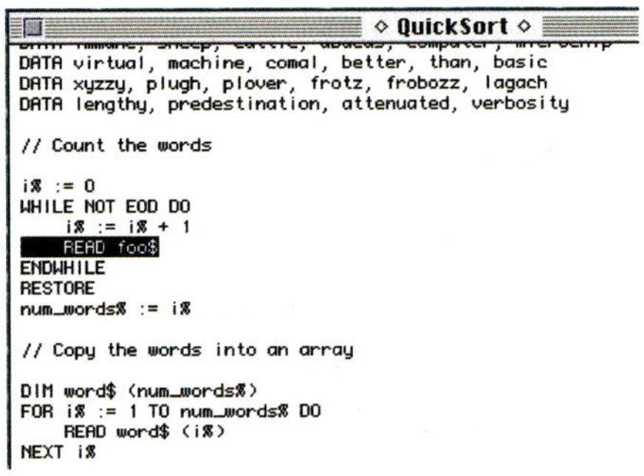

Figure 6.16 *COMAL for Mac OS™ – Trace facility*

A trace facility allows the user to go through the program one line at a time. This is called **single stepping**.

Another useful facility provided by some programming languages is the ability to set **breakpoints** or temporary halts in your program. While the program is paused in this way, it is possible to examine the values of the program's variables.

Manual or hand testing

One alternative to using a trace facility is **hand testing**. This is the process of going through the program code manually, in order to find mistakes. Proof reading is one method of hand testing and it is made easier using a structured listing. Another method of hand testing is to carry out a **dry run** using a **trace table**.

A **dry run** is usually carried out on a small part of a program (such as a procedure) at one time. To carry out a dry run you would begin by making a list of all the variables in the part of the program you are going to examine. This is called a **trace table**, and as you go through the program, it allows you to write down how the values of the variables change at each line.

For example

		counter	times	total	average
Line 250		25	2	5760	230.40
Line 260		45	3	13098	453.78

and so on ....

By comparing the values of the variables calculated in the program and the values which you have calculated yourself, you should be able to spot where the program is going wrong.

Structured listing

A program listing is a printout or hard copy of the program code. A structured listing is a program listing which uses indentations (formatting) to show some of the structure of the program. Program structures such as the beginning and end of procedures, control structures such as loops and decisions are usually all indented in a structured listing.

In addition to this, a structured listing may also highlight language keywords and variable names in some way. One form of highlighting keywords and variable names is to put the keywords into upper case lettering (capitals) and the variable names into lower case letters. Some software development environments, for instance *Codewarrior*™, uses different colours in its structured listings.

Indenting program structures in this way has two main advantages:

1. You can see at a glance where each of the program control structures begins and ends. This makes it easy to understand the structure of each part of the program

2. You are more likely to be able to spot mistakes in the program when you examine a structured listing as opposed to one which is unstructured. The indentations which form the control structures move to the right at the start of each control structure, and return to the same relative position at the end of the control structure. The highlighting of keywords and variables also helps you to spot mistakes, since you can see at a glance if the keywords and variables have been entered correctly. You can see some examples of structured listings in figure 6.17.

Key:
1 FOR ... NEXT loop
2 CASE ...OF
3 WHILE ... DO
4 PROC... ENDPROC
5 IF ... ENDIF

```
PROC display (numlist, REF array ()) CLOSED
   FOR counter := 1 TO numlist DO
      PRINT array (counter)
   NEXT counter
ENDPROC display
//
PROC input_item (REF item) CLOSED
   PRINT "Please enter the number to find"
   INPUT item
ENDPROC input_item
//
PROC find_item (item, length_of_list, REF array (), REF location, REF found) CLOSED
   found := FALSE
   exit := FALSE
   current := 1
   WHILE (NOT found) AND (current < length_of_list + 1) AND (exit = FALSE) DO
      CASE array (current) OF
         WHEN = item
            found := TRUE
            location := current
         WHEN < item
            exit := TRUE
            // item not in list
         WHEN > item
            current := current + 1
      ENDCASE
   ENDWHILE
ENDPROC find_item
//
PROC display_location (item, location, found) CLOSED
   IF found THEN
      PRINT "The item "; item; " was found at position "; location
   ELSE
      PRINT "The item "; item; " was not found in the list"
   ENDIF
ENDPROC display_location
```

COMAL for Mac OS™

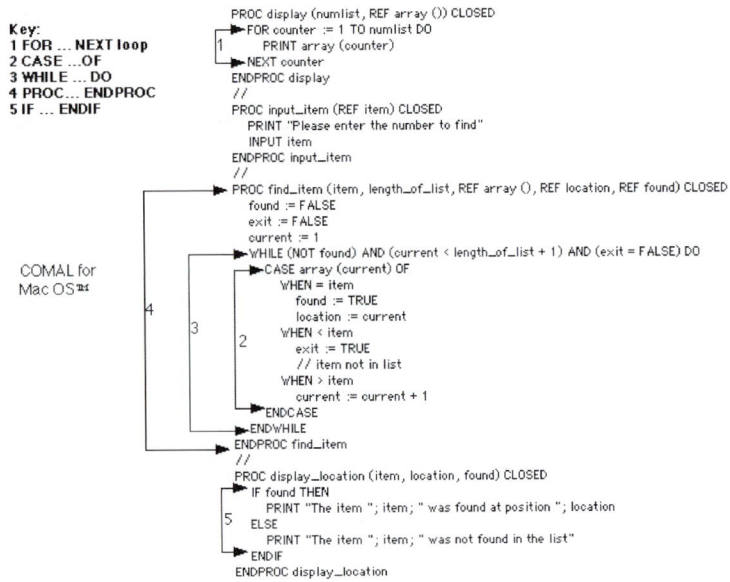

BBC BASIC™ - This language allows you to control the way the listing is displayed

```
800  IF A$<>"" THEN
810    Q$=ASK$(FNaddq("How can I tell it from "+artb$+B$),"Does it")
820    IF Q$<>"" THEN
830      C$=ANSWER$(FNsubstitute(Q$,arta$+A$),"No","Yes")
840      REM Re-arrange the data structure to include the new
850      REM question and animal
860      blank%=FNblank_node
870      PROCmake_node(blank%,"0",0,0,p%!f_str%+ram%)
880      CASE C$ OF
890        WHEN "Yes"
900          p%!f_yes%=FNnew_node(A$)-ram%
910          p%!f_no%=blank%-ram%
920        WHEN "No"
930          p%!f_no%=FNnew_node(A$)-ram%
940          p%!f_yes%=blank%-ram%
950      ENDCASE
960      block%=FNalloc(LEN(Q$))
970      $(block%)=Q$
980      p%!f_str%=block%-ram%
990      p%?f_type%=ASC"Q"
1000     PROCmodified(TRUE)
1010   ENDIF
1020 ENDIF
```

☒ Wrap lines

LIST Options
☒ Indent lines
☒ Indent structures
☐ Split lines at colons
☒ Keywords in bold

Graphics
☒ No text shading
☐ Integer scaling
☐ Invert screen

[Cancel] [OK]

Figure 6.17 *Structured listings*

5. Documentation

When documenting a program, **a technical guide** and a **user guide** must be produced.

Technical guide

A technical guide explains how to install the software on to a computer system. It lists the type of computer system(s) upon which the software will run, and the installation requirements. Installation requirements include the type and version of operating system, amount of free memory needed, amount of backing storage space required and type and clock speed of the processor. Additional operational requirements may be that the user should have particular items of hardware, such as speakers, or a scanner.

Software which is capable of being installed on two completely different platforms, such as Windows™ and Macintosh™ computers, is called **dual platform**. Many software companies will list the installation requirements on the outside of the box, under the clear shrink-wrap packaging, so that the user can look at the installation requirements before deciding to purchase the software. Note that it is important to read these requirements before opening the shrink-wrap, because once the packaging is open, you cannot return the software or get a refund unless the disk is faulty.

A technical guide may also explain how to edit or make changes to the software, or provide a troubleshooting guide.

User guide

A user guide explains how to operate the software once it is installed. User guides are sometimes divided into different parts. These may include some kind of 'getting started' notes, a tutorial guide to teach you how to use the software, and a manual or reference guide which gives a detailed explanation of every feature in the program.

It is common to supply only the briefest information in the form of printed material, with all the rest of the documentation being in electronic form, usually on the media which carries the software itself, such as a CD-ROM. The user may decide for himself whether or not to print out all of the documentation, or view it on screen. The documentation may also be provided on-line in the form of an on-line help and/or an on-line tutorial. On-line help is useful because you can call on it if you experience difficulties while using the package. Note that the on-line help referred to here is 'on-line' in the sense that it is part of, or accompanying the application. This means that you can get help while you are working through the program. This type of on-line help does not necessarily mean that your computer needs to be constantly connected to the Internet to use it.

If your computer system is connected to the Internet, many packages contain live links to the software companies' web pages where further help may be obtained. For example, you can carry out a search for help on a particular software feature, look at a list of FAQs (Frequently Asked Questions), join an on-line forum or user group dedicated to the software, or email the company with a specific question. Such support is normally conditional upon the user completing some form of software registration process. This may be simply done on-line via email or may involve posting some information back to the software company. Most companies only require the users name, contact details (email address) and type of hardware and operating system used in order to register as a user of the software.

Figure 6.18 *Documentation*

Additional documentation which is normally provided with the software, is some form of licence agreement and a serial number. Note that the licence agreement normally covers the use of the software on only one computer at a time, and places restrictions on copying or giving away the software to others. The unique serial number may be required to be entered at the installation stage. Can you suggest a reason for this?

6. Evaluation

Evaluation involves reviewing the solution against suitable criteria.

The criteria against which you should evaluate software are **robustness**, **reliability**, **portability**, **efficiency**, **maintainability**, **readability**, **fitness for purpose** and **user interface**.

Robustness

Is the software able to cope with errors during execution without failing?

If a peripheral such as a printer, jams or runs out of paper, then this should not cause the computer program to fail. In this example, a robust program will begin by asking the user whether or not a printer is actually connected, and if so, testing the printer to check that it is working properly before sending a print job to it. If the printer runs out of paper, the user should be advised to take appropriate action and the program should continue working instead of crashing.

Reliability

How well does the software operate without stopping due to design faults?

Reliable software should be free from design and coding bugs, and may be depended upon to provide correct results for all specified inputs.

Portability

Can the developed software be used on a computer other than that for which it was originally designed?

It is important to clarify the meaning of 'computer' as used in this definition. It would not be remarkable if software which works on an IBM personal computer would be capable of running on a DELL personal computer, since both of these machines would probably be running the same operating system (Windows™) and have the same or similar processor (made by Intel, AMD, Cyrix, DEC, etc.). It would be quite a different matter if the same software was able to run on a Macintosh computer under OS X, with a PowerPC processor. A particular combination of hardware, processor and operating system together is known as a hardware **platform**. In this case we are dealing with two different hardware platforms.

Portability is an important consideration for a software developer. It is less important for the programs which you will write during the course of this unit, since they will probably be run in a single software development environment.

Portability is important for software developers because the size and complexity of modern software means that it takes a great deal of time to write a major application, for instance a database or a computer game. If the software developer can sell the same program for more than one hardware platform, then they can make a great deal more money than if the program was confined to a single platform.

Computer games are a good example of the need for software portability. If a developer is able to write the source code for one version of a program, usually in a high level language, like C++, for, say, Windows™ computers, and then **cross-compile** a second version for the Macintosh platform using the *same source code*, then they can both save and make money. They will save money because they do not have to employ two different programming teams to develop software for both **platforms**. They will make more money by releasing the game simultaneously on both **platforms**, so that the number of potential customers is greatly increased. This is called **cross-platform development**.

Portability is also an issue for software run by large commercial organisations. Many of these types of programs remain in use for much longer than the original hardware on which they were first run. As the company updates its hardware, it will also have to **port** its software to the new hardware. This saves money because the company does not have to completely rewrite the software from scratch. This is an example of **adaptive maintenance**.

Efficiency

Does the software require excessive resources in order to run properly?

Efficiency means that your program should not require excessive resources in order to run, for example a large quantity of free memory or a great deal of backing storage space. Some application programs require hundreds of Megabytes of backing storage space in order to install them on your computer system. Because of this, such programs usually offer a range of installation options – a full or *complete installation*, *customised* or a *minimal installation*. The minimal installation is useful if your computer system has a limited amount of free backing storage space. The customised installation option allows the user to choose which parts of the software are installed.

Maintainability

How easy is it to correct and/or update the software in future?

Maintainability is the term used to describe how easy it is to update a program some time after it has been delivered. The different types of program maintenance are described in the next section in this chapter. One factor that helps program maintenance is **readability**.

Readability

How easy is it for another person to understand your program code?

Readability means that the design and the code in your programs should be easily understandable by other people. Using meaningful variable names, structured listings and internal documentation aids readability.

Fitness for purpose

Does the solution solve the original problem?

Does the program that you have written meet the software specification? You should carefully examine the software specification. Identify and account for any differences between what your program does and what is stated in the specification.

You should also consider the test data results at this point. While creating the test data, you calculated what the expected results should be. Do the actual results of testing match the expected results?

User Interface

the means of communication between the user and the computer, also called the *human computer interface* (HCI).

When evaluating the user interface in your solution, you should consider the *nature of the HCI, help screens, instruction screens, visual appeal, screen layout* and *prompts for the user.*

- **The nature of the human computer interface**. The most common form of communication between people is speech, but this is not yet in everyday use between people and computers, although voice recognition is becoming more widely available. A variety of user interfaces are currently employed on computer systems. These include the graphical user interface (GUI), menu selection interface and forms dialogue interface.

Figure 6.19 *GUI*

The most common *graphical user interface* is the WIMP (Window Icon Menu Pointer) environment. A *menu selection interface* is one in which the computer displays a list of options from which the user may choose. In a *forms dialogue interface* the computer outputs separate prompt and response fields for a number of options and the user may complete a number of fields before moving on. Forms dialogue interfaces are common methods of collecting personal data from the user, for instance, completing a response frame on a web page in order to purchase goods.

- **Help screens and instruction screens**. No matter how experienced a computer user may be, help is usually required when an unfamiliar program is encountered. If possible, your program should allow the user to access help or instructions from any point within the software.

It is becoming more common for commercial programs, especially application packages, to include *context-sensitive* help. A context sensitive help system will always be aware of what the user is currently doing, and will respond appropriately when help is sought. For instance, supposing you are using an integrated package and you open a new spreadsheet document, then call upon the help facility. The help system will assume that you want help on using a spreadsheet, and an appropriate screen will be displayed.

- **Visual appeal and screen layout.** If you want your program to be attractive to users, then you should pay careful attention to its visual appeal. This is particularly important if your program is designed to be used by young children, who will be attracted to a colourful, eye-catching display.

  Users always prefer a neat, uncluttered screen layout to one where the screen which is too 'busy'. The screen layout should make it obvious to the user what is happening in the program, with clear areas for input and output operations as required.

- **Prompts for the user.** A prompt is a character or message displayed on a screen to indicate that the user is expected to do something, usually to input data into the system, or to confirm a selected operation. The prompts in your programs should be clear and give some indication to the user regarding the nature of the expected response.

  For example:

  Please enter a number ... is NOT a very helpful prompt!

  Please enter a whole number in the range 1 to 100 and press <Enter> ... is much more helpful.

  In addition, prompts should give some visible (or audible) feedback to the user that the response has been received correctly. This is particularly important if the required response is a mouse click on an area of the screen.

7. Maintenance

Program **maintenance** involves changing a program, often quite some time after it has been written. The first type of maintenance we will look at is corrective maintenance.

Corrective maintenance

Corrective maintenance is amending software to correct errors.

Example

You may have read about the considerable amount of fuss that was made in the months leading up to 1 January 2000 regarding the 'Millennium bug'. In an effort to reduce memory and backing storage requirements in the early days of computers, programmers used only two digits, for example '99' to represent '1999'. The concern was that when the year 2000 happened, programs written in this way would assume that '00' meant 1900 instead of 2000, thus causing all sorts of difficulties. Many of these old programs were still in use in 1999, and a great deal of time, money and effort was spent in order to correct these problems. In some cases old software was completely replaced with new, but in other cases the old software was amended.

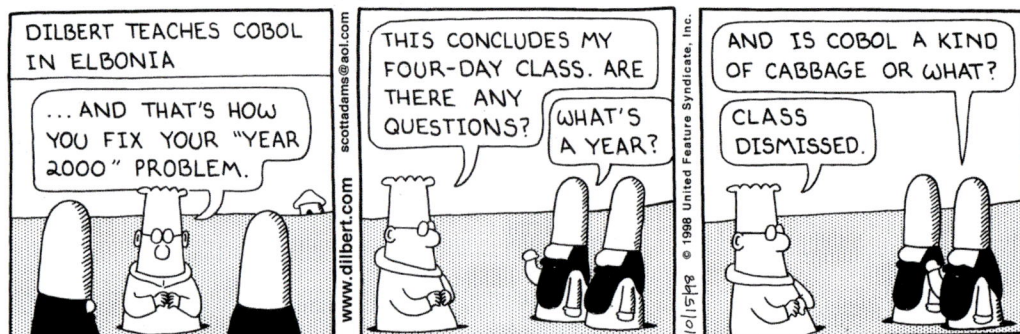

Figure 6.20 *Fixing the year 2000 problem*

One of the difficulties with the 'Millennium bug' was that the software was so old that the original programmers had long since retired, or in some cases, died. Although it is unlikely that any of your programs (at least, the ones that you write in this unit) will still be in use so long in the future, it makes it much easier to maintain a program if it has been well designed, well structured and well documented. Using internal documentation and a structured listing aids **maintainability**.

Two other types of program maintenance are **adaptive** and **perfective**.

Adaptive maintenance

Adaptive maintenance involves changing the software in response to changes either within or outwith the organisation which uses the software. For example, most desktop computers have replaced their CD-ROM drives with combined DVD/CD re-writer drives. This change required adaptive maintenance to the part of the operating system software which controls the drive.

Perfective maintenance

Perfective maintenance involves improving the software in order to enhance its performance. For example, a program may be modified to increase its speed of operation, perhaps by making better use of the processor's built-in instruction set, or by adding new features to the software, like additional transitions in a presentation package, or new tools in a photo-editing application.

Example of maintenance

When Apple changed its processors from the Motorola 680x0 family to PowerPC, this move required changes in the operating system software to make it run correctly on the new processors. At first only part of the operating system code was changed, just enough to get it to work (from version 7.1 → 7.5). As the operating system developed from version 7.5 → 8 → 9 → X, more and more of the operating system code was changed to run using PowerPC instructions, which work much faster than instructions designed to run on the 680x0 processor. Eventually the stage was reached where later versions of the operating system contained only PowerPC code and would no longer run on the old 680x0 processors.

This example shows both adaptive and perfective maintenance. It is an example of adaptive maintenance, because the first change allowed the original operating system to run on the new processor, while still retaining backwards compatibility with the old hardware. Later changes allowed the software to run even faster on the new processor, making this an example of perfective maintenance.

Some statistics show that up to seventy-five percent of an application's lifetime cost is for maintenance.

Figure 6.21 *Maintenance*

The need for documentation at each stage of the Software Development Process

Documentation is needed at each stage of the Software Development Process:

- Analysis – the documentation at this stage consists of the software specification. The software specification is important because it is the basis of all of the remaining stages of the software development process.
- Design – the documentation consists of the description of the program design in an appropriate design notation, and the design of the user interface. This description is important because it is the 'bridge' between the software specification and the code.
- Implementation – the documentation at this stage is the program listing(s), complete with internal commentary. This is important because it explains the purpose of each part of the code, and therefore eases the process of maintenance.
- Testing – the documentation at this stage includes the test plan, and the results of testing. This is important because it demonstrates whether or not the program does what it was designed to do.
- Documentation – this stage has the technical guide and the user guide. These are important because they explain how to install and operate the software.

- Evaluation – the acceptance test report, the results of evaluation against suitable criteria. This is important because it means that the program has been written to the satisfaction of the client, and that the software company can then be paid for their work.
- Maintenance – documentation at this stage is a log of changes made to the program code, together with the date and the new version number of the program. This is important because it will be updated constantly throughout the life of the software in order to inform programmers about earlier changes that have been made.

Personnel involved in software development

The **project manager** is the person within the software company who – overseas the whole project; makes sure the correct personnel are involved; checks that time limits are not overrun; communicates with the client. In a professional programming situation, a **systems analyst** (who is unlikely to be the programmer) would interview the **client** (the person or company for whom the program is to be written) to discuss the problem and take observation notes in the workplace. It would be possible for the client to explain any aspects of the problem statement which were not perfectly clear. The systems analyst would look at how the existing system operates and study examples of the type of information that the system already uses. Questionnaires may be used to help gather this information. The systems analyst would also study any literature that was available describing the previous system. This process is called the *requirements elicitation*. The client would have to agree to the precise software specification document, and this document now has the **status of a legal contract** between the client and the software company. The role of the **programmer** is to design and write the program code, working from the software specification. One other **purpose of the software specification document** is for it to be used as the basis for all the remaining stages of the software development process, including measuring the performance of the final program. An **independent test group** may do this.

Specialised companies known as **independent test groups** have been set up in order to test software. These groups of people are not associated with the software company or the programmers who wrote the software, and so can be relied upon to provide an unbiased opinion. An independent test group may carry out the following sequence of operations while testing software:

- Examine the source code, object code, test plan and results of testing already carried out by the software developer.
- Document additional tests to be carried out if appropriate.
- Re-test the software, repeating all the original tests and performing any additional tests.
- Document any errors found and communicate these to the software developer for correction.
- Receive corrected code from the developer.
- Repeat all tests on the corrected code.

This sequence of operations will be repeated (iteration) until all test results are acceptable, or it is decided that any remaining problems do not require to be fixed.

The iterative nature of the software development process

Iteration simply means repetition or doing something over again. The software development process described in this chapter is said to be iterative.

Example

Suppose you are writing a program. You have read and understood the whole of this chapter and the following three chapters as well! You have a good understanding of the stages involved in the software development process and you have applied them well to the program that you are working on just now. Do you think it is likely that your program will work the first time that you type the code into the computer? Supposing that it does work the first time, will it withstand rigorous testing without failing? Is the program design all correctly explained? It is unlikely that every part of your program or its design will be perfect first time around. (Remember the farmer's program at the beginning of this chapter!) You will probably find it necessary to revisit different parts of the software development process, whether it is implementation, design, or whatever, either to correct any mistakes or to improve your solution. So, each stage of the software development process may be revisited or repeated. This is the **iterative** nature of the software development process.

In short, the iterative nature of the software development process could be described using pseudocode like this:

```
REPEAT
    Analysis
    Design
    Implementation
    Testing
    Documentation
    Evaluation
UNTIL your software meets the specification
```

Questions

1. What is the software development process?
2. The software development process is said to be *iterative* in nature. Explain what is meant by the term *iterative*, when applied to the software development process.
3. At which stage of the software development process should a programmer consider.
   a. the software specification?
   b. the inputs, processes and outputs?
   c. internal documentation?
4. What is the process of planning the solution to a problem called?
5. What is internal documentation?
6. What is field testing?
7. a. What name is given to the pre-release version of a piece of software?
   b. Why might a software company distribute this version?
8. What is the purpose of a test report?
9. What is an evaluation?

10. List three questions that the programmer should ask at the evaluation stage in the software development process.

11. What is program maintenance?

12. Choose one program you have written, and comment on how easy it would be for someone in next session's Higher class to maintain.

13. Name and describe one *design methodology* with which you are familiar.

14. Which design methodology *begins with* writing modules or procedures?

15. Name and describe one *design notation* with which you are familiar.

16. What is the difference between *design methodology* and *design notation*?

17. What is the purpose of test data?

18. Name three types of test data.

19. Look back at the questions on problem analysis on pages 118 and 119. Choose one of the problems dealing with numerical data and one of the problems dealing with textual data. Create a set of test data for each of the two problems you have chosen.

20. What is exhaustive testing?

21. a. What is a structured listing?
    b. Explain one way in which a structured listing can aid the programmer.

22. What is:
    a. a run-time error?
    b. a linking error?
    c. a syntax error?

23. a. How can a logical error be detected in a program?
    b. Give an example of either a piece of program code or an algorithm which contains a logical error.

24. What features does your chosen software development environment contain which can help you to find errors in your programs?

25. What is hand testing?

26. Describe one situation where an error would be generated from the operating system during the run-time of a program.

27. Why is portability of particular economic importance as a software characteristic?

28. a. What is meant by the term hardware platform?
    b. Describe one hardware platform that you have used in this unit.

29. Why is efficiency a desirable characteristic of software?

30. Why does the software specification have the status of a legal contract?

31. Give an example of what could happen if the software specification was not correct.

32. List the personnel involved in the software development process.

33. Who carries out the requirements elicitation?

34. What techniques are used at the requirements elicitation?

35. Who is in overall charge of the software development process?

36. Which personnel are not employed by the software company?

37. State two forms of modular design.

38. Why is pseudocode said to be language independent?

39. Name one graphical design notation and draw a diagram of it.

40. What terms does pseudocode use to indicate the flow of data between program modules?

41. What features affect the portability of software?

42. State two items that should be considered in a test plan.

43. Why can it be true to say that '*you can never ensure that a program is totally correct*'?

44. What stage of the software development process may involve *printing a snapshot of selected variables*?

45. State two events that form part of the sequence of operations that an independent test group would carry out.

46. What is debugging?

47. Give one example of a statement syntax error and one of a structure syntax error.

• Key points •

- **Analysis** is the understanding of the problem and the conversion of a problem outline into a precise software specification which should include problem inputs, processes and outputs.
- **Design** involves the careful planning of a solution to the problem using a recognised design methodology, for example top-down design using structure diagrams or pseudocode.
- **Implementation** is changing the program design into instructions that the computer can understand and the production of internal documentation.
- **Testing** is to ensure that a piece of software performs correctly (i.e. meets the software specification).
- **Documentation** of a program includes a user guide and a technical guide. All other stages of the software development process also need some form of documentation.
- **Evaluation** involves reviewing the solution against suitable criteria.
- **Maintenance** involves making changes in the form of corrections or updates to the program at some time in the future and is made easier by good practice in software development.
- **Iteration** is revisiting or repeating one or more steps in the software development process in order to improve the solution.
- **Personnel** involved in software development are the client, systems analyst, project manager, programmer and independent test group.
- **Design methodology** is the approach that the programmer takes to the design of the solution.
- **Top-down design** involves looking at the overall problem and breaking it down into a series of steps.
- **Stepwise refinement** takes each step and breaks it down as far as possible, until each step can be turned into a single line of program code.
- **Design notation** is the way of representing the design of a program. Pseudocode and Structure charts are two design notations.

- **Test data** is a set of data used to make sure that your program actually solves the problem it is supposed to (i.e. meets the software specification).
- **Systematic testing** involves using a test plan.
- **Comprehensive testing** means that all your programs should be tested as thoroughly as possible.
- **Structured listing** is a program listing which uses indentations (formatting) to show some of the structure of the program.
- **Error reporting** is the communication and explanation of errors, in the software, to the user.
- **Robustness** is the ability of software to cope with errors during execution without failing.
- **Reliability** is how well software operates without stopping due to design faults.
- **Portability** is the ability of software to be used on a computer other than that for which it was originally designed.
- **Efficiency** is when the software does not require excessive resources in order to run.
- **Maintainability** is how easy it is to correct or update the software in future.
- **Readability** is how easy it is for another person to understand your program code.
- **Fitness for purpose** is when the solution solves the original problem.
- **User interface** looks at the nature of the HCI, help screens, instruction screens, visual appeal, screen layout and prompts for the user.
- **Corrective maintenance** is fixing bugs or mistakes.
- **Adaptive maintenance** is changing the software in response to changes in the hardware or operating system.
- **Perfective maintenance** is adding new features to a program.

7 Software Development Languages and Environments

Procedural, declarative, event-driven and scripting languages

Programming languages may be classified according to their type. The types of programming language include:

1. Procedural
2. Declarative
3. Event-driven
4. Scripting

1. Procedural languages

A **procedural language** is one in which the user sets out a list of instructions in the correct sequence (an **algorithm**) in order to solve a problem.

A procedural language typically has the following features:

- Data storage using variables of different types
- Arithmetic and logical operations
- Program control using sequence, repetition and selection
- Subprograms or procedures
- Data flow using parameters

You can read more about these features in chapter 8.

A program written in a procedural language has a definite start and finish point.

The sequence of instructions:

1. get numbers
2. calculate average
3. display average
4. END

is a typical algorithm which may be implemented using a procedural language.

When a program written in a procedural language is run, the sequence of instructions is followed from the beginning of the program to the end in the programmed order.

For this reason, procedural languages are also known as *imperative* languages, since the word imperative in the context of computer languages means giving or expressing commands.

TrueBASIC, COMAL and Pascal are examples of procedural languages.

2. Declarative languages

The use of a **declarative language** is very different from the use of a procedural language. Instead of giving a concise list of instructions set out in the correct order, a declarative language states 'what has to be done' rather than ' how to do it'.

Declarative languages like Prolog, contain sets of statements or clauses, like this:

```
cold (snow)         means that snow is cold
cold (ice)          means that ice is cold
hot (molten lava)   means that molten lava is hot
```

which can be used to describe facts,

and rules, like:

```
melts(X,Y) :        means that X melts Y if
hot(X),cold(Y)      X is hot and Y is cold
```

These facts and rules together can be used to answer questions or **queries**, like this:

```
?hot (molten lava)      which asks the question, is
                        molten lava hot? to which
                        the answer should be yes!
?melts (molten lava,ice)  ... and so on
```

The facts and rules described in a declarative language program are known as the **knowledge base**. When a query is entered, the declarative language looks for a solution contained in the knowledge base.

One feature of declarative languages is **recursion**. Recursion in a declarative language is equivalent to repetition or looping in a procedural language. Recursion involves a rule referring to, or calling itself. Recursion must be used with care, because it is easy to enter an infinite loop, and if this happens, the program may cause the computer to 'hang' or perhaps crash with an 'out of memory' error.

3. Event-driven languages

An event-driven language is provided with a program which helps you to design the user interface by placing graphics objects on screen. Because of this, it is much quicker to design a program with a graphical user interface when using an event-driven language.

Programs written in event-driven languages have no definite start or end. When the program is running, the user interacts with the event-driven language by selecting from a choice of screen objects, like buttons, menus or windows. Clicking on one of these objects activates the program code associated with that object.

The action of clicking on or selecting a screen object is called an event, and the event is detected by the program, hence the name **event-driven language**.

The code below is written in the Visual Basic language in order to detect a click on the object 'cmdStartLoop' and carry out an action on the window 'picDisplay'.

```
Private Sub cmdStartLoop_Click()
        picDisplay.Cls
        For loop_counter = 1 To 5
                picDisplay.Print "John"
        Next loop_counter
End Sub
```

Can you work out what action the code is designed to perform after the click event has taken place?

An event-driven language program is very similar in operation to a menu-driven operating system with a graphical user interface, in the sense that the operating system is always running in the computer and waiting for the user to select from a menu.

Visual Basic, Delphi (Visual Pascal), Real Basic and HyperTalk (HyperCard) are examples of event-driven languages. You can see screenshots and listings of code from some Visual Basic programs in chapters 8 and 9.

4. Scripting languages

Features of a scripting language
Scripting languages may be divided into two types:

(a) those which are embedded within an application package and which make use of only those commands which are available within the package
(b) those which work with the operating system and across and between suitable (**scriptable**) applications.

Uses of a scripting language
The provision of a scripting language allows the user to tailor an application package to carry out additional operations other than those provided in the original menus. Scripting languages use commands from application packages in order to do this.

Examples of scripting languages include *Visual Basic for Applications* (**VBA**), *JavaScript* and *Perl*. Some of these languages are described later on in this chapter.

An expert user of an application package would use a scripting language to automate a repetitive task that had to be carried out. Programs written using a scripting language are often called **macros**. Once programmed, a macro may be activated by clicking on a button or by selecting from a menu.

A **macro** is a set of keystrokes and instructions that are recorded, saved, and assigned to a single key or a combination of keys. When the key code is typed, the recorded keystrokes and instructions are carried out.

Creating a macro

A macro may be created either by recording a sequence of keystrokes and mouse actions, or by entering a suitable script in an appropriate language into an editor. The screenshot in figure 7.1 shows the code and the sample output associated with a simple macro.

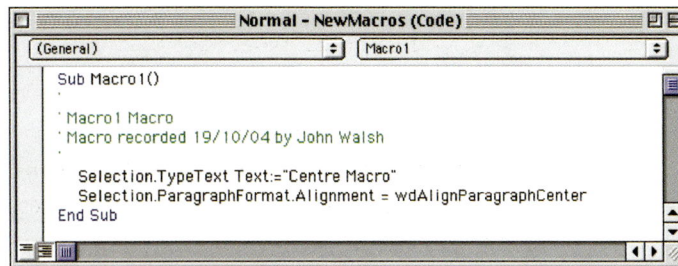

Figure 7.1 *Creating a macro in Microsoft Word*

This macro, in Microsoft Excel, creates a simple spreadsheet which may be used to add two numbers.

```
Sub Example()
'
' Example Macro
' Macro recorded 17/4/00 by John Walsh
'
' Keyboard Shortcut: Option+Cmd+Shift+A
'
    Range("B2").Select
    ActiveCell.FormulaR1C1 = "number one"
    Range("B3").Select
    ActiveCell.FormulaR1C1 = "number two"
    Range("C5").Select
    ActiveCell.FormulaR1C1 = "=SUM(R[-3]C:R[-2]C)"
    Range("B5").Select
    ActiveCell.FormulaR1C1 = "total"
End Sub
```

Figure 7.2 *Sample output from Excel macro*

Editing a macro

A macro may be edited by making changes to its code and saving the new version. The screenshot below shows the macro in figure 7.1 after it has been edited. What changes have been made? What will the edited macro do?

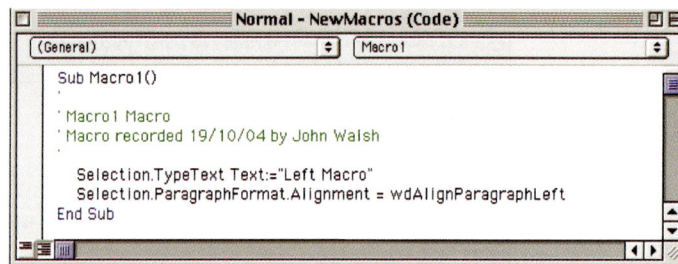

Figure 7.3 *Editing a macro in Microsoft Word*

The need for scripting languages

The need for scripting languages arises from the requirement to be able to make changes to the commands or menus, or to automate tasks within an application package or an operating system.

The benefits of scripting languages

The benefits of scripting languages are that they allow application packages to be enhanced with additional commands, automate tasks for an expert user and allow a beginner to perform tasks that they would not otherwise be able to undertake.

Translator programs

A **translator** is a computer program used to convert program code from one language to another, for example, from a high level language to machine code. Translators are used because it is very difficult to write programs directly in machine code. It is much easier for the programmer to write the program in a high level language and then have it changed into machine code by a translator program. There are three types of translator programs **assemblers**, **compilers** and **interpreters**. This unit deals only with compilers and interpreters.

The function of a compiler

A **compiler** translates a high level language program, the **source code**, into machine code which is the **object code**. The compiler changes each single high level language instruction into several machine code instructions. Compilation involves analysing the language structure of the source program, checking to see

if it is correct, and producing machine code. These separate compilation stages are known as **lexical analysis**, **syntax analysis** and **code generation**.

Lexical analysis

In the **lexical analysis** stage, each recognised keyword in the source code is changed into a token. This tokenising process resembles the representation of characters by their ASCII values, in that each token is a unique code. The keyword PRINT, for instance, has the token 1111 0001 (decimal 241) and IF has the token 11100111 (decimal 231). Any errors detected at this stage are reported.

Syntax analysis

During the **syntax analysis** stage, the language statements are checked against the rules or grammar of the language. This grammar checking process is known as **parsing** and the part of the compiler program that carries it out is the **parser**. Typical **syntax errors** that might be detected and reported by the parser are missing brackets from an arithmetical expression or inverted commas from a PRINT statement.

Code generation

Finally, the **code generation** stage produces the object code, which is a machine code representation of the source code.

After compilation is complete, the object code can then be run. The object code runs very fast because it is in the computer's own language, machine code. The object code program may be saved and run separately. The source code should also be saved, because, without it, it is impossible to edit the program since the object code, once produced, cannot be easily changed.

Machine code is the computer's own language and is specific to the processor being used. This means that a machine code program which runs on an *Intel Pentium* processor will be unlikely to work on a computer with an *IBM PowerPC* as its processor. Machine code programs are not **portable**, although by using a special type of compiler called a **cross-compiler**, it is possible to produce separate machine code translations of a high level language program, each of which will run on a different processor.

The programming language Pascal is an example of a language which is normally compiled before it can be run.

The function of an interpreter

An **interpreter** translates and runs a high level language program one instruction (or statement) at a time. No object code is produced. Interpreted programs run slower than compiled or assembled programs because each line must be translated every time the program is run. An interpreter will report any mistakes (syntax errors) in the code as it is being developed, rather than waiting until the end of the translation the way compilers do. For this reason, interpreted programming languages are popular with students and others who are learning to program. Programming languages such as True BASIC and COMAL are normally interpreted, although nowadays most languages are also provided with a compiler, which is capable of generating a stand-alone version of the user's program.

The efficiency of compilers and interpreters

Using an interpreter is a single process, unlike using a compiler, which requires the program to be compiled separately and then run. For these reasons, interpreted programming languages are popular with students and others who are learning to program. Unlike compilers, it is not possible to save the translated version which is produced by an interpreter since each program line is executed immediately upon translation. Interpreted programs tend to use more memory than compiled programs because the interpreter must also be present in the computer's memory when the program is run.

Table 7.1 *Comparing interpreted programs and compiled programs*

Interpreted programs	Compiled programs
Run slow	Run fast
Report mistakes immediately	Report mistakes at end of compilation
Translate and run is a single process	Translate and run are separate processes
Cannot save translated version	Can save object code
Interpreter required to run the code	Compiler not required to run the code

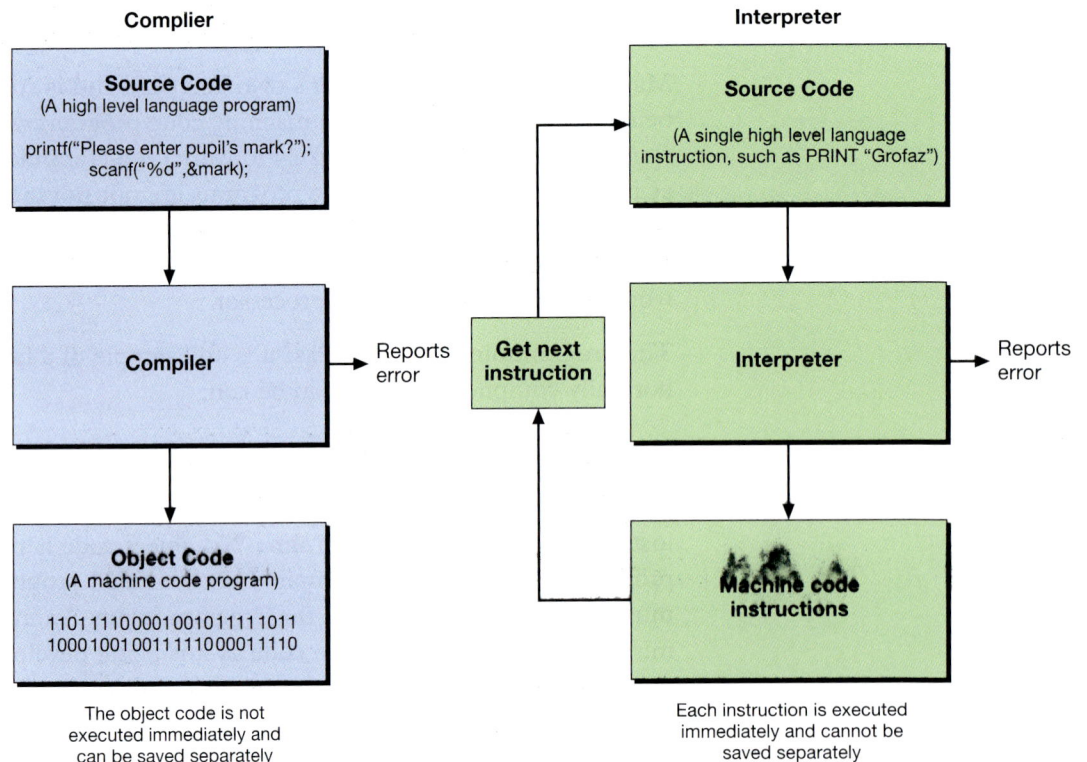

Figure 7.4 *Compiler and Interpreter*

The uses of compilers and interpreters

When an interpreted program is being created, both the source code and the interpreter are required to write, edit, test and use the completed program.

When a compiled program is being created, the source code and the compiler are needed at the writing and editing stages; the source code, object code and compiler are required at the testing stage, and only the object code is required to use the completed program.

Run-time version and stand alone code

Compilers are capable of producing an object code translation of a program which may be saved and run separately from the source code, i.e. it *stands alone* or is independent of the translator program. This object code is sometimes called the *run-time* version because all the user can do is run the finished program, rather than edit it. Commercial programs which are sold (or otherwise distributed) are always copies of the object code.

When you buy a commercial program, all you are buying is the right to run the object code (normally on a single computer). Programmers and software companies never allow the source code for their programs into the public domain. Can you suggest why this is the case?

Text editors

A **text editor** allows the programmer to enter and edit the source code for a program. Most text editors have special features which make the programmer's task easier. In a windows (WIMP) environment, the text editor usually has a dedicated window where the user can enter code. Figure 7.5 shows a screen shot of a text editor.

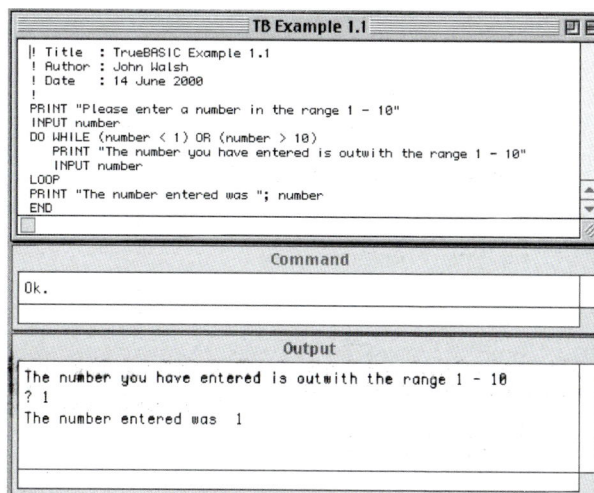

```
                        TB Example 1.1

|! Title  : TrueBASIC Example 1.1
 ! Author : John Walsh
 ! Date   : 14 June 2000
 !
 PRINT "Please enter a number in the range 1 - 10"
 INPUT number
 DO WHILE (number < 1) OR (number > 10)
    PRINT "The number you have entered is outwith the range 1 - 10"
    INPUT number
 LOOP
 PRINT "The number entered was "; number
 END

                         Command

 Ok.


                          Output

 The number you have entered is outwith the range 1 - 10
 ? 1
 The number entered was  1
```

Figure 7.5 *Text editor*

Some text editors help the programmer by anticipating what you are typing and will help complete a program statement. This is called *predictive typing*. Figure 7.6 shows predictive typing in Visual Basic.

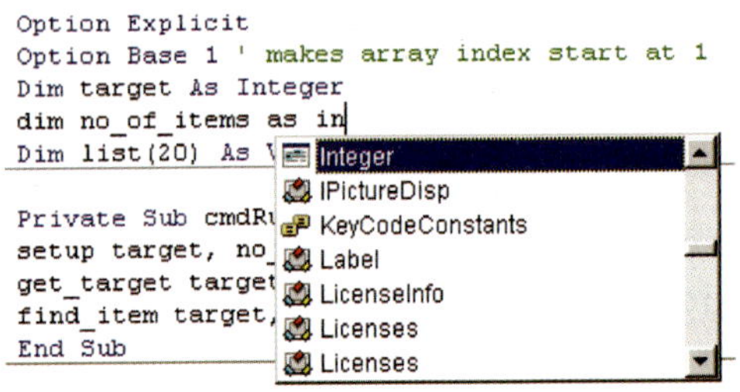

```
Option Explicit
Option Base 1 ' makes array index start at 1
Dim target As Integer
dim no_of_items as in
Dim list(20) As V  ▭ Integer
                   🖼 IPictureDisp
                   📇 KeyCodeConstants
Private Sub cmdRt    🖼 Label
setup target, no_    🖼 LicenseInfo
get_target target    🖼 Licenses
find_item target,    🖼 Licenses
End Sub
```

Figure 7.6 *Predictive typing*

Another type of editor is a link editor – see below.

Module libraries

A **module library** is part of a **software library**. A software library is a collection of software held permanently accessible on backing storage. A software library will typically include complete programs, a module library and a set of machine code routines, which may be loaded into user programs when required.

The use of module libraries

Using a module library speeds up the whole software development process because time is saved in design, implementation, testing and documentation.

- **Saving time in design**. Using a module library saves time in program design because the design has already been done when the module was created in the first place.
- **Saving time in implementation**. A programmer would not write a procedure to sort numbers each time this was required in a new program, the procedure would simply be loaded from a module library.
- **Saving time in testing**. All of the modules in a module library are already tested and known to be free from errors. This also speeds up the software development process because these modules do not need to be tested again.
- **Saving time in documentation**. Each module in a module library is already fully documented. For instance, there will be a list of the parameters required by the module.

Linking modules

If machine code routines from a software library have to be added to a compiled program, then this is carried out by a piece of software called a **linker**, or **link editor**. Errors in the linking process are called linking errors (see chapter 6). Look at figure 7.7, which shows a module library and a linker.

Software libraries also have an important part to play in cross-platform development. This is when a single program is compiled in different versions to run under different operating systems.

Modules are considered to be part of the *software hierarchy*. The software hierarchy starts at the bottom with the simplest form of software which is closest to the processor, namely machine code. The hierarchy continues through assembly language, high level language, fourth generation language, to application packages.

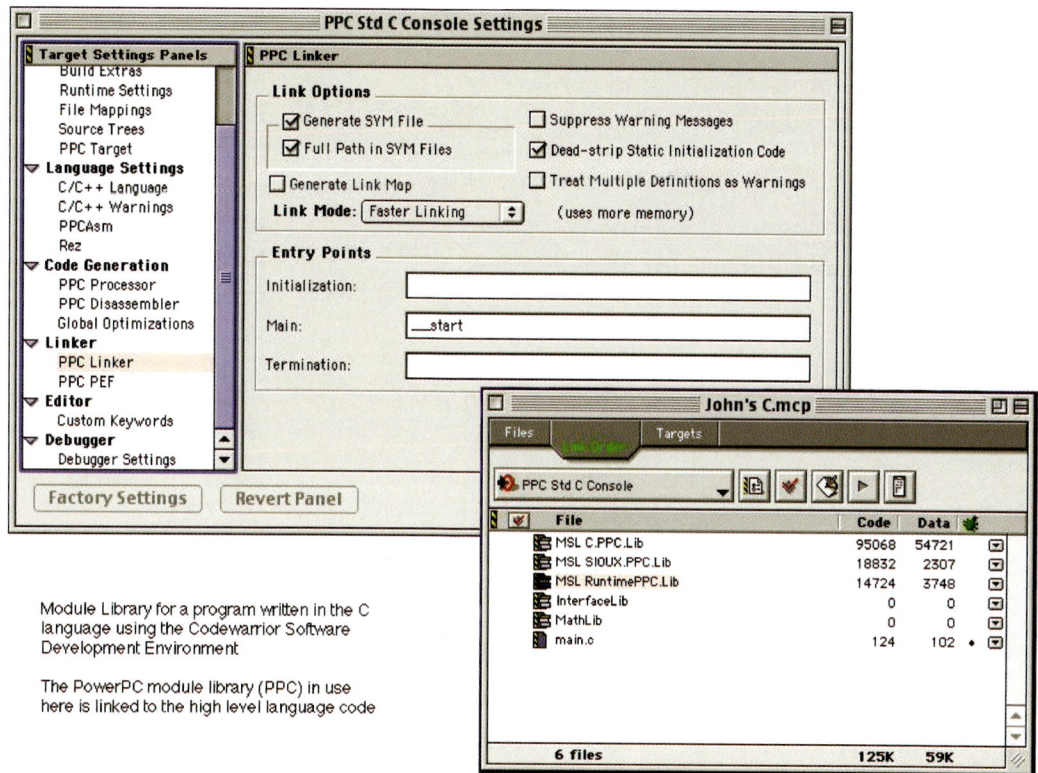

Module Library for a program written in the C
language using the Codewarrior Software
Development Environment

The PowerPC module library (PPC) in use
here is linked to the high level language code

Figure 7.7 *A module library and a linker*

Questions

1. Name four types of programming language.
2. What is a procedural language?
3. List three typical features of procedural languages.
4. Why is sequence important in procedural languages?
5. Name one procedural language.
6. What is a declarative language?
7. Name one declarative language.
8. Give one example of a fact in a declarative language which states that:
   a. tea is hot
   b. ice cream is cold.
9. What two items make up the knowledge base in a declarative language?
10. What is an event-driven language?
11. What particular type of program do event-driven languages make it easy to design?
12. Why is an event-driven language so called?
13. Name one event-driven language.
14. What use is a scripting language?
15. What is a macro?
16. Describe one method of creating a macro.
17. Explain the need for scripting languages.
18. Describe one benefit of scripting languages.
19. What was the main stimulus in the development of high level languages?
20. What is a translator program?
21. Why are translator programs necessary?
22. What is the function of a compiler?
23. What is source code?
24. What is object code?
25. Which translator program does not produce object code?
26. What happens during:
    a. lexical analysis?
    b. syntax analysis?
    c. code generation?
27. Name one programming language which may be:
    a. compiled
    b. interpreted.
28. Why are machine code programs not portable?
29. What use is a cross-compiler?
30. What is the function of an interpreter?
31. Compare the relative efficiency of compilers and interpreters. Draw a table to show your answers.

32. Describe a programming situation where a compiler would be preferable to an interpreter and one situation where an interpreter would be preferable to a compiler.

33. Why should the source code of a program be retained by the programmer, even after the program is complete?

34. Why do programmers not sell the source code?

35. What is a *stand-alone* version of your program?

36. State one benefit of being able to produce a *stand-alone* version of your code.

37. What is a module library?

38. Explain how a module library may speed up the following stages of the software development process:
  a. design
  b. implementation
  c. testing
  d. documentation.

39. What is a text editor?

• Key points •

- The types of programming language include: procedural, declarative, event-driven and scripting

- A procedural language is one in which the user sets out a list of instructions in the correct sequence (an algorithm) in order to solve a problem.

- A declarative language may be thought of as the opposite of a procedural language. Instead of giving a concise list of instructions set out in the correct order, a declarative language states 'what to do' rather than 'how to do it'.

- An event-driven language is provided with a program which helps you to design the user interface by placing graphics objects on screen. The action of clicking on, or selecting, a screen object is called an event, and the event is detected by the program, hence the name event-driven language.

- A scripting language allows the user to tailor an application package to carry out additional operations other than those provided in the original menus. Scripting languages use commands from application packages in order to do this.

- Programs written using a scripting language are often called macros. Once programmed, a macro may be activated by clicking on a button or by selecting from a menu. A macro is a set of keystrokes and instructions that are recorded, saved, and assigned to a single key or a combination of keys. When the key code is typed, the recorded keystrokes and instructions are carried out.

- The need for scripting languages arises from the requirement to be able to make changes to the commands or menus, or to automate tasks within an application package or an operating system.

- The benefits of scripting languages are that they: allow application packages to be enhanced with additional commands, automate tasks for an expert user and allow a beginner to perform tasks that they would not otherwise be able to undertake.

- A translator converts a computer program from one language to another (for example, from a high level language to a low level language). Compilers and interpreters are types of translator programs.

- A compiler translates a high level language program (the source code), into machine code (the object code).

- An interpreter translates and runs a high level language program one instruction or statement at a time. No separate object code is produced. Interpreted programs run slower than compiled programs because each line must be translated every time the program is run.

- Module libraries are pre-defined routines which support and speed up the software development process. Using a module library speeds up the whole software development process because time is saved in design, implementation, testing and documentation.

8 High Level Programming Language Constructs

To construct something is to build it or put it together out of a set of parts. The term **high level programming language** constructs refers to those parts which make up a high level programming language.

This chapter provides a description and examples of the following features of a high level programming language:

- Procedures/sub-routines
- User-defined functions
- Modularity
- Parameter passing (in, out, in/out)
- Call by reference/value
- Local and global variables, scope
- Real, integer and Boolean variables and one-dimensional arrays
- String operations
- Formatting of input/output
- Multiple outcome selection

In addition, some of the *basic features of a software development environment* are dealt with, in order to provide a reminder to candidates of earlier work, and support to those candidates who may not have done any programming before embarking upon this course.

We will also look at two of the main themes of the course, **Syntax and semantics** and later in the chapter, **Objects** and **Operations**.

Syntax and semantics

The **syntax** of a programming language (or software development environment) is the way in which you give instructions to the computer. Each programming language has its own syntax. Look at, and compare, the various program implementations later on in this chapter. You can see that each programming language has its own way of doing the same thing. However, the syntax of each programming instruction that you give must be precise, or the computer will not understand the instruction and you will have made a **syntax error**. See chapter 7 for more about syntax errors.

The **semantics** of a particular instruction is its meaning or its effect, that is, what it does.

Example of a range of different syntaxes, all with the same semantics

Syntax	Semantics
PRINT "Hello World !" *printf ("Hello World !");* *PR "Hello World !* *picDisplay.Print "Hello World !"* *writeln (output, "Hello World !");*	*These examples all display the text "Hello World !"*

Example of the same syntax, but different semantics:

Syntax	Semantics
number = 10	In Visual Basic, give the value 10 to the variable called number
number = 10	In COMAL, this is part of a condition e.g. IF number = 10 THEN .....

Note: Syntax is the way in which you give instructions to the computer using a software development environment. Semantics is the meaning or effect of these instructions.

Modularity

Modularity means that when a program is designed and written, it is divided into smaller sections called **subprograms** or **sub-routines**. Subprograms may be called in any order in a program, and they may be reused many times over. Each subprogram performs a particular task within the program. Subprograms may be written at the same time as the rest of the program or they may be pre-written. Pre-written subprograms are known as **library modules**. See chapter 7 for further details on the use of module libraries.

High level procedural languages use two types of modules or subprograms. These are **procedures** and **functions**.

Procedures

Before a procedure may be used in a program, it must be **defined**. Defining a procedure gives it a name, and also allows the programmer to state which data the procedure requires to have sent to it from the program. Data is passed to a procedure using **parameters**. When a procedure receives data, it carries out an operation using the data, and makes results available to the program. These results may simply be displayed on screen from within the procedure, or they may be passed back out of the procedure to another procedure, again using parameters. A procedure is said to **produce an effect**.

Example of a procedure:

Procedure definition (using COMAL)

```
PROC sum (number_one, number_two, REF total) CLOSED
      total := number_one + number_two    – note formal parameters
      PRINT total
ENDPROC sum
```

Note that in COMAL, the keyword CLOSED ensures that all the variables inside a procedure are LOCAL to that procedure.

Procedure call

sum (first_number, second_number, answer) – note *actual parameters*

Functions

A function is similar to a procedure, but **returns a single value** to a program. Like a procedure, a function must be defined and given a name before it can be used in a program. The name of the function is used to represent a variable containing the value to be returned.

Example of a function:

Function definition (in COMAL)

FUNC area_of_circle (radius) CLOSED   – note the *parameter* in a
   *area := PI * radius * radius*   function is sometimes
   RETURN area   called the **argument**
ENDFUNC area_of_circle

Function call

area := area_of_circle (number)

The function *area_of_circle* described above, is known as a **user-defined function**. A user-defined function is a function which is created within a program rather than being already present or **pre-defined** as part of the normal syntax of a programming language.

If you study the program documentation for the particular programming language that you are using, you can find examples of pre-defined functions.

Example of a pre-defined function in COMAL:

The SQR function returns the square root of a number

*number := 4
root := SQR (number)
PRINT root*

2

Author's note: In this book the terms procedures/sub-routines/subprograms and modules are interchangeable.

Objects and operations

An **operation** is a process which is carried out on an item of data (in a program).

An **object** is the item of data which is involved in the process.

There are several types of operations.

Arithmetical operations

Arithmetical operations are calculations involving numeric data (objects). The set of **arithmetic operators** includes add, subtract, multiply and divide. These operators are represented in many programming languages by using the symbols **+**, **−**, ***** and **/**.

Examples of arithmetical operations:

number_one + number_two   *– the objects are number_one and number_two, the operation is add*

19 – 54   *– the objects are 19 and 54, the operation is subtract*

String operations

String operations can process string data. String operations include joining strings, known as **concatenation**, and selecting parts of strings, known as **substrings**.

Examples of string operations:

PRINT "house" + "boat"   *– would produce the result 'houseboat'. This is **concatenation**.*

word\$:= "mousetrap"

PRINT word\$ (: 5)   *– would produce the result 'mouse'. This is selecting a **substring**.*

PRINT LEN (word\$)   *– would produce the result 9 (the length of the string 'mousetrap')*

Note: Some languages use '&' instead of '+' for concatenation

Some other string operations include:

- Changing strings to numbers and numbers to strings
- Changing characters into their ASCII values and ASCII values into characters
- Changing case – 'j' to 'J' and vice versa
- Removing blank spaces from a string

(Some languages may not contain specific keywords for all of these operations)

Relational operations

Relational operations use **relational operators** to compare data and produce a Boolean answer of true or false. The set of relational operators includes :

=   *equals*
>   *greater than*
<   *less than*
>=   *greater than or equal to*
<=   *less than or equal to*
<>   *is not equal to*

Relational operators can be used in program control structures such as selection and repetition.

Examples of relational operations:

> IF value >= 7 THEN .....

> WHILE month < 12 .....

Logical operations

Logical operations are also called **Boolean operations** because they use logical operators to produce a Boolean result such as *true* or *false*. The set of **logical operators** includes AND, OR and NOT. Logical operations are usually combined with relational operations in program control structures (see above).

Examples of logical operations:

> (target = found) AND (items remaining >0)

> WHILE NOT found ....

> REPEAT .... UNTIL false

Formatting of input/output

Formatting of input/output is arranging the appearance of the data on the screen when input or output is taking place. Each high level language has its own syntax for the formatting of program input and output. In *COMAL* and *True BASIC*, for example, *PRINT TAB* and *PRINT USING* are used to format output.

```
PRINT "The total of the numbers entered is "; TAB (40);
total
The total of the numbers entered is 13.652
PRINT USING "##.##" : total
13.65
```

Visual Basic also uses *PRINT TAB*. However, in *Visual Basic*, the keyword *FORMAT$* may be used to produce a similar effect to *PRINT USING*.

```
FORMAT$(3.4, "0.00")
3.40
```

Basic features of a software development environment

The features of a software development environment include:

1. Control
2. Data storage
3. Data flow

We will now consider each of these features in turn. These features will be described and implemented in the particular context of a high level procedural language being used as the software development environment.

The design notation which we will use to describe these features will be **pseudocode**, which we first met in chapter 6. Pseudocode uses ordinary English terms rather than the special keywords used in high level languages. Pseudocode is therefore **language independent**. Pseudocode is particularly useful for designing high level language programs because each line of pseudocode translates directly into a single line of code in a high level language.

Note that when example algorithms are given, the details are limited to cover the structure being shown. None of the algorithms in this chapter necessarily represents a complete program design.

1. Control

There are three basic control structures used in procedural languages. These are **sequence**, **selection** and **repetition**.

Sequence

Sequence simply means the order in which things are done. For example – remove clothes, take shower, dry off, put on clothes – is a sequence of operations. Putting these operations into the wrong order could cause a few problems. Just so with programming, the sequence or order in which you give instructions to the computer is important.

The purpose of sequence
The purpose of sequence is to ensure that instructions given to the computer in the form of a computer program are carried out (or **executed**) in the correct order.

Consider the following example algorithm, given in pseudocode:

    algorithm to add two numbers
    1. ask user for first number
    2. take in first number
    3. ask user for second number
    4. take in second number
    5. add two numbers to find total
    6. display total

Figure 8.1 *Sequence is important!*

This example will work correctly if, and only if, the steps are followed in the correct sequence, and none of the steps is missed out.

What would happen if the following algorithm were used?

    1. ask user for first number
    2. take in first number
    3. add two numbers to find total
    4. ask user for second number
    5. display total

Figure 8.2 *Ballot box*

Selection

Selection means making a choice, or deciding something. Selection is based on one or more **conditions**, used together with a control structure such as IF or CASE. Conditions have values, they may be either **true** or **false**.

Example:

age=18 – is a **simple condition**.

Month >= 1 AND Month <= 12 – is a **complex condition** (two or more simple conditions linked by AND, OR, NOT).

These conditions may be used together with a suitable control structure in order to carry out selection, like this :

```
IF age=18 THEN
    I can vote
ELSE
    I can't vote
END IF
IF Month >= 1 AND Month <= 12 THEN
    process date
ELSE
    display error message
END IF
```

In each case, the condition is tested, and if true, then the appropriate selection is made. Selection allows the sequence of execution of program statements to be changed. This has the effect of increasing the number of possible pathways that may be followed through a program. Look back at chapter 6 for more about program pathways.

The purpose of selection

The purpose of selection is to allow a choice to be made in a program, like changing the order or sequence of execution of program statements. Selection may be carried out by using a control structure and one or more conditions. In each case, the condition is tested, and if true, then the appropriate selection is made. The purpose of the condition is to allow the selection process to take place within the particular control structure in use.

Two control structures are commonly used to allow selection. These are **IF**...THEN..ELSE...END IF and CASE ... OF... WHEN... END CASE. The IF structure is suitable for use when a single selection (or a limited number of selections) is to be made. The **CASE** structure allows **multiple outcome selections** to be made in a program. Only one of several statements is executed in a CASE structure, depending on the data being processed at the time. The other statements are not executed.

The general form of the **IF** structure is:

```
IF condition is true THEN
    do something
ELSE
    do something different
END IF
```

Like the loop control structures which we discussed earlier, IF structures may be nested.

Here are some examples of algorithms which use IF structures :

pass mark algorithm

```
1. IF pupil's test mark is greater than or equal to 50 THEN display pass message
```

pass or fail algorithm

```
1. IF pupil's test mark is greater than or equal to 50 THEN
2.    display pass message
3.    ELSE
4.    display fail message
5. END IF
```

Grade algorithm using IF

```
1. IF pupil's test mark is greater than or equal to 80 THEN
2.    grade is grade 1
3. ELSE
4.    IF pupil's test mark is greater than or equal to 60 THEN
5.       grade is grade 2
6.    ELSE
7.       IF pupil's test mark is greater than or equal to 40 THEN
8.          grade is grade 3
9.       ELSE
10.         IF pupil's test mark is greater than or equal to 20 THEN
11.            grade is grade 4
12.         ELSE
13.            IF pupil's test mark is greater than or equal to 10 THEN
14.               grade is grade 5
15.            ELSE
16.               grade is grade 6
17.            END IF
18.         END IF
19.      END IF
20.   END IF
21. END IF
```

From the example above, you can see how complicated a nested IF structure may become, when **multiple outcome selections** have to be made. It is much more elegant to use a CASE structure in situations like this.

The general form of the **CASE** structure is:

```
CASE variable OF
   WHEN comparison with variable is true
      do something
   WHEN comparison with variable is true
      do something
   WHEN comparison with variable is true
      do something
   WHEN comparison with variable is true
      do something
   WHEN comparison with variable is true
      do something
   OTHERWISE
      do something
END CASE
```

When programming using a CASE structure, it should be noted that, even if more than one condition is true for a given variable, only the statement(s) following the first of the true conditions will be carried out. Careful thought needs to be given to the order in which the conditions appear to ensure that your program works in the way you intend.

Here are some examples of algorithms which use the CASE structure:

```
* Holiday algorithm using CASE*
1. CASE destination OF
2.    WHEN town
3.       take credit card
4.    WHEN pool
5.       take swimming costume
6.    WHEN beach
7.       take bucket and spade
8.    WHEN hillwalking
9.       take rucksack + food
10.   WHEN disco
11.      take ID card
12.   OTHERWISE
13.      watch TV
14. END CASE
```

```
* Teacher's Algorithm using CASE*
1. CASE day OF
2.     WHEN Monday
3.        give S1 homework
4.     WHEN Tuesday
5.        give S2 homework
6.     WHEN Wednesday
7.        give S3 homework
8.     WHEN Thursday
9.        give S4 homework
10.       WHEN Friday
11.          give S5/6 homework
12.       OTHERWISE
13.          mark homework
14.    END CASE
```

```
*Grade algorithm using CASE*  – compare with *Grade algorithm using IF* (above)
1. CASE pupil's test mark OF
2.     WHEN greater than or equal to 80
3.        grade is grade 1
4.     WHEN greater than or equal to 60
5.        grade is grade 2
6.     WHEN greater than or equal to 40
7.        grade is grade 3
8.     WHEN greater than or equal to 20
9.        grade is grade 4
10.       WHEN greater than or equal to 10
11.          grade is grade 5
12.       OTHERWISE
13.          grade is grade 6
14.    END CASE
```

Repetition

Repetition means repeating or doing something over and over again. Another term we met in chapter 6 which means the same as repetition is iteration. Repetition involves using a loop. Loops may be either conditional or fixed. Fixed loops may also be called unconditional or count-controlled loops and conditional loops may be called condition-controlled loops.

The purpose of repetition

The purpose of repetition is to allow statements in a program to be repeated as many times as is necessary.

Fixed loops

The purpose of a fixed loop is to repeat a set of program statements for a predetermined number of times. Fixed loops are controlled by a variable called a **loop counter**. The purpose of a loop counter is to count up the number of times the loop structure is to be repeated between the two limits set at the start of the loop. The loop counter may also be used for calculations inside the loop or be displayed in order to count entries, for example.

The general form of a fixed loop is:

> FOR *counter equals start number TO finish number .... STEP stepsize*
>   *do something*
> NEXT *counter*

Here are some examples of algorithms which use fixed loops:

Figure 8.3 *Repetition*

```
*algorithm to display a name five times*

1. start loop FOR one TO five times – this loop counts between the two fixed
                                      limits (one and five)
2.    display a name
3. end loop
```

```
*algorithm to display one name a number of times*

1. ask user how many times name is required      - this loop counts for a
                                                   variable number of times
2. take in the number of times name is required  - depending upon the value
                                                   stored
3. start loop FOR one TO number of times          - in the variable "number of
                                                   times"
4.    display a name
5. end loop
```

One feature of fixed loops in some programming languages is that they can increase or decrease in steps other than one. The purpose of the next example is to display all the even numbers from 2 to 30.

```
*algorithm showing a fixed loop with steps*

1. start loop FOR two TO thirty times STEP 2
2.    display loop counter
3. end loop
```

Loops may occur inside other loops – these are called **nested loops**.

```
1. start down loop FOR one TO five times
2.    start across loop FOR ten TO twenty times
3.       display a star character (using down and across in TAB)
4.    end across loop
5. end down loop
```

Conditional loops

The purpose of a conditional loop is to manage the situation where the number of times repetition must take place is not known in advance. Statements inside this type of loop may be carried out once, many times or not at all, depending upon one or more test conditions which are attached to the control structure of the loop.

The advantages of using conditional loops are:

- the amount of data to be processed need not be known in advance
- a mathematical calculation can continue until an answer is found
- more than one exit condition may be used, for example the loop could continue until the result is obtained or an error is found (See the Linear search algorithm in Chapter 9 for an example of this).

There are two types of conditional loop, each taking its name from the position of the test condition, either at the start or at the end of the loop. These are called **test at start** and **test at end**.

The program statement(s) inside a conditional loop with test at start *may not be run at all* if the test condition is not met. The program statement(s) inside a conditional loop with test at end *is always run at least once*. When this type of loop (conditional with test at end) is used for repeated data entry, like taking in a list of names or numbers, **a terminating value** or **sentinel value** is often used. The terminating value should be carefully chosen to be different from the 'real' data which is being entered.

The general form of a conditional loop with **test at start** is:

> *WHILE condition is true*
> > *do something*
> *END WHILE*

The general form of a conditional loop with **test at end** is:

> *REPEAT*
> > *do something*
> *UNTIL condition is true*

Here are some examples of algorithms which use conditional loops:

take in a word algorithm with test at end

```
1. loop REPEAT
2.    ask user to enter a word
3.    take in a word
4. UNTIL the word "end" is entered
```

– the word "end" is called the
– **terminating value** which
– tells the loop when to stop

Press space bar to continue algorithm

```
1. loop REPEAT
2.    display message "Press space bar"
3.    take in a character
4. UNTIL the character " " is entered
```

Quiz question algorithm

```
1. get question
2. get correct answer
3. loop REPEAT
4.    ask question
5.    take in response
6. UNTIL response equals correct answer
```

Sum numbers algorithm using a running total

```
1. set total to zero
2. set number to zero
3. loop REPEAT
4.    make total equal to total + number
5.    ask user to enter a number
6.    take in a number
7. UNTIL number equals -999 - in this case the number -999 is the terminating value
8. display total
```

algorithm with test at start

```
1. take in a word
2. loop WHILE the word is NOT 'end'
3.    take in a word
4. end loop
```

Other types of loops

A third type of loop, which hopefully, you will not encounter too often when in your chosen software development environment, is an **infinite loop**. An infinite loop is a loop from which there is no exit and the instructions in the loop will continue to be repeated forever. Depending on the software and computer system in use, you may be able to exit from an infinite loop by pressing the <ESCAPE> key on the keyboard, and so regain control. An infinite loop is usually caused by a **logical error** in a program. Look back at the section on logical errors in chapter 6 for an example of an infinite loop. If the infinite loop cannot be interrupted in this way, the computer is said to be **hung** and may need to be **reset**, either by pressing a combination of keys, such as <CONTROL-ALT-DELETE> (IBM) or <CONTROL-COMMAND-POWER> (or ESCAPE to end the task) (Macintosh), or by pressing the reset button on the computer.

2. Data storage

Variables

Data is stored in a computer's memory in storage locations. Each storage location in the computer's memory has a unique address. (See chapter 1 for more about storage locations). A **variable** is the name that a programmer uses to identify a storage location. (This is much more convenient than using a memory address – compare *number* with *90987325.*) By using a variable name a programmer can store, retrieve and handle data without knowing what the data will be. Variable names, procedure and function names are sometimes also called **identifiers**, because they are used to identify that particular item.

- **Local and global variables**. Two types of variables are **global variables** and **local variables**. Global variables may be used anywhere in a program but local variables are defined only for use in one part of a program (a subprogram – normally a function or a procedure). Local variables only come into existence when that procedure is entered and the data that they contain is lost when the processing of that procedure is complete. Using local variables reduces the unplanned effects of the same variable name being used in another part of the program and accidentally being changed. Global variables should only be used for data that needs to be shared between different procedures within a program, because they are accessible to any part of the whole program. It is good practice to declare global variables at the start of a program.

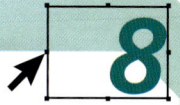

Look further on in this chapter for the implementation of an algorithm which shows the difference between local and global variables. The algorithm for this example is not shown here because looking at the algorithm on its own is not particularly helpful. In order to understand this properly, you need to look at the implementation and the sample output. The sample output shows that the values of the local variables (*sum* and *product*) within the calculate procedure have no effect on the values of the global variables (also called *sum* and *product*) outside the calculate procedure, i.e. throughout the rest of the program.

- **Scope of variables**. The **scope** of a variable is the range of statements for which a variable is valid. So, the scope of a local variable is the subprogram it is used in. This means that in a large programming project, where a number of programmers are writing separate subprograms, there is no need to be concerned about using different (or similar) local variable names, since they cannot have any effect outside their scope.

Data types

The data types stored by a program may be a number, a character, a string, a date, an array, a sound sample, a video clip or indeed, any kind of data. Some high level languages, such as C++, allow programmers to specify their own data types – these are called user-defined data types.

Some of the more important data types are listed below:

- **Alphanumeric data** – may include letters, digits and punctuation. It includes both the character and string data types. **Character data** is a single character represented by the character set code, e.g. ASCII (American Standard Code for Information Interchange). **String data** is a list of characters, e.g. a word in a sentence.
- **Numeric data** – may consist of **real data** or **integer data**. Real data includes ALL numbers, both whole and fractional. Integer data is a subset of real data which includes only whole numbers, either positive or negative.
- **Date data** – is when data is in a form representing a valid date e.g. 29/2/2000 is valid date data, 30/2/2000 is not.
- **Boolean** or **logical data** – may only have two values, *true* or *false*. Boolean data is used in a program's control structures (see Selection and Repetition, earlier in this chapter).
- **Sample data** – consists of digitally recorded **sound data** (e.g. MP3) and **video data** (e.g. a video clip – MPEG). These are complex data types which contain enough data to allow a subprogram or application to reproduce the original data

One factor which may influence a programmer's choice of software development environment is the range of data types available. For example, C++ has at least six different numeric data types, whereas some versions of the BASIC language may only have the two numeric data types described above.

Structured data types

Structured data types include **arrays**.

A set of data items *of the same type* grouped together using a single variable name is called an **array**. Each part of an array is called an **element**. Each element in an array is identified by the **variable name** and a **subscript** (**element number** or **index**).

An array of names might look like this:

> *name (1)* -- John
> *name (2)* -- Helen
> *name (3)* -- Peter
> *name (4)* -- Mary

This array has four parts. Element number 3 of this array is the name 'Peter'.

Arrays which have one number as their subscript are called **one-dimensional arrays**. Arrays may have more than one dimension, and, in that case, would have a separate subscript number for each dimension, e.g. point (x,y) would refer to a two-dimensional array of points. When programming using arrays, it is necessary to declare the name of the array and its size at the start of the program, so that the computer may set aside the correct amount of memory space for the array. For instance, to set aside space for an array called apples with a size of 15 in BASIC, Pascal and C:

> *DIM apples% (15)   VAR apples : array [1..15] of integer;   int apples [15];*

Here is an example of an algorithm which makes use of arrays for data storage:

---

algorithm to read names and marks into two arrays

```
1. set array counter to zero
2. set aside space for ten pupils names in the array name []
3. set aside space for ten pupils marks in the array mark []
4. loop REPEAT
5.    add one to array counter
6.    READ value into name array [counter]
7.    READ value into mark array [counter]
8. UNTIL end of data is reached
```

Notes on the above algorithm:
> *End of data is a useful feature, present in some high level languages. When there is no more data to be read, end of data is set to true, causing the loop to stop. End of file is a similar feature, although file handling is outwith the scope of this unit. If you know in advance the number of data items to be read, a terminating condition such as counter equals ten may be used. If the data contains a terminating value, such as −1, then mark equals −1 may be used as the terminating condition for the loop.*

3. Data flow

The movement of data (or the data flow) between subprograms is implemented by using **parameters**. Data structures (such as variables) which are only passed into subprograms to be used are known as **in** parameters. Variables which are passed into a subprogram and are changed or updated are referred to as **in/out** parameters. Variables which are only passed out of subprograms are known as **out** parameters.

Parameters

A **parameter** is information about a data item being supplied to a subprogram (function or procedure) when it is called into use. When the subprogram is used, the calling program must pass parameters to it. This is called **parameter passing**.

Let's take as an example a validation procedure which checks that a number is within a certain range. Suppose this procedure is called *validate*, and that the variable we wish to pass to this procedure is *test*, which has a value input by the user.

```
begin program
ask for test mark
take in test mark                        This is the calling program
validate (test)                          (or main program)
end program

begin procedure validate (number)
   loop WHILE number is outwith range
      prompt to reenter number           This is the subprogram
      take in the number                 (procedure)
   end loop
end procedure
```

- **Actual and formal parameters**. The parameter test contains the value that is being passed into the procedure validate – the parameter test is called the **actual parameter**.

  number is the name of the parameter which is used in the procedure definition, so *number* is called the **formal parameter**.

Remember: Parameters which are passed into a procedure (or function) when it is called from any other part of the program are called the actual parameters. Parameters used in the procedure or function are the formal parameters.

- **Value and reference parameters**. Parameters can be passed either by **value** or by **reference**. The method used depends upon whether the parameter is going into or in/out of a procedure (or function). Parameters are passed by **value** when a parameter is passed **into** a procedure but does not require to be passed back out again (to be used in another procedure). Parameters are passed by **reference** when the parameter requires to be passed in to a procedure, **updated** and then passed back out of the procedure again. One exception to this rule exists for the array data structure only. When an **array** is being passed as a parameter, it is always passed by **reference**. Note that in some software development environments, parameters passed by reference are called **variable parameters**.

Describing the data flow

It is necessary to describe the data flow in a program in order to work out how the parameters should be passed between the main program and any subprograms and between the subprograms themselves.

Consider the following algorithm and refinement, which describe a solution to the problem 'Count the number of five letter words in a list':

```
Algorithm                                    Data Flow

1. initialise
2. take in list of words and count number of five letter words
                                    (in/out: no_of_5_letter_words)

3. display result                   (in: no_of_5_letter_words)

Refinement

1.1 set number of five letter words to zero

2.1   loop REPEAT                   (in/out: no_of_5_letter_words)
2.2      take in a word
2.3      IF the word has five letters THEN add one to the number of five letter
         words
2.4   UNTIL the word "stop" is entered

3.1   display number of words with five letters   (in: no_of_5_letter_words)
```

The parameter being passed in the above example is the variable **no_of_5_letter_words**, which, at the end of the program, will contain the value representing the number of words found to have five letters. You can see an implementation of this algorithm in the next section.

Remember: in and out when referring to data flow within a program is between procedures – it does not correspond to program inputs and outputs.

Here is an example algorithm to show the effect of passing parameters by value and by reference:

(You should look at the implementations of this algorithm later in this chapter to help you understand this example.)

```
1. set one actual parameter to first
2. set one actual parameter to second
3. display the values of the parameters at the start of the program
4. exchange the parameters              (in/out: first_actual, second_actual)
5. display the values of the parameters at the end of the program

Refinement

4.1 make swap equal to the first parameter
4.2 make the first parameter equal to the second parameter
4.3 make the second parameter equal to the value in swap
```

In the following sections A to C, we will look at the means of implementing some of the algorithms listed earlier in this chapter, and give examples in a variety of different procedural high level languages. You should compare each example shown below with its related algorithm in the previous section. A number of implementations in other software development environments are also shown for comparison purposes where appropriate. (section D)

Section A : COMAL implementations

1. Control

Sequence

Program implementation based on *algorithm to add two numbers*

```
// Title : COMAL Example 1
// Author : John Walsh
// Date : 15 April 2000
//
PRINT "Please enter the first number ";
INPUT number_one
PRINT "Please enter the second number ";
INPUT number_two
total := number_one + number_two
PRINT "The total is "; total
END
```

Sample Output

Please enter the first number ? 19
Please enter the second number ? 54
The total is 73

Selection – IF ...THEN

Program implementation based on *pass or fail algorithm*

```
// Title : COMAL Example 2
// Author : John Walsh
// Date : 15 April 2000
//
PRINT "Please enter pupil's mark ";
INPUT mark
IF mark >= 50 THEN
PRINT "Pass"
ELSE
PRINT "Fail"
ENDIF
END
```

Please enter pupil's mark ? 49
Fail
Please enter pupil's mark ? 50
Pass
Please enter pupil's mark ? 51
Pass

Program implementation based on *Grade algorithm using IF*

```
// Title : COMAL Example 3
// Author : John Walsh
// Date : 15 April 2000
//
PRINT "Please enter pupil's mark ";
INPUT mark
IF mark >= 80 THEN
   PRINT "Grade 1"
ELSE
   IF mark >= 60 THEN
      PRINT "Grade 2"
   ELSE
      IF mark >= 40 THEN
         PRINT "Grade 3"
      ELSE
         IF mark >= 20 THEN
            PRINT "Grade 4"
         ELSE
            IF mark >= 10 THEN
               PRINT "Grade 5"
            ELSE
               PRINT "Grade 6"
            ENDIF
         ENDIF
      ENDIF
   ENDIF
ENDIF
END
```

Sample Output

Please enter pupil's mark ? 80

Grade 1

Please enter pupil's mark ? 60

Grade 2

Please enter pupil's mark ? 40

Grade 3

Please enter pupil's mark ? 20

Grade 4

Please enter pupil's mark ? 10

Grade 5

Please enter pupil's mark ? 9

Grade 6

Selection – CASE ... OF

Program implementation based on *Grade algorithm using CASE*

```
// Title : COMAL Example 4
// Author : John Walsh
// Date : 15 April 2000
//
PRINT "Please enter pupil's mark ";
INPUT mark
CASE mark OF
   WHEN >= 80
      PRINT "Grade 1"
   WHEN >= 60
      PRINT "Grade 2"
   WHEN >= 40
      PRINT "Grade 3"
   WHEN >= 20
      PRINT "Grade 4"
   WHEN >= 10
      PRINT "Grade 5"
   OTHERWISE
      PRINT "Grade 6"
ENDCASE
END
```

Repetition – Fixed loops

Program implementation based on *algorithm to display a name five times*

```
// Title : COMAL Example 5
// Author : John Walsh
// Date : 15 April 2000
//
FOR loop_counter := 1 TO 5 DO
   PRINT "John"
NEXT loop_counter
END
```

Program implementation based on *algorithm to display one name a number of times*

```
// Title : COMAL Example 6
// Author : John Walsh
// Date : 15 April 2000
//
PRINT "Please enter the number of times a name is required"
INPUT number_of_times
FOR loop_counter := 1 TO number_of_times DO
   PRINT "John"
NEXT loop_counter
END
```

Sample Output

Please enter the number of times a name is required

? 3

John

John

John

Program implementation based on *algorithm showing a fixed loop with steps*

```
// Title : COMAL Example 7
// Author : John Walsh
// Date : 15 April 2000
//
FOR loop_counter := 2 TO 30 STEP 2 DO
   PRINT loop_counter
NEXT loop_counter
END
```

Sample Output

2

4

6

8

10

12

14

16

18

20

22

24

26

28

30

Program implementation based on *tab algorithm showing nested loops*

```
// Title : COMAL Example 8
// Author : John Walsh
// Date : 15 April 2000
//
FOR down := 1 TO 5 DO
   FOR across := 10 TO 20 DO
      PRINT TAB (across, down); "*"
   NEXT across
NEXT down
END
```

Sample Output

```
**********
**********
**********
**********
**********
```

Repetition – Conditional loops

Program implementation based on *take in a word algorithm with test at end*

```
// Title : COMAL Example 9
// Author : John Walsh
// Date : 1 May 2000
//
timesinloop := 0
REPEAT
   timesinloop := timesinloop + 1
   PRINT "Please enter a word (or END to finish) ";
   INPUT word$
UNTIL word$ = "END" OR word$ = "end"
PRINT "Program ended"
PRINT "The number of times in the loop is "; timesinloop
END
```

Sample Output

Please enter a word (or END to finish) ? Conditional

Please enter a word (or END to finish) ? loop

Please enter a word (or END to finish) ? with

Please enter a word (or END to finish) ? test

Please enter a word (or END to finish) ? at

Please enter a word (or END to finish) ? end

Program ended

The number of times in the loop is 6

Please enter a word (or END to finish) ? end

Program ended

The number of times in the loop is 1

*Note that the code in a conditional loop with test at end is always run at least once.
Note that this example shows a COMPLEX condition.*

Program implementation based on *Sum numbers algorithm using a running total*

```
// Title : COMAL Example 10
// Author : John Walsh
// Date : 15 April 2000
//
total := 0
number := 0
REPEAT
   total := total + number
   PRINT "Please enter a number (-999 to finish)";
   INPUT number
UNTIL number = -999
PRINT "The total of the numbers entered is "; total
PRINT "Program ended"
END
```

Sample Output

Please enter a number (−999 to finish)? −999
The total of the numbers entered is 0
Program ended
Please enter a number (-999 to finish)? 6
Please enter a number (-999 to finish)? 7
Please enter a number (-999 to finish)? 1
Please enter a number (-999 to finish)? −999
The total of the numbers entered is 14
Program ended

Note that this example shows a SIMPLE condition.

Program implementation based on *algorithm with test at start*

```
// Title : COMAL Example 11
// Author : John Walsh
// Date : 1 May 2000
//
timesinloop := 0
PRINT "Please enter a word ";
INPUT word$
WHILE NOT ((word$ = "end") OR (word$ = "END")) DO
   timesinloop := timesinloop + 1
   PRINT "Please enter a word ";
   INPUT word$
ENDWHILE
PRINT "Program ended"
PRINT "The number of times in the loop is "; timesinloop
END
```

Sample Output

Please enter a word ? Conditional
Please enter a word ? loop
Please enter a word ? with
Please enter a word ? test
Please enter a word ? at
Please enter a word ? start
Please enter a word ? end
Program ended
The number of times in the loop is 6

Please enter a word ? end
Program ended
The number of times in the loop is 0

Note that the code in a conditional loop with test at start need not be run at all if the condition is not met.
Note that this example shows a COMPLEX condition.

2. Data storage

Program implementation based on *algorithm to read names and marks into two arrays*

```
// Title : COMAL Example 12
// Author : John Walsh
// Date : 16 April 2000
//
array_counter := 0
DIM pupil_name$ (10)
DIM pupil_mark% (10)
REPEAT
   array_counter := array_counter + 1
   READ pupil_name$ (array_counter)
   READ pupil_mark% (array_counter)
UNTIL EOD
END
//
DATA Harjinder, 76, Paul, 68, Jennifer, 56
DATA David, 52, Siobhan, 89, Cecilia, 75
DATA Angus, 61, Sarah, 93, Anwar, 92
```

Note: No Sample output from this program

Program implementation based on *local and global variables*

```
// Title : COMAL Example 13
// Author : John Walsh
// Date : 15 May 2000
//
sum% := 0  // global variables
product% := 0
first_number% := 13
second_number% := 33
//
calculate (first_number%, second_number%)
//
PRINT sum%, product%
END
//
PROC calculate (number_one%, number_two%)
   LOCAL sum%, product% // set up two local variables
   sum% := number_one% + number_two%
   product% := number_one% * number_two%
   PRINT sum%, product%
ENDPROC calculate
```

The sample output shows that the values of the local variables (sum and product) within the calculate procedure have no effect on the values of the global variables (also called sum and product) outside the calculate procedure, i.e. throughout the rest of the program.

3. Data Flow

Program implementation based on *Count the number of five letter words in a list*

Note that the single parameter (*no_of_5_letter_words%*) which is passed in this program is passed out by reference from the *take_in_list_of_words* procedure and passed by value into the *display_result* procedure.

```
// Title : COMAL Example 14
// Author : John Walsh
// Date : 14 May 2000
//
initialise
take_in_list_of_words (no_of_5_letter_words%)
display_result (no_of_5_letter_words%)
END
//
PROC initialise
   // This procedure initialises all parameters
   word$ := ""
   no_of_5_letter_words% := 0
ENDPROC initialise
//
PROC take_in_list_of_words (REF no_of_5_letter_words%) CLOSED
   // This procedure counts the words that have five letters
   REPEAT
      INPUT "Please enter a word (stop to finish) " : word$
      IF LEN (word$) = 5 THEN no_of_5_letter_words% := no_of_5_letter_words% + 1
   UNTIL word$ = "stop"
ENDPROC take_in_list_of_words
//
PROC display_result (no_of_5_letter_words%) CLOSED
   PRINT "The number of words with five letters is "; no_of_5_letter_words%
ENDPROC display_result
```

Sample Output

Please enter a word (stop to finish) hello
Please enter a word (stop to finish) stop
The number of words with five letters is 1
Please enter a word (stop to finish) stop
The number of words with five letters is 0
Please enter a word (stop to finish) Giraffe
Please enter a word (stop to finish) Zebra
Please enter a word (stop to finish) Gnu
Please enter a word (stop to finish) Oryx
Please enter a word (stop to finish) Snake
Please enter a word (stop to finish) stop
The number of words with five letters is 2

Program implementation based on algorithm – passing parameters by value and by reference:

```
// Title : COMAL Example 15
// Author : John Walsh
// Date : 16 April 2000
//
first_actual$ := "First"
second_actual$ := "second"
//
PRINT "Values at start of program are :"
PRINT "first_actual$ = "; first_actual$
PRINT "second_actual$ = "; second_actual$
//
exchange (first_actual$, second_actual$)
//
PRINT "Values at end of program are :"
PRINT "first_actual$ = "; first_actual$
PRINT "second_actual$ = "; second_actual$
END
//
PROC exchange (REF formal_one$, REF formal_two$)   // Remove REF to pass by value
   LOCAL swap$
   swap$ := formal_one$
   formal_one$ := formal_two$
   formal_two$ := swap$
ENDPROC exchange
```

Values at start of program are :
first_actual$ = First
second_actual$ = Second
Values at end of program are :
first_actual$ = Second
second_actual$ = First

Notes on the above code:

(a) The values are exchanged correctly when passed by reference.

(b) Here is the sample output from the same program with the REF removed:
i.e. PROC exchange (formal_one$, formal_two$)

Values at start of program are :
first_actual$ = First
second_actual$ = Second
Values at end of program are :
first_actual$ = First
second_actual$ = Second

Note that the values are not exchanged and remain as per the original.

Section B : Visual Basic implementations

1. Control
Sequence

Program implementation based on *algorithm to add two numbers*

```
'Title : Visual Basic Example 1
'Author : John Walsh
'Date : 25 May 2000
'
Option Explicit
Dim number_one As Integer, number_two As Integer, total As Integer

Private Sub cmdEnd_Click()
End
End Sub
Private Sub cmdEnterNumbers_Click()
number_one = InputBox("Please enter the first number")
number_two = InputBox("Please enter the second number")
total = number_one + number_two
picDisplay.Print Tab(20); "The total is "; total
End Sub
```

Sample Output

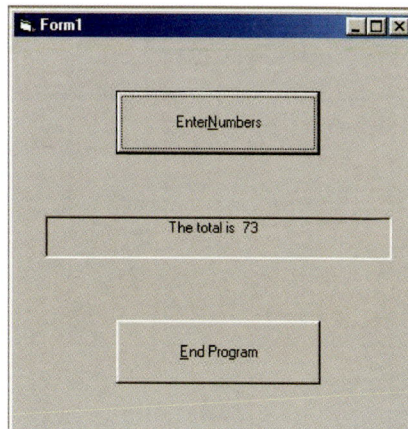

Figure 8.4 *Sample output of Visual Basic Example 1*

Selection – IF ...THEN

Program implementation based on *pass or fail algorithm*

```
'Title : Visual Basic Example 2
'Author : John Walsh
'Date : 25 May 2000
'

Option Explicit
Dim mark As Integer

Private Sub cmdEnterMark_Click()
picDisplay.Cls
mark = InputBox("Please enter the mark")
If mark >= 50 Then
    picDisplay.Print Tab(25); "Pass"
Else
    picDisplay.Print Tab(25); "Fail"
End If
End Sub
Private Sub cmdEnd_Click()
End
End Sub
```

Sample Output

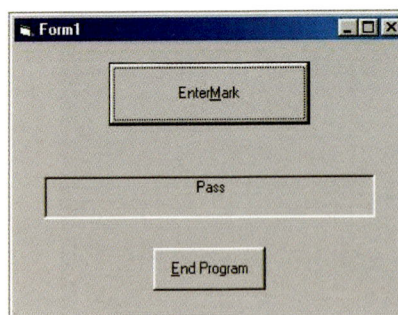

Figure 8.5 *Sample output of Visual Basic Example 2*

Program implementation based on *Grade algorithm using IF*

```
'Title : Visual Basic Example 3
'Author : John Walsh
'Date : 25 May 2000
'
Option Explicit
Dim mark As Integer

Private Sub cmdEnterMark_Click()
picDisplay.Cls
mark = InputBox("Please enter pupil's mark")

If mark >= 80 Then
   picDisplay.Print Tab(25); "Grade 1"
Else
   If mark >= 60 Then
      picDisplay.Print Tab(25); "Grade 2"
   Else
      If mark >= 40 Then
         picDisplay.Print Tab(25); "Grade 3"
      Else
         If mark >= 20 Then
            picDisplay.Print Tab(25); "Grade 4"
         Else
            If mark >= 10 Then
               picDisplay.Print Tab(25); "Grade 5"
            Else
               picDisplay.Print Tab(25); "Grade 6"
            End If
         End If
      End If
   End If
End If
End Sub

Private Sub cmdEnd_Click()
End
End Sub
```

Sample Output

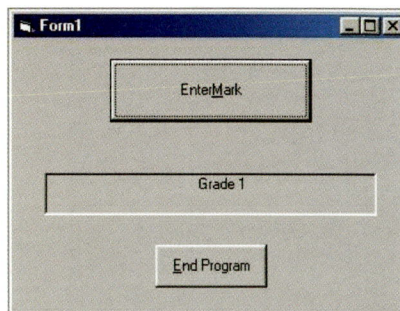

Figure 8.6 *Sample output of Visual Basic Example 3*

Selection – CASE ... OF

Program implementation based on *Grade algorithm using CASE*

```
"Title : Visual Basic Example 4
'Author : John Walsh
'Date : 26 May 2000
'
Option Explicit
Dim mark As Integer

Private Sub cmdEnterMark_Click()
picDisplay.Cls
mark = InputBox("Please enter pupil's mark")

Select Case mark
Case Is >= 80
picDisplay.Print Tab(25); "Grade 1"
Case Is >= 60
picDisplay.Print Tab(25); "Grade 2"
Case Is >= 40
picDisplay.Print Tab(25); "Grade 3"
Case Is >= 20
picDisplay.Print Tab(25); "Grade 4"
Case Is >= 10
picDisplay.Print Tab(25); "Grade 5"
Case Else
picDisplay.Print Tab(25); "Grade 6"
End Select
End Sub

Private Sub cmdEnd_Click()
End
End Sub
```

Sample Output

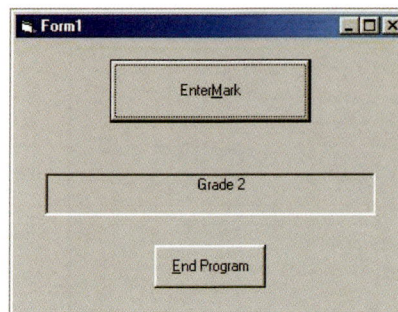

Figure 8.7 *Sample output of Visual Basic Example 4*

Repetition – Fixed loops

Program implementation based on *algorithm to display a name five times*

```
'Title : Visual Basic Example 5
'Author : John Walsh
'Date : 26 May 2000
'

Option Explicit
Dim loop_counter As Integer

Private Sub cmdStartLoop_Click()
picDisplay.Cls
For loop_counter = 1 To 5
   picDisplay.Print "John"
Next loop_counter
End Sub

Private Sub cmdEnd_Click()
End
End Sub
```

Sample Output

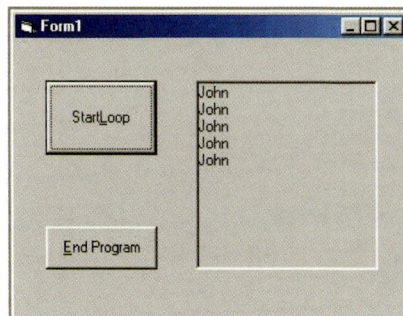

Figure 8.8 *Sample output of Visual Basic Example 5*

Program implementation based on *algorithm to display one name a number of times*

```
'Title : Visual Basic Example 6
'Author : John Walsh
'Date : 27 May 2000
'
Option Explicit
Dim loop_counter As Integer, number_of_times As Integer

Private Sub cmdTakeNames_Click()
picDisplay.Cls
number_of_times = InputBox("Please enter the number of times a name is
required")
For loop_counter = 1 To number_of_times
    picDisplay.Print "John"
Next loop_counter
End Sub

Private Sub cmdEnd_Click()
End
End Sub
```

Sample Output

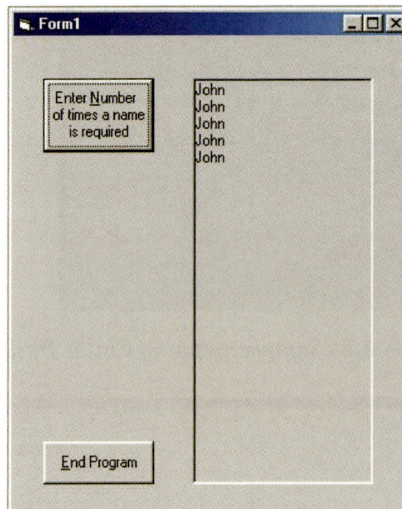

Figure 8.9 *Sample output of Visual Basic Example 6*

Program implementation based on *algorithm showing a fixed loop with steps*

```
'Title : Visual Basic Example 7
'Author : John Walsh
'Date : 27 May 2000
'
Option Explicit
Dim loop_counter As Integer

Private Sub cmdDisplayNumbers_Click()
picDisplay.Cls
For loop_counter = 2 To 30 Step 2
   picDisplay.Print loop_counter
Next loop_counter
End Sub


Private Sub cmdEnd_Click()
End
End Sub
```

Sample Output

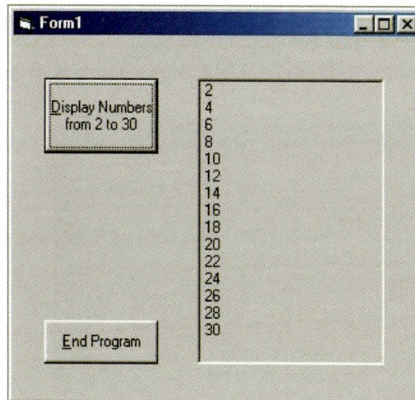

Figure 8.10 *Sample output of Visual Basic Example 7*

Program implementation based on *tab algorithm showing nested loops*

```
'Title : Visual Basic Example 8
'Author : John Walsh
'Date : 27 May 2000
'
Option Explicit
Dim across As Integer, down As Integer

Private Sub cmdPrintStars_Click()
picDisplay.Cls
For down = 1 To 5
   For across = 10 To 20
      picDisplay.Print Tab(across); "*"; 'Note – only one TAB parameter allowed
   Next across
Next down                               'so this example is not directly equivalent
End Sub


Private Sub cmdEnd_Click()
End
End Sub
```

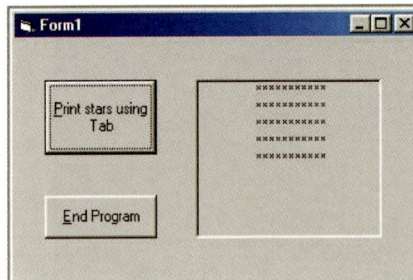

Figure 8.11 *Sample output of Visual Basic Example 8*

Repetition – Conditional loops

Program implementation based on *take in a word algorithm with test at end*

```
'Title : Visual Basic Example 9
'Author : John Walsh
'Date : 27 May 2000
'
Option Explicit
Dim word As String, timesinloop As Integer

Private Sub cmdEnterWords_Click()
'picDisplay.Cls – is disabled for the sample output
timesinloop = 0
Do
   timesinloop = timesinloop + 1
   word = InputBox("Please enter a word (or END to finish)")
   picDisplay.Print word
Loop Until word = "END" Or word = "end"
picDisplay.Print "Loop ended"
picDisplay.Print "The number of times in the loop is "; timesinloop
End Sub

Private Sub cmdEnd_Click()
picDisplay.Cls
End
End Sub
```

Sample Output

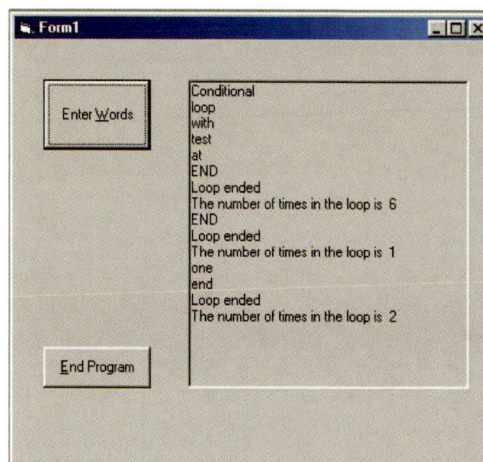

Figure 8.12 *Sample output of Visual Basic Example 9*

*Note that the code in a conditional loop with test at end is always run at least once.
Note that this example shows a COMPLEX condition.*

Program implementation based on *Sum numbers algorithm using a running total*

```
'Title : Visual Basic Example 10
'Author : John Walsh
'Date : 28 May 2000
'
Option Explicit
Dim total As Integer, number As Integer

Private Sub cmdEnterNumbers_Click()
'picDisplay.Cls
total = 0
number = 0
Do
    total = total + number
    number = InputBox("Please enter a number (-999 to finish)")
    picDisplay.Print number
Loop Until number = -999
picDisplay.Print "The total of the numbers entered is "; total
End Sub

Private Sub cmdEnd_Click()
picDisplay.Cls
End
End Sub
```

Sample Output

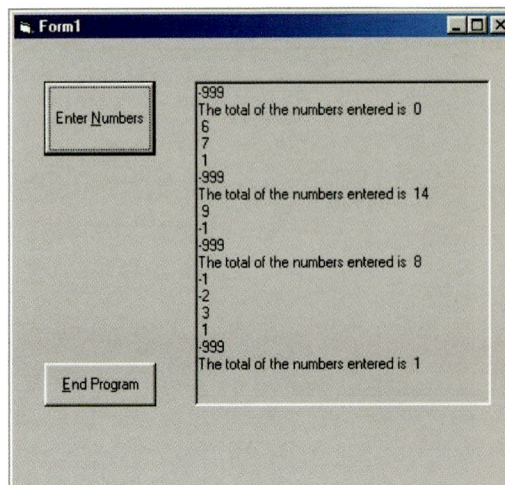

Figure 8.13 *Sample output of Visual Basic Example 10*

Note that this example shows a SIMPLE condition.

Program implementation based on *algorithm with test at start*

```
'Title : Visual Basic Example 11
'Author : John Walsh
'Date : 28 May 2000
'
Option Explicit
Dim word As String, timesinloop As Integer

Private Sub cmdEnterWords_Click()
'picDisplay.Cls - is disabled for the sample output
timesinloop = 0
word = InputBox("Please enter a word (or END to finish)")
picDisplay.Print word
Do While Not ((word = "end") Or (word = "END"))
   timesinloop = timesinloop + 1
   word = InputBox("Please enter a word (or END to finish)")
   picDisplay.Print word
Loop
picDisplay.Print "Loop ended"
picDisplay.Print "The number of times in the loop is "; timesinloop
End Sub

Private Sub cmdEnd_Click()
picDisplay.Cls
End
End Sub
```

Sample Output

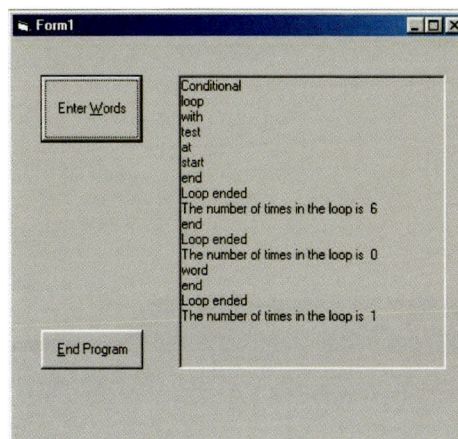

Figure 8.14 *Sample output of Visual Basic Example 11*

Note that the code in a conditional loop with test at start need not be run at all if the condition is not met.

Note that this example shows a COMPLEX condition.

2. Data storage

Program implementation based on *algorithm to read names and marks into two arrays*

```
'Title : Visual Basic Example 12
'Author : John Walsh
'Date : 29 May 2000
'
Option Explicit
Option Base 1 " makes array index start at 1
Dim array_counter As Integer
Dim pupil_name(10) As String
Dim pupil_mark(10) As Integer

Private Sub cmdFillArray_Click()
array_counter = 0
LstNames.AddItem "Harjinder"
LstMarks.AddItem 76
LstNames.AddItem "Paul"
LstMarks.AddItem 68
LstNames.AddItem "Jennifer"
LstMarks.AddItem 56
LstNames.AddItem "David"
LstMarks.AddItem 52
LstNames.AddItem "siobhan"
LstMarks.AddItem 89
Do
   array_counter = array_counter + 1
   pupil_name(array_counter) = LstNames.List(array_counter)
   'Val changes a string into an integer value
   pupil_mark(array_counter) = Val(LstMarks.List(array_counter))
   'ListCount is the number of items in the list
Loop Until array_counter = LstNames.ListCount
End Sub

Private Sub cmdEnd_Click()
End
End Sub
```

Sample Output

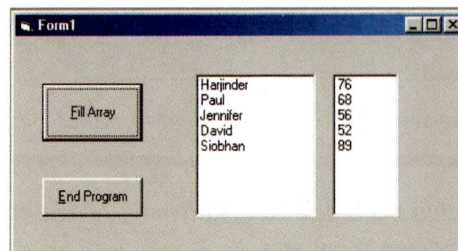

Figure 8.15 *Sample output of Visual Basic Example 12*

Program implementation based on *local and global variables*

```
'Title : Visual Basic Example 13
'Author : John Walsh
'Date : 29 May 2000
'

Option Explicit
Dim sum As Integer, product As Integer
Dim first_number As Integer, second_number As Integer

Private Sub cmdRunProgram_Click()
sum = 0   'global variables
product = 0
first_number = 13
second_number = 33
'
calculate first_number, second_number
'
PicDisplay.Print sum, product
End Sub

Private Sub calculate(ByVal number_one, ByVal number_two)
   Dim sum As Integer, product As Integer 'local variables
   sum = number_one + number_two
   product = number_one * number_two
   PicDisplay.Print sum, product
End Sub

Private Sub cmdEnd_Click()
End
End Sub
```

Sample Output

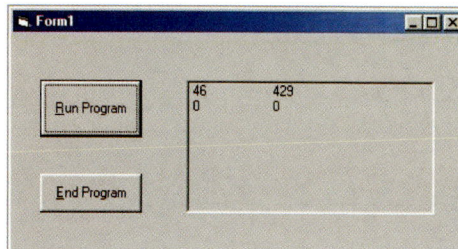

Figure 8.16 *Sample output of Visual Basic Example 13*

The sample output shows that the values of the local variables (sum and product) within the calculate procedure have no effect on the values of the global variables (also called sum and product) outside the calculate procedure, i.e. throughout the rest of the program.

3. Data Flow

Program implementation based on *Count the number of five letter words in a list*

Note that the single parameter (no_of_5_letter_words) which is passed in this program is passed out by reference from the take_in_list_of_words procedure and passed by value into the display_result procedure.

```
'Title : Visual Basic Example 14
'Author : John Walsh
'Date : 29 May 2000
'
Option Explicit
Dim word As String, no_of_5_letter_words As Integer

Private Sub cmdRunProgram_Click()
Call initialise
Call take_in_list_of_words(no_of_5_letter_words)
Call display_result(no_of_5_letter_words)
End Sub

Private Sub initialise()
    'This procedure initialises all parameters
    word = ""
    no_of_5_letter_words = 0
    PicDisplay.Cls
End Sub

Private Sub take_in_list_of_words(ByRef no_of_5_letter_words)
    'This procedure counts the words that have five letters
    Do
       word = InputBox("Please enter a word (stop to finish)")
       PicDisplay.Print word
       If Len(word) = 5 Then no_of_5_letter_words = no_of_5_letter_words + 1
    Loop Until word = "stop"
End Sub

Private Sub display_result(ByVal no_of_5_letter_words)
    PicDisplay.Print "The number of words with five letters is ";
    no_of_5_letter_words
End Sub

Private Sub cmdEnd_Click()
PicDisplay.Cls
End
End Sub
```

Sample Output

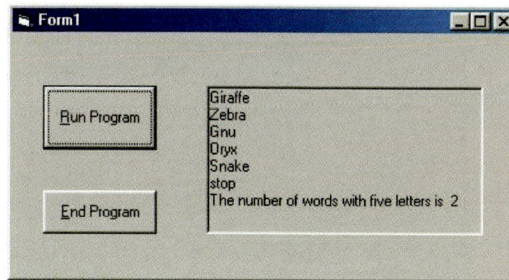

Figure 8.17 *Sample output of Visual Basic Example 14*

Program implementation based on algorithm – passing parameters by value and by reference:

```
'Title : Visual Basic Example 15
'Author : John Walsh
'Date : 30 May 2000
'
Option Explicit
Dim first_actual As String, second_actual As String

Private Sub cmdRunProgram_click()
first_actual = "First"
second_actual = "second"
'
PicDisplay.Print "Values at start of program are :"
PicDisplay.Print "first_actual = "; first_actual
PicDisplay.Print "second_actual = "; second_actual
'
exchange first_actual, second_actual
'
PicDisplay.Print "Values at end of program are :"
PicDisplay.Print "first_actual = "; first_actual
PicDisplay.Print "second_actual = "; second_actual
End Sub

Private Sub exchange(ByRef formal_one, ByRef formal_two)
'Change parameters to ByVal and no swap occurs
Dim swap As String
swap = formal_one
formal_one = formal_two
formal_two = swap
End Sub

Private Sub cmdEnd_Click()
PicDisplay.Cls
End
End Sub
```

Sample Output

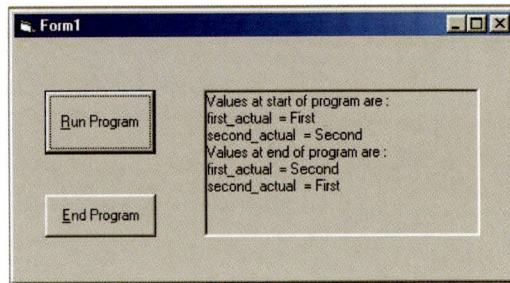

Values at start of program are :
first_actual = First
second_actual = Second
Values at end of program are :
first_actual = Second
second_actual = First

Run Program

End Program

Figure 8.18 *Sample output of Visual Basic Example 15*

Section C: TrueBASIC implementations

1. Control

Sequence

Program implementation based on *algorithm to add two numbers*

```
! Title : TrueBASIC Example 1
! Author : John Walsh
! Date : 19 May 2000
!
PRINT "Please enter the first number ";
INPUT number_one
PRINT "Please enter the second number ";
INPUT number_two
LET total = number_one + number_two
PRINT "The total is "; total
END
```

Sample Output

Sample output
Please enter the first number ? 19
Please enter the second number ? 54
The total is 73

Selection – IF ...THEN

Program implementation based on *pass or fail algorithm*

```
! Title : TrueBASIC Example 2
! Author : John Walsh
! Date : 19 May 2000
!
PRINT "Please enter pupil's mark ";
INPUT mark
IF mark >= 50 THEN
   PRINT "Pass"
ELSE
   PRINT "Fail"
END IF
END
```

Sample Output

Sample output
Please enter pupil's mark ? 49
Fail
Please enter pupil's mark ? 50
Pass
Please enter pupil's mark ? 51
Pass

Program implementation based on *Grade algorithm using IF*

```
! Title : TrueBASIC Example 3
! Author : John Walsh
! Date : 19 May 2000
!
PRINT "Please enter pupil's mark ";
INPUT mark
IF mark >= 80 THEN
   PRINT "Grade 1"
ELSE
   IF mark >= 60 THEN
      PRINT "Grade 2"
   ELSE
      IF mark >= 40 THEN
         PRINT "Grade 3"
```

```
      ELSE
         IF mark >= 20 THEN
            PRINT "Grade 4"
         ELSE
            IF mark >= 10 THEN
               PRINT "Grade 5"
            ELSE
               PRINT "Grade 6"
            END IF
         END IF
      END IF
   END IF
END IF
END
```

Sample Output

```
Please enter pupil's mark ? 80
Grade 1
Please enter pupil's mark ? 60
Grade 2
Please enter pupil's mark ? 40
Grade 3
Please enter pupil's mark ? 20
Grade 4
Please enter pupil's mark ? 10
Grade 5
Please enter pupil's mark ? 9
Grade 6
```

Selection – CASE … OF

Program implementation based on *Grade algorithm using CASE*

```
! Title : TrueBASIC Example 4
! Author : John Walsh
! Date : 19 May 2000
!
PRINT "Please enter pupil's mark ";
INPUT mark
SELECT CASE mark
CASE IS >= 80
   PRINT "Grade 1"
```

```
CASE IS >= 60
   PRINT "Grade 2"
CASE IS >= 40
   PRINT "Grade 3"
CASE IS >= 20
   PRINT "Grade 4"
CASE IS >= 10
   PRINT "Grade 5"
CASE ELSE
   PRINT "Grade 6"
END SELECT
END
```

Sample Output

Please enter pupil's mark ? 80
Grade 1
Please enter pupil's mark ? 60
Grade 2

Repetition – Fixed loops

Program implementation based on *algorithm to display a name five times*

```
! Title : TrueBASIC Example 5
! Author : John Walsh
! Date : 19 May 2000
!
FOR loop_counter = 1 TO 5
   PRINT "John"
NEXT loop_counter
END
```

Sample Output

John
John
John
John
John

Program implementation based on *algorithm to display one name a number of times*

```
! Title : TrueBASIC Example 6
! Author : John Walsh
! Date : 19 May 2000
!
PRINT "Please enter the number of times a name is required"
INPUT number_of_times
FOR loop_counter = 1 TO number_of_times
    PRINT "John"
NEXT loop_counter
END
```

Sample Output

Please enter the number of times a name is required
? 3
John
John
John

Program implementation based on *algorithm showing a fixed loop with steps*

```
! Title : TrueBASIC Example 7
! Author : John Walsh
! Date : 19 May 2000
!
FOR loop_counter = 2 TO 30 STEP 2
    PRINT loop_counter
NEXT loop_counter
END
```

Sample Output

```
2
4
6
8
10
12
14
16
18
20
22
24
26
28
30
```

Program implementation based on *tab algorithm showing nested loops*

```
! Title : TrueBASIC Example 8
! Author : John Walsh
! Date : 19 May 2000
!
FOR down = 1 TO 5
   FOR across = 10 TO 20
      PRINT TAB (across, down); "*"
   NEXT across
NEXT down
END
```

Sample Output

```
**********
**********
**********
**********
**********
```

Repetition – Conditional loops

Program implementation based on *take in a word algorithm with test at end*

```
! Title : TrueBASIC Example 9
! Author : John Walsh
! Date : 19 May 2000
!
LET timesinloop = 0
DO
   LET timesinloop = timesinloop + 1
   PRINT "Please enter a word (or END to finish) ";
   INPUT word$
LOOP UNTIL word$ = "END" OR word$ = "end"
PRINT "Program ended"
PRINT "The number of times in the loop is "; timesinloop
END
```

Sample Output

Please enter a word (or END to finish) ? Conditional
Please enter a word (or END to finish) ? loop
Please enter a word (or END to finish) ? with
Please enter a word (or END to finish) ? test
Please enter a word (or END to finish) ? at
Please enter a word (or END to finish) ? end
Program ended
The number of times in the loop is 6

Please enter a word (or END to finish) ? end
Program ended
The number of times in the loop is 1

*Note that the code in a conditional loop with test at end is always run at least once.
Note that this example shows a COMPLEX condition.*

Program implementation based on *Sum numbers algorithm using a running total*

```
! Title : TrueBASIC Example 10
! Author : John Walsh
! Date : 19 May 2000
!
LET total = 0
LET number = 0
DO
   LET total = total + number
   PRINT "Please enter a number (-999 to finish)";
   INPUT number
LOOP UNTIL number = -999
PRINT "The total of the numbers entered is "; total
PRINT "Program ended"
END
```

Sample Output

Please enter a number (−999 to finish)? -999
The total of the numbers entered is 0
Program ended
Please enter a number (−999 to finish)? 6
Please enter a number (−999 to finish)? 7
Please enter a number (−999 to finish)? 1
Please enter a number (−999 to finish)? −999
The total of the numbers entered is 14
Program ended

Note that this example shows a SIMPLE condition.

Program implementation based on *algorithm with test at start*

```
! Title : TrueBASIC Example 11
! Author : John Walsh
! Date : 20 May 2000
!
LET timesinloop = 0
PRINT "Please enter a word (stop to finish) ";
INPUT word$
DO WHILE NOT ((word$ = "end") OR (word$ = "END"))
   LET timesinloop = timesinloop + 1
   PRINT "Please enter a word ";
   INPUT word$
LOOP
PRINT "Program ended"
PRINT "The number of times in the loop is "; timesinloop
END
```

Sample Output

Please enter a word ? Conditional
Please enter a word ? loop
Please enter a word ? with
Please enter a word ? test
Please enter a word ? at
Please enter a word ? start
Please enter a word ? end
Program ended
The number of times in the loop is 6

Please enter a word ? end
Program ended
The number of times in the loop is 0

Note that the code in a conditional loop with test at start need not be run at all if the condition is not met.

Note that this example shows a COMPLEX condition.

2. Data storage

Program implementation based on *algorithm to read names and marks into two arrays

```
! Title : TrueBASIC Example 12
! Author : John Walsh
! Date : 20 May 2000
!
LET array_counter = 0
DIM pupil_name$ (10)
DIM pupil_mark (10)
DO while more data
   LET array_counter = array_counter + 1
   READ pupil_name$ (array_counter)
   READ pupil_mark (array_counter)
LOOP
!
DATA Harjinder, 76, Paul, 68, Jennifer, 56
DATA David, 52, Siobhan, 89, Cecilia, 75
DATA Angus, 61, Sarah, 93, Anwar, 92
END
```

Note: No Sample output from this program

Program implementation based on *local and global variables*

```
! Title : TrueBASIC Example 13
! Author : John Walsh
! Date : 20 May 2000
!
LET sum = 0     ! global variables
LET product = 0
LET first_number = 13
LET second_number = 33
!
CALL calculate (first_number, second_number)
!
PRINT sum, product
END
!
SUB calculate (number_one, number_two)
   LOCAL sum, product  ! set up two local variables
   LET sum = number_one + number_two
   LET product = number_one * number_two
   PRINT sum, product
END SUB
```

The sample output shows that the values of the local variables (sum and product) within the calculate procedure have no effect on the values of the global variables (also called sum and product) outside the calculate procedure, i.e. throughout the rest of the program.

3. Data flow

Program implementation based on *Count the number of five letter words in a list*

Note that the single parameter (no_of_5_letter_words) which is passed in this program is passed out by reference from the take_in_list_of_words procedure and passed by value into the display_result procedure.

```
! Title : TrueBASIC Example 14
! Author : John Walsh
! Date : 20 May 2000
!
CALL initialise
CALL take_in_list_of_words (no_of_5_letter_words) ! pass by reference
CALL display_result ((no_of_5_letter_words)) ! pass by value - note(())
END
!
SUB initialise
   ! This procedure initialises all parameters
   LET word$ = ""
   LET no_of_5_letter_words = 0
END SUB
!
SUB take_in_list_of_words (no_of_5_letter_words)
   ! This procedure counts the words that have five letters
   DO
      PRINT "Please enter a word (stop to finish) ";
      INPUT word$
      IF LEN (word$) = 5 THEN LET no_of_5_letter_words = no_of_5_letter_words + 1
   LOOP UNTIL word$ = "stop"
END SUB
!
SUB display_result (no_of_5_letter_words)
   PRINT "The number of words with five letters is "; no_of_5_letter_words
END SUB
```

Sample Output

Please enter a word (stop to finish) hello
Please enter a word (stop to finish) stop
The number of words with five letters is 1
Please enter a word (stop to finish) stop
The number of words with five letters is 0
Please enter a word (stop to finish) Giraffe
Please enter a word (stop to finish) Zebra
Please enter a word (stop to finish) Gnu
Please enter a word (stop to finish) Oryx
Please enter a word (stop to finish) Snake
Please enter a word (stop to finish) stop
The number of words with five letters is 2

Program implementation based on algorithm – passing parameters by value and by reference:

```
! Title : TrueBASIC Example 15
! Author : John Walsh
! Date : 20 May 2000
!
LET first_actual$ = "First"
LET second_actual$ = "second"
!
PRINT "Values at start of program are :"
PRINT "first_actual$ = "; first_actual$
PRINT "second_actual$ = "; second_actual$
!
CALL exchange (first_actual$, second_actual$) ! use ((first_actual$),
                                                    (second_actual$))
!                                             ! to pass parameters by value
!
PRINT "Values at end of program are :"
PRINT "first_actual$ = "; first_actual$
PRINT "second_actual$ = "; second_actual$
END
!
SUB exchange (formal_one$, formal_two$)
   LOCAL swap$
   LET swap$ = formal_one$
   LET formal_one$ = formal_two$
   LET formal_two$ = swap$
END SUB
```

Notes on the above code
(a) The values are exchanged correctly when passed by reference
(b) Here is the sample output from the same program when parameters passed by value:
i.e. CALL exchange ((first_actual$), (second_actual$))

Values at start of program are :
first_actual$ = First
second_actual$ = Second
Values at end of program are :
first_actual$ = First
second_actual$ = Second

Note that the values are not exchanged and remain as per the original.

Section D : Miscellaneous implementations – General purpose packages, InterModeller

1. Control

Sequence

Program implementation based on *algorithm to add two numbers*

```
Excel example 1

This macro, in Microsoft Excel, creates a simple spreadsheet, which may be used
to add two numbers

Sub Example()
'
' Example Macro
' Macro recorded 17/4/00 by John Walsh
'
' Keyboard Shortcut: Option+Cmd+Shift+A
'
   Range("B2").Select
   ActiveCell.FormulaR1C1 = "number one"
   Range("B3").Select
   ActiveCell.FormulaR1C1 = "number two"
   Range("C5").Select
   ActiveCell.FormulaR1C1 = "=SUM(R[-3]C:R[-2]C)"
   Range("B5").Select
   ActiveCell.FormulaR1C1 = "total"
End Sub
```

Sample Output

B	C
number one	19
number two	54
total	=SUM(C2:C3)

	A	B	C	D	E	F
1		Program implementation based on algorithm to add two numbers				
2						
3		number one	19			
4		number two	54			
5						
6		total	73			

Figure 8.19 *Sample output of Excel example 1*

Selection – CASE … OF

Program implementation based on *Holiday algorithm in the InterModeller Expert System Shell*

```
This solution uses Backward rules.

' Take bucket and spade ' = true IF
   ' What is your destination ? ' = Beach.

Take ID card = true IF
   ' What is your destination ? ' = Disco.

Take rucksack + food = true IF
   ' What is your destination ? ' = Hillwalking.

Watch TV = true IF
   ' What is your destination ? ' = None of these.

Take swimming costume = true IF
   ' What is your destination ? ' = Pool.

Take credit card = true IF
   ' What is your destination ? ' = Town.
```

Sample Output

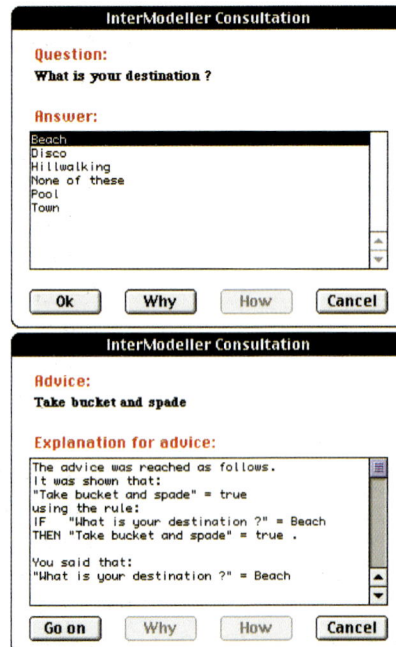

Figure 8.20 *Sample output of a program based on holiday algorithm in the InterModeller expert system shell*

Questions

1. Explain what is meant by:
   a. syntax
   b. semantics.
   Use an example from the software development environment that you have been studying in this unit to help explain your answer.

2. Look at the following statements taken from different software development environments:
   number :+ 1
   number ++ 1
   Both of these statements mean the same, i.e. add one on to (increment) the variable *number*.
   Using these statements as examples, explain the difference between syntax and semantics.

3. What is modularity?

4. What is the difference between a *procedure* and a *function*?

5. a. What is a user-defined function?
   b. Give one example of a user-defined function.

6. Which type of parameter (*value* or *reference*) allows data from a procedure to be passed back out to a program?

7. What is an
   a. operation?
   b. object?

8. What type of operation is known as:
   a. concatenation?
   b. substrings?

9. Give two examples each of:
   a. logical operators
   b. arithmetical operators
   c. relational operators.

10. What is meant by the term *formatting of input/output*?

11. Look at the following statement in a programming language:
    total = first_number + second_number
    What would the value total hold if *first_number* = 18, *second_number* = 20, and
    a. *first_number*, *second_number* and *total* are numeric variables?
    b. *first_number*, *second_number* and *total* were all string variables?

12. List three features of a software development environment.

13. a. Which control structures are likely to be found in a procedural language?

    b. Choose one of these control structures and explain how it works.

14. Give one example of a *simple condition* and one example of a *complex condition*.

15. Explain why a *condition* and a *control structure* are both necessary for selection.

16. What is meant by the following terms:
    a. variable?
    b. local variable?
    c. global variable?
    d. scope?
    e. data type?

17. What is the scope of a:
    a. local variable?
    b. global variable?

18. Which control structures may use Boolean data?

19. Which structured data type uses elements and subscripts?

20. State one advantage of using an array rather than unique variable names when programming.

21. What is a parameter?

22. a. When should parameters be passed into a subprogram:
       i. by value?
       ii. by reference?
    b. What is the exception to this rule?

23. a. Explain the purpose of the following control structures in a program:
       i. sequence
       ii. repetition
       iii. selection.
    b. What control structure may be implemented using a loop?
    c. What is a *nested* loop?

24. a. What type of error is present in the following algorithm?
       set counter to zero
       loop REPEAT
       add one to counter
       UNTIL counter equals zero
    b. What term is used to describe the situation to which such an error may lead?

25. State one advantage of using a conditional loop structure.

26. State an advantage of using test at start as opposed to *test at end* in a conditional loop structure.

27. **a.** What is the purpose of a *terminating value?*
   b. Give an example of an algorithm where such a value is used.

28. Give an example of a situation in which a CASE structure would be used in preference to an IF structure.

29. Write algorithms for the following problem outlines, showing refinements as appropriate:
   a. Take in a first name and a second name and display them.
   b. Calculate the area of a circle given the radius as input (πr^2).
   c. Take in ten test marks and calculate the average mark.
   d. Take in a sentence and display it fifty times.
   e. Take in a name and ask the user how many times the name is to be displayed, and then display the name.
   f. Take in five names using a loop with a terminating value.
   g. A pass or fail algorithm for up to twenty pupils' marks.
   h. Input validation for months 1–12 with a suitable message.
   i. A quiz with ten questions and a score at the end.
   j. Calculate the result of doubling a number ten times. The number should start at 1.
   k. The number of weeds on a football pitch doubles every month. If there are 200 weeds today, how many weeds will there be in a year?
   l. You have a bank account with £100 in it. How much money will you have in ten years if the annual interest is 5%?

30. Why is it helpful to describe the data flow in a program alongside the design notation?

31. Consider the following algorithm:
```
CASE mark OF
WHEN >= 50
display grade 3
WHEN >= 60
display grade 2
WHEN >= 70
display grade 1
END CASE
```
   a. What would be the output from a program based on this algorithm if *mark* = 70?
   b. Rewrite this algorithm to give the correct result.

32. What is the purpose of the OR which links the two conditions in COMAL example 9?

33. Look at the following program in COMAL:
```
// 99 bottles of beer
// COMAL for MacOS version
// by John Walsh
// November 2000
//
FOR count% := 99 TO 1 STEP -1 DO
bottles (count%, TRUE)
bottles (count%, FALSE)
PRINT "Take one down, pass it
around."
bottles (count% - 1, FALSE)
NEXT count%
END
//
PROC bottles (number%, wall) CLOSED
PRINT number%;
text$ := "bottle"
IF number% <> 1 THEN
text$ := text$ + "s"
ENDIF
PRINT text$; "of beer";
IF wall THEN
PRINT "on the wall";
ENDIF
PRINT "."
ENDPROC bottles
```
   a. Suggest what the output will be when this program is run.
   b. If you have access to the COMAL language, enter the code and run it.

34. This program is one translation of a program about '99 Bottles of Beer on the Wall'. Versions of this program have been translated into nearly every known programming language. Listings of all of these program versions have been collected together on a web site at http://www.99-bottles-of-beer.net/. Have a look at the site and make a note of the current total number of programming language versions available. At the time of writing this book, there were over 600 versions. You should look for a version of the program in your own particular software development environment.

35. Look at the following screenshot in Figure 8.21. Which control structure involves iteration?

Figure 8.21 *Iteration*

• Key points •

- The syntax of a programming language is the way in which you give instructions to the computer.
- The semantics of a particular instruction is its meaning or its effect.
- Modularity means that when a program is designed and written, it is divided into smaller sections called subprograms or sub-routines.
- High level procedural languages use two types of modules or subprograms. These are procedures and functions.
- A procedure is said to produce an effect, a function returns a single value to a program.

- A user-defined function is a function which is created within a program rather than being already present or pre-defined as part of a programming language.
- An operation is a process which is carried out on an item of data (in a program).
- An object is the item of data which is involved in the process.
- Arithmetical operations are calculations involving numeric data.
- String operations include joining strings, known as concatenation, and selecting parts of strings, known as substrings.

- Relational operations use relational operators to compare data and produce a Boolean answer of *true* or *false*.
- Each high level language has its own syntax for the formatting of program input and output.
- There are three basic control structures used in procedural languages – sequence, selection and repetition.
- Sequence is the order in which things are done.
- Repetition is doing something over again e.g. in a loop, either conditional or fixed.
- Selection is making a choice e.g. control structure + condition(s).
- The IF structure is suitable for use when a single selection (or a limited number of selections) is to be made.
- The CASE structure allows multiple outcome selections to be made in a program.
- A variable is the name that a programmer uses to identify a storage location.
- Two types of variables are global variables and local variables.
- Global variables may be used anywhere in a program but local variables are defined only for use in one part of a program (a subprogram).
- The scope of a variable is the range of statements for which a variable is valid.
- The data types stored by a program may be a number, a character, a string, a date, a file, an array, a sound sample, a video clip or indeed, any kind of data.
- Numeric data – may consist of real type data or integer type data.
- Real type data includes ALL numbers, both whole and fractional.
- Integer type data is a subset of real type data which includes only whole numbers, either positive or negative.
- Boolean or Logical data – may only have two values, *true* or *false*. Boolean data is used in a program's control structures.
- A set of data items *of the same type* grouped together using a single variable name is called an array.
- Each part of an array is called an element.
- Each element in an array is identified by the variable name and a subscript.
- The movement of data (or the data flow) between subprograms is implemented by using parameters.
- A parameter is information about a data item being supplied to a subprogram.
- When a subprogram is used, the calling program must pass parameters to it – this is parameter passing.
- Data structures (such as variables) which are only passed into subprograms are known as in parameters.
- Variables which are passed into a subprogram and are changed or updated are referred to as out parameters.
- Variables which are only passed out of subprograms are known as in/out parameters.
- Parameters can be passed either by value or by reference.
- Parameters are passed by value when a parameter is passed into a procedure but does not require to be passed back out again.
- Parameters are passed by reference when the parameter requires to be passed in to a procedure, updated and then passed back out of the procedure again.
- When an array is being passed as a parameter, it is always passed by reference.

Differences between Acornsoft COMAL and COMAL for MacOS

All of the *COMAL* programs in this book were written in *COMAL for MacOS*. They are easily portable to *Acornsoft COMAL* with the addition of line numbers, % changes to # and by placing spaces in the keywords as shown in the table below.

COMAL for MacOS	Acornsoft COMAL
ENDIF	END IF
ENDPROC	END PROC
ENDWHILE	END WHILE
ENDCASE	END CASE
ENDFUNC	END FUNC
integer%	integer#

Integer variables – *Acornsoft COMAL* identifies integer variables with a # suffix. *COMAL for MacOS* will accept either a # or a % sign, but in either case, it defaults to displaying a % sign.

Line numbers – *COMAL for MacOS* does not use line numbers

Systems specific keywords such as – AUTO, RENUMBER, MODE, VDU, SOUND, COLOUR, DRAW, ENVELOPE etc. are not supported in *COMAL for MacOS* and are not used in this book.

9 Standard Algorithms

An **algorithm** is a sequence of instructions that can be used to solve a problem.

In this chapter the following standard algorithms are described and implemented:

1. Input validation
2. Linear search
3. Counting occurrences
4. Finding maximum and minimum (Finding min/max)

In some cases more than one algorithm is described within each category. The algorithms that you need to know about are shown in **bold type**. The input validation algorithm is Intermediate 2 level content. It is included here for completeness.

1. Input validation

Input validation is the process of checking that the input is acceptable or within a certain range. Some form of validation is required when checking user input to a program. For example, valid dates in the year 2007 could range from 1/1/2007 to 31/12/2007. Ages of pupils in the fifth year at school might have a range of 15 to 17 years. A well-written program should validate all user input.

There are a variety of possible input validation algorithms:

```
1.1 loop - REPEAT
1.2   ask user for data input
1.3   take in the data
1.4 end loop - UNTIL data is within range
```

This is sometimes called a validation loop (Note the structured listing)

This is not very user-friendly, since it does not give any indication to the user of what might be wrong with any rejected input. The user may think that they are entering a list of data rather than being repeatedly asked to re-enter an invalid item. Adding an IF statement makes this algorithm more useful.

```
1.1 loop - REPEAT
1.2   ask user for data input
1.3   take in the data
1.4    IF data is outwith range THEN display error message
1.5 end loop - UNTIL data is within range
```

Or, alternatively, enter the data first, and if the user correctly inputs the valid data on the first occasion, the validation loop need not be entered at all:

```
1.1 ask user for data input
1.2 take in the data
1.3 loop WHILE data input is outwith range
1.4  prompt to re-enter data
1.5  take in the data
1.6 end loop
```

Some software development environments, such as high level languages, may automatically provide some form of input validation. For instance, entering a string (text value) into a program designed to accept a numeric input will provide the user with a re-entry prompt because of a variable type error.

Please enter a number
? w
Bad value.
? 1.2

2. Linear search

A linear search algorithm is used to find an item of data (the target value) in a list.

This algorithm reports if the item has been found and its location. However, it does not tell the user if the target value is not in the list, nor does it find more than one occurrence of the target value in a list (see the count occurrences algorithm below).

```
2.1 ask user for target value
2.2 take in target value
2.3 loop - FOR each item in the list
2.4   IF current item = target value THEN
2.5      display found message
2.6      display item and its location in the list
2.7   END IF
2.8 end loop - NEXT item
```

The following algorithm may be used in order to tell the user that the target value is not in the list if the search is unsuccessful. A Boolean variable called 'found' is set to FALSE at the start of the search and is only set to TRUE if the target value is found. (Remember: A Boolean variable can only have one of two values *true* or *false*.)

```
2.1   set the value of found to be FALSE
2.2   ask user for target value
2.3   take in target value
2.4   loop - FOR each item in the list
2.5      IF current item = target value THEN
2.6         set the value of found to be TRUE
2.7         note the location of the target in the list
2.8      END IF
2.9   end loop - NEXT item
2.10  IF found is TRUE THEN
2.11     display found message
2.12     display item and its location in the list
2.13     ELSE
2.14     display item not found message
2.15  END IF
```

Both of the above linear search algorithms will work on a list in any order. If the list is sorted in, say, descending order, then it becomes possible to stop the search as soon as the current item being examined is smaller than the target item.

For example, when searching the ordered list: 99, 88, 65, 54, 32, 23, for the target value 90, then you can stop searching once the value 88 is reached, since 90 is larger than 88.

In a short list like this, such an algorithm would not be of much benefit, but if a long list containing, say, 10,000 items was being searched then it would reduce the average search time.

The following linear search algorithm takes advantage of such an ordered list. It uses an additional variable called 'exit' which is set to FALSE at the start of the search and is only set to TRUE when the current item being examined is smaller than the target item.

```
2.1   set the value of found to be FALSE
2.2   set the value of exit to be FALSE
2.3   start at first item in list
2.4   ask user for target value
2.5   take in target value
2.6   loop - WHILE (found is FALSE) AND (end of list not reached) AND (exit is
      FALSE)
2.7               CASE current item OF
2.8                  WHEN = target value
2.9                     set the value of found to be TRUE
2.10                    note the location of the target in the list
2.11                    display item and its location in the list
2.12                  WHEN < target value
```

```
2.13                   set the value of exit to be TRUE
2.14                   display item not found message
2.15               WHEN > target value
2.16                   move to next location in list
2.17          END CASE
2.18 end loop - END WHILE
```

If you know in advance that the list you are searching is sorted in order, then it is much more efficient to use a different algorithm called a binary search. The binary search algorithm is more efficient than the linear search algorithm because it usually requires fewer comparisons to find an item in a list. However, the binary search algorithm is outwith the scope of this unit on Software Development.

3. Counting occurrences

A counting occurrences algorithm will count how many times a value appears in a list.

```
3.1  set the number of times item found (hits) to zero
3.2  ask user for the target value
3.3  take in the target value
3.4  loop - FOR each item in the list
3.5     IF current item = target value THEN
3.6        add 1 to number of hits
3.7     END IF
3.8  end loop - NEXT item
3.9  display number of times item found (hits)
```

Compare this algorithm with the first linear search algorithm above.

The following algorithm may be used where the list to be searched is stored as data within the program:

```
3.1  set the number of times item found (hits) to zero
3.2  ask user for the target value
3.3  take in the target value
3.4  loop - REPEAT
3.5     READ in the current item from the list of data
3.6     IF current item = target value THEN
3.7        add 1 to number of hits
3.8     END IF
3.9  end loop - UNTIL end of data has been reached
3.10 display number of times item found (hits)
```

4. Finding maximum and minimum

The maximum value is the highest value in a list. Here is one possible method of finding the maximum value. Note that it will only work correctly if the maximum value in the list is greater than or equal to zero.

```
4.1   set the maximum value to be zero
4.2   loop - REPEAT
4.3     READ in the current item from the list of data
4.4     IF the current item is greater than the maximum value THEN
4.5       set the maximum value to be equal to the current item
4.6     END IF
4.7   end loop - UNTIL end of data has been reached
4.8   display maximum value
```

A better method is to set the maximum value to the first item in the list, like this:

```
4.1   READ in the first item from the list
4.2   set the maximum value to be equal to the first item
4.3   loop - REPEAT
4.4     READ in the next item from the list of data
4.5     IF the current item is greater than the maximum value THEN
4.6       set the maximum value to be equal to the current item
4.7     END IF
4.8   end loop - UNTIL end of data has been reached
4.9   display maximum value
```

The minimum value is the smallest value in a list. This algorithm will find the minimum value in a list:

```
5.1   READ in the first item from the list
5.2   set the minimum value to be equal to the first item
5.3   loop - REPEAT
5.4     READ in the next item from the list of data
5.5     IF the current item is less than the minimum value THEN
5.6       set the minimum value to be equal to the current item
5.7     END IF
5.8   end loop - UNTIL end of data has been reached
5.9   display minimum value
```

Algorithms for finding the maximum and minimum value in a list are useful when sorting a list of items into order. However, the sort algorithm is outwith the scope of this unit on Software Development.

Implementation of standard algorithms

Each of the algorithms is implemented in *COMAL*, *TrueBasic* and *Visual Basic*. Note that no implementation for finding the minimum value is given, since it is very similar to finding the maximum. You should implement this algorithm in your chosen software development environment. See the questions at the end of this chapter.

COMAL implementations

```
// Title : COMAL Example 1.1
// Author : John Walsh
// Date : 14 June 2000
//
PRINT "Please enter a number in the range 1 - 10"
INPUT number%
WHILE number% < 1 OR number% > 10 DO
   PRINT "The number you have entered is outwith the range 1 - 10 Please re-
   enter"
   INPUT number%
ENDWHILE
PRINT "The number entered was "; number%
END
```

Sample Output

```
Please enter a number in the range 1 - 10
? 1
The number entered was 1
Please enter a number in the range 1 - 10
? 10
The number entered was 10
Please enter a number in the range 1 - 10
? 5
The number entered was 5
Please enter a number in the range 1 - 10
? 0
The number you have entered is outwith the range 1 - 10 Please re-enter
? 3
The number entered was 3
```

```
// Title : COMAL Example 2.1
// Author : John Walsh
// Date : 17 June 2000
//
// Program to demonstrate the Linear Search algorithm
//
setup
get_target (target%)
find_item (target%, no_of_items%, list% ())
END
//
PROC setup
   // set initial values of variables
   no_of_items% := 20
   target% := 0
   item% := 0
   // fill list with 20 numbers
   DIM list% (20)
   REPEAT
      item% := item% + 1
      READ list% (item%)
   UNTIL item% = no_of_items%
   //
   DATA 1, 23, 53, 12, 71, 45, 99, 3, 12, 10
   DATA 67, 19, 54, 41, 46, 100, 56, 58, 11, 19
   //
ENDPROC setup
//
PROC get_target (REF target%) CLOSED
   // ask user for target value
   PRINT "Please enter a number to find"
   INPUT target%
ENDPROC get_target
//
PROC find_item (target%, no_of_items%, REF list% ()) CLOSED
   // look for the target value in the list
   FOR position% := 1 TO no_of_items% DO
      IF list% (position%) = target% THEN
         PRINT "Item found"
         PRINT "The item"; target%; "was found at position"; position%; "in the list"
      ENDIF
   NEXT position%
ENDPROC find_item
```

```
Please enter a number to find
? 24
Please enter a number to find
? 23
Item found
The item 23 was found at position 2 in the list
Please enter a number to find
? 12
Item found
The item 12 was found at position 4 in the list
Item found
The item 12 was found at position 9 in the list
Please enter a number to find
? 1
Item found
The item 1 was found at position 1 in the list
```

```
// Title : COMAL Example 3.1
// Author : John Walsh
// Date : 17 June 2000
//
// Program to demonstrate the Counting Occurrences algorithm
//
setup
get_target (target%)
count_occurrences (no_of_items%, target%, list% ())
END
//
PROC setup
   // set initial values of variables
   no_of_items% := 20
   target% := 0
   item% := 0
   // fill list with 20 numbers
   DIM list% (20)
   REPEAT
      item% := item% + 1
      READ list% (item%)
   UNTIL item% = no_of_items%
   //
```

```
    DATA 1, 23, 53, 12, 71, 45, 99, 3, 12, 10
    DATA 67, 19, 54, 41, 46, 100, 56, 58, 11, 19
    //
ENDPROC setup
//
PROC get_target (REF target%) CLOSED
    // ask user for target value
    PRINT "Please enter a number to find"
    INPUT target%
ENDPROC get_target
//
PROC count_occurrences (no_of_items%, target%, REF list% ()) CLOSED
    no_of_hits% := 0 // set number of hits to zero
    // count occurrences of the target value in the list
    FOR position% := 1 TO no_of_items% DO
        IF list% (position%) = target% THEN
            no_of_hits% := no_of_hits% + 1
        ENDIF
    NEXT position%
    PRINT "The target value"; target%; "was found"; no_of_hits%; "times in the list"
ENDPROC count_occurrences
```

Sample Output

Please enter a number to find
? 24
The target value 24 was found 0 times in the list
Please enter a number to find
? 23
The target value 23 was found 1 times in the list
Please enter a number to find
? 12
The target value 12 was found 2 times in the list
Please enter a number to find
? 1
The target value 1 was found 1 times in the list

```
// Title : COMAL Example 4.1
// Author : John Walsh
// Date : 17 June 2000
//
// Program to demonstrate the Finding Maximum algorithm
//
setup
find_maximum (item%, list% ())
END
//
PROC setup
   // set initial values of variables
   item% := 1
   // set aside space for 20 numbers in the list
   DIM list% (20)
   //
   DATA 1, 23, 53, 12, 71, 45, 99, 3, 12, 10
   DATA 67, 19, 54, 41, 46, 100, 56, 58, 11, 19
   //
ENDPROC setup
//
PROC find_maximum (item%, REF list% ()) CLOSED
   // find the maximum value in the list
   READ list%(item%)
   maximum% := list% (item%)
   REPEAT
      item% := item% + 1
      READ list% (item%)
      IF list% (item%) > maximum% THEN
         maximum% := list% (item%)
      ENDIF
   UNTIL EOD
   PRINT "The maximum value in the list is "; maximum%
ENDPROC find_maximum
```

Sample Output

The maximum value in the list is 100

TrueBASIC implementations

```
! Title : TrueBASIC Example 1.1
! Author : John Walsh
! Date : 14 June 2000
!
PRINT "Please enter a number in the range 1 - 10"
INPUT number
DO WHILE (number < 1) OR (number > 10)
    PRINT "The number you have entered is outwith the range 1 - 10 Please re-
    enter"
    INPUT number
LOOP
PRINT 'The number entered was "; number
END
```

Sample Output

```
Please enter a number in the range 1 - 10
? 1
The number entered was 1
Please enter a number in the range 1 - 10
? 10
The number entered was 10
Please enter a number in the range 1 - 10
? 5
The number entered was 5
Please enter a number in the range 1 - 10
? 0
The number you have entered is outwith the range 1 - 10 Please re-enter
? 3
The number entered was 3
```

```
! Title : TrueBASIC Example 2.1
! Author : John Walsh
! Date : 30 June 2000
!
! Program to demonstrate the Linear Search algorithm
!
DIM list(20)
CALL set_up(target,no_of_items,list())
CALL GET_TARGET(target)
```

```
CALL FIND_ITEM((target),(no_of_items),list())
END
!
SUB set_up(target,no_of_items,list())
   ! set initial values of variables
   LET no_of_items = 20
   LET target = 0
   LET item = 0
   ! fill list with 20 numbers
   DO
      LET item = item + 1
      READ list (item)
   LOOP UNTIL item = no_of_items
   !
   DATA 1, 23, 53, 12, 71, 45, 99, 3, 12, 10
   DATA 67, 19, 54, 41, 46, 100, 56, 58, 11, 19
   !
END SUB
!
SUB get_target(target)
   ! ask user for target value
   PRINT "Please enter a number to find"
   INPUT target
END SUB
!
SUB find_item(target,no_of_items,list())
   ! look for the target value in the list
   FOR position = 1 TO no_of_items
      IF list (position) = target THEN
         PRINT "Item found"
         PRINT "The item"; target; "was found at position"; position; "in the list"
      END IF
   NEXT position
END SUB
```

```
! Title : TrueBASIC Example 3.1
! Author : John Walsh
! Date : 2 July 2000
!
! Program to demonstrate the Counting Occurrences algorithm
!
DIM list(20)
CALL set_up (no_of_items,target,list())
CALL GET_TARGET(target)
CALL count_occurrences ((no_of_items), (target), list ())
END
!
SUB set_up (no_of_items,target,list())
   ! set initial values of variables
   LET no_of_items = 20
   LET target = 0
   LET item = 0
   ! fill list with 20 numbers
   DO
      LET item = item + 1
      READ list (item)
   LOOP UNTIL item = no_of_items
   !
```

```
   DATA 1, 23, 53, 12, 71, 45, 99, 3, 12, 10
   DATA 67, 19, 54, 41, 46, 100, 56, 58, 11, 19
   !
END SUB
!
SUB get_target(target)
   ! ask user for target value
   PRINT "Please enter a number to find"
   INPUT target
END SUB
!
SUB count_occurrences (no_of_items,target,list())
   LET no_of_hits = 0  ! set number of hits to zero
   ! count occurrences of the target value in the list
   FOR position = 1 TO no_of_items
      IF list (position) = target THEN
         LET no_of_hits = no_of_hits + 1
      END IF
   NEXT position
   PRINT "The target value"; target; "was found"; no_of_hits; "times in the list"
END SUB
```

Sample Output

Please enter a number to find
? 24
The target value 24 was found 0 times in the list
Please enter a number to find
? 23
The target value 23 was found 1 times in the list
Please enter a number to find
? 12
The target value 12 was found 2 times in the list
Please enter a number to find
? 1
The target value 1 was found 1 times in the list

```
! Title : TrueBASIC Example 4.1
! Author : John Walsh
! Date : 2 July 2000
!
! Program to demonstrate the Finding Maximum algorithm
!
DIM list(20)
CALL find_maximum(list())
END
!
SUB find_maximum(list())
    ! find the maximum value in the list
    !
    DATA 1, 23, 53, 12, 71, 45, 99, 3, 12, 10
    DATA 67, 19, 54, 41, 46, 100, 56, 58, 11, 19
    !
    LET item = 1
    READ list (item)
    LET maximum = list (item)
    DO while more data
       LET ITEM = item + 1
       READ list (item)
       IF list (item) > maximum THEN
          LET maximum = list (item)
       END IF
    LOOP
    PRINT "The maximum value in the list is "; maximum
END SUB
```

Sample Output

The maximum value in the list is 100

Visual Basic implementations

```
'Title : Visual Basic Example 1.1
'Author : John Walsh
'Date : 14 June 2000
'
Option Explicit
Dim number As Integer


Private Sub cmdEnterNumbers_Click()
'picDisplay.Cls
number = InputBox('Please enter a number in the range 1 - 10')
Do While (number < 1) Or (number > 10)
   number = InputBox("The number you have entered is outwith the range 1 - 10
   Please re-enter")
Loop
picDisplay.Print "The number entered was "; number
End Sub


Private Sub cmdEnd_Click()
picDisplay.Cls
End
End Sub
```

Sample Output

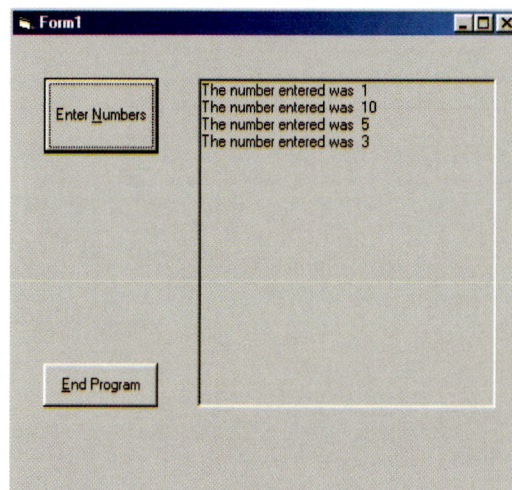

Figure 9.1 *Sample output from Visual Basic Example 1.1*

```
'Title : Visual Basic Example 2.1
'Author : John Walsh
'Date : 4 July 2000
'
'Program to demonstrate the Linear Search algorithm
'
Option Explicit
Dim target As Integer
Dim no_of_items As Integer
Dim list(20) As Variant

Private Sub cmdRunProgram_Click()
setup target, no_of_items, list()
get_target target
find_item target, no_of_items, list()
End Sub

Private Sub setup(ByRef target, ByRef no_of_items, ByRef list())
' set initial values of variables
target = 0
no_of_items = 0
' fill list with 20 numbers
LstMarks.AddItem 1
LstMarks.AddItem 23
LstMarks.AddItem 53
LstMarks.AddItem 12
LstMarks.AddItem 71
LstMarks.AddItem 45
LstMarks.AddItem 99
LstMarks.AddItem 3
LstMarks.AddItem 12
LstMarks.AddItem 10
LstMarks.AddItem 67
LstMarks.AddItem 19
LstMarks.AddItem 54
LstMarks.AddItem 41
LstMarks.AddItem 46
LstMarks.AddItem 100
LstMarks.AddItem 56
LstMarks.AddItem 58
LstMarks.AddItem 11
LstMarks.AddItem 19
Do
    'Val changes a string into an integer value
```

```
   list(no_of_items) = Val(LstMarks.list(no_of_items))
   'ListCount is the number of items in the list
   no_of_items = no_of_items + 1
Loop Until no_of_items = LstMarks.ListCount
End Sub


Private Sub get_target(ByRef target)
target = InputBox("Please enter a number to find")
End Sub


Private Sub find_item(ByVal target, ByVal no_of_items, ByRef list())
Dim position As Integer
   ' look for the target value in the list
   ' visual basic arrays start from 0, so add 1 to give correct position
   For position = 0 To no_of_items - 1
     If list(position) = target Then
        picDisplay.Print "Item found"
        picDisplay.Print "The item"; target; "was found at position"; position +
        1; " in the list"
     End If
   Next position
End Sub


Private Sub cmdEnd_Click()
picDisplay.Cls
End
End Sub
```

Sample Output

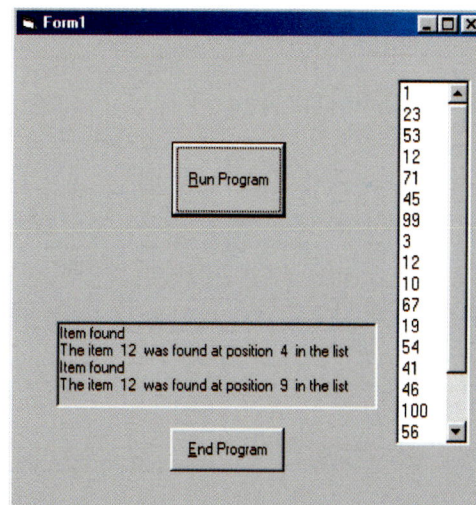

Figure 9.2 *Sample output from Visual Basic Example 2.1*

```
'Title : Visual Basic Example 3.1
'Author : John Walsh
'Date : 5 July 2000
'
'Program to demonstrate the Counting Occurrences algorithm
'
Option Explicit
Dim target As Integer
Dim no_of_items As Integer
Dim list(20) As Variant

Private Sub cmdRunProgram_Click()
setup target, no_of_items, list()
get_target target
count_occurrences target, no_of_items, list()
End Sub

Private Sub setup(ByRef target, ByRef no_of_items, ByRef list())
' set initial values of variables
target = 0
no_of_items = 0
' fill list with 20 numbers
LstMarks.AddItem 1
LstMarks.AddItem 23
LstMarks.AddItem 53
LstMarks.AddItem 12
LstMarks.AddItem 71
LstMarks.AddItem 45
LstMarks.AddItem 99
LstMarks.AddItem 3
LstMarks.AddItem 12
LstMarks.AddItem 10
LstMarks.AddItem 67
LstMarks.AddItem 19
LstMarks.AddItem 54
LstMarks.AddItem 41
LstMarks.AddItem 46
LstMarks.AddItem 100
LstMarks.AddItem 56
LstMarks.AddItem 58
LstMarks.AddItem 11
LstMarks.AddItem 19
Do
    'Val changes a string into an integer value
    list(no_of_items) = Val(LstMarks.list(no_of_items))
```

```
    'ListCount is the number of items in the list
    no_of_items = no_of_items + 1
Loop Until no_of_items = LstMarks.ListCount
End Sub

Private Sub get_target(ByRef target)
target = InputBox("Please enter a number to find")
End Sub

Private Sub count_occurrences(ByVal target, ByVal no_of_items, ByRef list())
Dim position As Integer
Dim no_of_hits As Integer
no_of_hits = 0
    ' count occurrences of the target value in the list
    ' visual basic arrays start from 0
    For position = 0 To no_of_items - 1
        If list(position) = target Then
            no_of_hits = no_of_hits + 1
        End If
    Next position
    picDisplay.Print "The target value"; target; "was found"; no_of_hits; "times in the list"
End Sub

Private Sub cmdEnd_Click()
picDisplay.Cls
End
End Sub
```

Sample Output

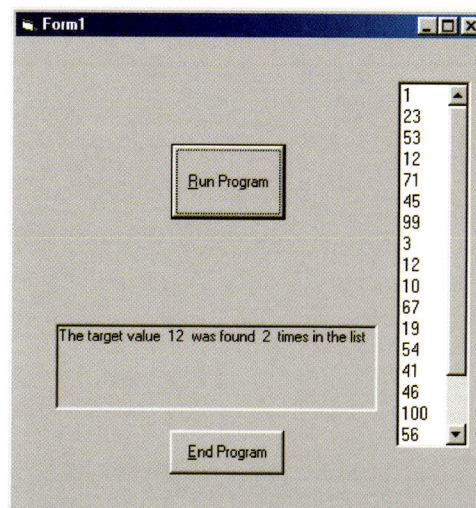

Figure 9.3 *Sample output from Visual Basic Example 3.1*

```
'Title : Visual Basic Example 4.1
'Author : John Walsh
'Date : 5 July 2000
'
'Program to demonstrate the Finding Maximum algorithm
'
Option Explicit
Dim target As Integer
Dim no_of_items As Integer
Dim list(20) As Variant

Private Sub cmdRunProgram_Click()
setup no_of_items, list()
find_maximum no_of_items, list()
End Sub

Private Sub setup(ByRef no_of_items, ByRef list())
' set initial values of variables
no_of_items = 0
' fill list with 20 numbers
LstMarks.AddItem 1
LstMarks.AddItem 23
LstMarks.AddItem 53
LstMarks.AddItem 12
LstMarks.AddItem 71
LstMarks.AddItem 45
LstMarks.AddItem 99
LstMarks.AddItem 3
LstMarks.AddItem 12
LstMarks.AddItem 10
LstMarks.AddItem 67
LstMarks.AddItem 19
LstMarks.AddItem 54
LstMarks.AddItem 41
LstMarks.AddItem 46
LstMarks.AddItem 100
LstMarks.AddItem 56
LstMarks.AddItem 58
LstMarks.AddItem 11
LstMarks.AddItem 19
Do
    'Val changes a string into an integer value
    list(no_of_items) = Val(LstMarks.list(no_of_items))
    'ListCount is the number of items in the list
```

```
     no_of_items = no_of_items + 1
Loop Until no_of_items = LstMarks.ListCount
End Sub

Private Sub find_maximum(ByVal no_of_items, ByRef list())
Dim maximum As Integer
Dim item As Integer
' find the maximum value in the list
' visual basic arrays start from 0
maximum = list(0)
   For item = 1 To no_of_items - 1
      If list(item) > maximum Then
         maximum = list(item)
      End If
   Next item
   picDisplay.Print "The maximum value in the list is "; maximum
End Sub

Private Sub cmdEnd_Click()
picDisplay.Cls
End
End Sub
```

Sample Output

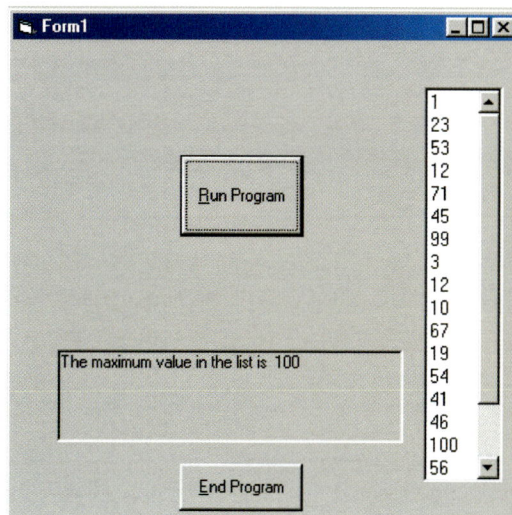

Figure 9.4 *Sample output from Visual Basic Example 4.1*

Questions

1. At which stage in the software development process is an algorithm produced?

2. Which algorithm would you use to:
   a. check program input?
   b. find an item in a list?
   c. count how many times an item appears in a list?
   d. find the highest and lowest values in a list?

3. a. Which design notation is used to represent the algorithms in this chapter?
   b. Suggest why this design notation was chosen.
   c. Choose one of the algorithms from this chapter and show how it would be represented using a structure diagram design notation – look back at chapter 6 for examples of a structure diagram.

4. Which algorithm described in this chapter would be likely to appear in a robust program?

5. Look at both the linear search and the count occurrences algorithms. State one difference and one similarity between these two algorithms.

6. Look at the linear search algorithms. What advantage is provided by using an ordered list?

7. Why does the input validation algorithm use a conditional (REPEAT / WHILE) rather than an unconditional (FOR) loop structure?

8. Write a new algorithm which finds *both* the minimum and maximum values in a list.

9. Look back at the algorithms described in this chapter whose implementations are NOT shown. Choose one of these algorithms and implement it in your chosen software development environment.

10. Look at the sample output of the linear search program.
    a. What happens if the target item is not in the list?
    b. Rewrite the program to give a suitable message if the target item is not found.

11. The data used in the linear search program ranges from 1 to 100. Change the linear search algorithm by adding input validation.

12. The finding maximum implementation is shown. Implement the finding minimum algorithm.

13. In both the finding maximum and finding minimum algorithms, why is it not a good idea to set the maximum or minimum to zero at the start?

• Key points •

- **Input validation** is used to check that data input is within a certain (acceptable) range.
- **Linear search** is used to find an item of data (the target value) in a list.
- **Counting occurrences** is used to count how many times a value appears in a list.
- **Finding maximum and minimum** is used to find the maximum and minimum values in a list.

Appendix

Questions

1. You are a *beta* tester for the latest version of *Web Wanderer*, *Skylon's* latest browser. You are testing the program and your computer 'freezes' or 'hangs'.

   a. Referring to a computer system with which you are familiar, state two possible courses of action you might follow, either of which would recover the computer from the above situation.

   b. You manage to recover the computer, and you post a message on the *Web Wanderer* discussion group, looking for a solution. iamapain@herd.org reads your query and replies, stating that the *beta* version of *Web Wanderer* requires 256 *Megabytes* of free *RAM*. What is free RAM?

   c. Your machine has a *total* of 256 *Megabytes* of RAM.

      i. Explain why this may be insufficient RAM to run the software.

      ii. State two possible methods of solving the problem of insufficient RAM.

      iii. State one advantage and one disadvantage for each of these methods

   d. You finally get the *Web Wanderer* software to work, and wish to print out the Frequently Asked Questions (FAQ) from the *Web Wanderer* discussion site. Your printer is slow, taking five minutes to print, and you are unable to use the computer until the print job is complete. Explain one way of solving the problem of being unable to use the machine while printing.

2. Cecilia takes a colour photograph with her *Dakko* 3 *Megapixel* digital camera. The camera stores its images on a *128 Megabyte flash card*. The camera can store a maximum of 90 images on this card at the maximum resolution. She transfers the photograph from the camera to her computer and saves it on the hard disk. The file size of the photograph is *7 Megabytes*. Her sister Siobhan uses a graphics package to edit the original photograph, and uses one of the options available in the graphics package, which changes the photograph to greyscale. When the editing is complete, she saves the new version of the photograph to hard disk. The file size remains at 7 *Megabytes*.

   a. What is the maximum resolution of the Dakko camera?

   b. What is a Megapixel?

Figure 10.1 *Cecilia's colour photograph*

c. Explain why the file size stayed the same after the photograph was changed from colour to greyscale.

d. What is a flash card?

e. Given that the typical file size of an image is 7 Megabytes, explain how it is possible for a 128 Megabyte flash card to hold a maximum of 90 images.

f. State one way in which the images on the flash card may be downloaded to a computer.

3. A computer magazine, *PC Globe*, carries out a comparative test of two desktop machines, the *Dandelion Pro* with its 1.5 *Ghz Amoeba* processor and the *Buttercup Expert* with its 1.5 *Ghz Beastie* processor. Here are the results of the tests.

a. What is a MFLOP?

b. Name another unit which may be used to measure the performance of a computer system.

c. What is an application-based test?

d. What important information about the application-based tests is NOT provided here?

e. Both of the above systems have the same processor clock rate. What do the results of these tests tell us about using the processor clock rate as a measure of system performance?

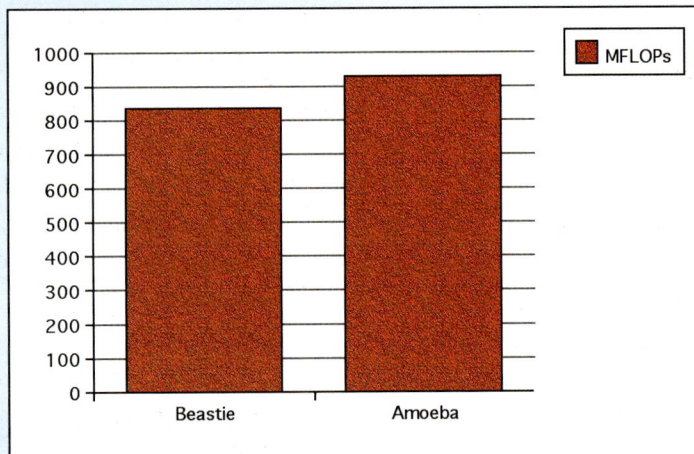

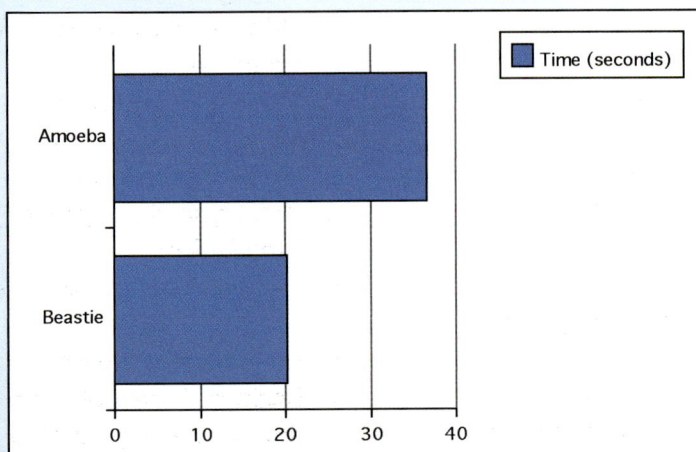

Figure 10.2 *Amoeba and Beastie test results*

f. *Timorous Technology*, the manufacturers of the *Beastie* processor, have announced that their new processor chip, the *Panic*, is to have a dual core. In reply, *Unicell Devices*, the manufacturers of the *Amoeba* processor, say that their new *Paramecium* processor chip, will have double the cache memory of the *Panic*. Suggest what a comparative test of the two new processors might show, and give a reason to support your suggestion for the results that may be achieved by each of the new processors.

4. Cladophora Computer Industries (CCI) is replacing its mainframe computer system and terminals with a *peer-to-peer* network using desktop computers and laptops.

   a. What is a peer-to-peer network?

   b. James is an employee of CCI, and his boss, Frances, asks him if he would like to take one of the old mainframe terminals to use at home. James refuses this offer and says that the terminal would be of no use to him.

      i. What is a mainframe terminal?

      ii. Why did James refuse the offer?

      iii. Frances asks James if he would like to borrow one of the new computers to work at home. James is not sure which type of computer to take and asks you to advise him. Choose one type of computer for James and give two reasons for your choice.

   c. The company orders two 24-port hubs to create this peer-to-peer network.

      i. What is a hub?

      ii. Should the company buy switches instead of hubs? If so, why?

   d. Frances tells James that the company has chosen a star topology rather than a bus topology for the network.

      i. What is a topology?

      ii. State one benefit of a star topology over a bus topology.

   e. James' brother Michael says that the company would be better off changing from a peer-to-peer network to a client-server network.

      i. State one item of hardware and one item of software which would be required to implement this change.

      ii. State one advantage of a client-server network over a peer-to-peer network.

   f. Each of the company's laptop computers has a wireless network interface card. What other item of hardware would the company need to allow wireless networking to take place?

5. Look at the following advertisement and answer the questions which follow:

WonderPic – amazing new graphics package from Excelsior software. Ideal for use with digital camera or scanner output! Powerful import and export facilities!

Complete with WonderScript programming language and script library. Versions available for all major platforms, including Windows, Macintosh and Linux operating systems.

WonderPic requires a 1 Gigahertz processor (2 Gigahertz preferred), Windows XP, Mac OSX or Linux, 300 Megabytes of free RAM minimum, 170 Megabytes of storage space for installation, 16 bit colour display (24 bit for true colour), mouse or graphics tablet. Bonus graphics library of GIF Clip Art downloadable from our web site when you register your purchase.

   a. **i.** What type of graphics package is WonderPic likely to be?

      ii. What information in the advertisement suggests this?

   b. What is meant by 'powerful import and export facilities'?

   c. Name two standard data formats that you would expect the WonderPic application to be able to recognise.

   d. What type of programming language is WonderScript?

   e. Of what benefit to the user is a script library?

   f. What is true colour?

   g. Registered users of this software can download a graphics library. Name one additional benefit of software registration for the user and one benefit for the company.

h. The graphics library consists of GIF files.
- i. What is GIF?
- ii. Suggest why the company used GIF instead of TIFF for the downloadable library.

6. The *Skylon* software house has developed *Skydisk Scanner*, a new disk repair and recovery program. The company decides to sell its software via the Internet rather than by distributing it on disk or CD-ROM.

a. What are the advantages to the company of selling its software via the Internet instead of on disk or CD-ROM?

b. Helen's hard disk has developed a fault and she decides to buy Skydisk Scanner to fix her disk. Skydisk Scanner is a utility program. What is a utility program?

c. She logs on to the company's web site using her sister Cecilia's computer in order to access the Internet. Why does Helen use her sister's computer rather than her own?

d. Helen enters her credit card number in order to pay for the software. The web site uses encryption to provide a secure electronic transaction. What is encryption?

e. Helen downloads the software by clicking on a link on the web page called *scan.zip*. When the download is complete, the file *scan.zip* is saved to the computer's hard disk. Helen tries to open the file *scan.zip* and a message appears – 'This is a compressed file'. What type of software will Helen use to solve this problem?

f. Helen manages to solve the problem and finds the following three files – *Readme.txt*, *Scanner.exe* and *Startup.sys*. What type of program will Helen use to open the file Readme.txt?

g. The file *Readme.txt* contains instructions on how to use the software. One of the instructions tells Helen that the files Scanner.exe and Startup.sys should be transferred to CD-ROM before use. Why does Helen need to transfer these files to CD-ROM rather than floppy disk?

h. What item of hardware will Helen require to use in order to transfer the files to CD-ROM?

i. The instructions also say that the CD-ROM should be used as a start-up disk in order to repair Helen's hard disk. What is a start-up disk?

j. What additional software must be present on the CD-ROM in order for it to be used as a start-up disk?

Glossary

acceptance test report An acceptance test report forms a contractual document within which acceptance of software is agreed between the programmer and the client for whom the software has been written

acceptance testing The beta testing stage of the software development process

actual parameters Parameters which are contained in a procedure call

adaptive maintenance Adaptive maintenance is changing the software in response to changes in the hardware or operating system

address bus The address bus carries the address information from the processor to the main memory and any other devices attached to the bus. The address bus is unidirectional

addressability The ability of the processor to identify each storage location is called its addressability

ADSL Asymmetric Digital Subscriber Line. A means of allowing broadband access over a normal telephone line

algorithm A set of instructions used to solve a problem

alphanumeric data Data consisting of text and numbers

analogue to digital conversion takes place in an interface

analysis Analysis is the understanding of the problem and the conversion of a problem outline into a precise software specification which should include problem inputs, processes and outputs

application based tests Tests which show how a computer system is likely to perform when it is being used to carry out ordinary tasks, for example, spell check a 100 page document

argument A parameter in a function is called an argument

arithmetic and logic unit (ALU) The part of the processor where all of the calculating and decision-making takes place

arithmetical operations Arithmetical operations are calculations involving numeric data. Arithmetic operators are +, -, / and *

array A set of data items of the same type grouped together using a single variable name is called an array

array parameter When an array is being passed as a parameter, it is always passed by reference

artefact A flaw or defect in a digital image, usually produced as a result of compression

ASCII ASCII is a seven-bit code, allowing for 128 different characters

attributes (of object) A list of numbers which describes a vector graphic

bandwidth Bandwidth is a measure of the quantity of data which may be carried by a communications channel at any one time

benchmark A measure of the performance of a computer system

beta version The pre-release version of a program is called the beta version

binary system A number system which has only two numbers, 0 and 1

bit depth The number of bits used to represent a pixel in bit mapped graphics

bit mapped graphics Bit mapped packages paint pictures by changing the colour of the pixels which make up the screen display

blocked process A process which cannot use the processor's time because it is busy with an input or output task

blocks (of a file) The way in which a file is stored on a backing storage medium such as a disk

Bluetooth Bluetooth is the name for IEEE 802.15.1 wireless standard, with a range of up to 10 metres and a bandwidth of 1 Mbps

Blu-ray A type of data storage using a blue coloured laser beam

Boolean data Boolean or Logical data – may only have two values, true or false. Boolean data is used in a program's control structures

boot sector virus A virus which infects a disk-based operating system when the computer starts up

bootstrap loader The bootstrap loader's function is to load the rest of the operating system from disk when the computer is switched on

bottom-up design A design methodology which begins with writing procedures and blocks of code

breakpoints A temporary halt in a program, used while debugging in order to take a snapshot of selected variables

browsers A program which is used to surf the World Wide Web

buffer A buffer is an area of memory used for the transfer of the data between the computer and a peripheral. A buffer provides temporary storage of data and is an essential component of any interface

bus A set of wires which carries data between the processor and the other components

Glossary | 251

bus topology A network topology in which all of the nodes are connected to a central line or bus

cache memory Cache memory holds frequently accessed instructions and allows fast access to them

camouflage A strategy used by a virus to evade detection by an anti-virus program

CAT(egory) 5 A type of cable used for data transmission in a local area network

CD-ROM server A computer which allows users on a client-server network access to CD-ROMs. Sometimes called a jukebox

central node A node at the centre of a star topology

channel A link between two nodes on a network, or any type of communications channel

channel failure The breakdown of a communications channel

checksum (virus detection) A checksum is performed on an uninfected program. Repeating the calculation on a suspect program allows the anti-virus software to test if the program has been changed, and if so, it will issue a warning that the program may be infected with a virus

client A workstation on a client-server network

client server network A client-server network is a method of organisation in which client workstations make use of resources available on one or more servers

clock The clock line carries a series of clock pulses at a constant rate in order to keep the processor and its related components in step with one another

clock speed The rate at which the clock generates pulses

code generation The code generation stage produces the object code, which is a machine code representation of the source code

colour depth The number of bits used to represent a pixel in bit mapped graphics

colour gradient A gradual change from one colour to another

Command Language Interpreter (CLI) The Command Language Interpreter is the layer of the operating system, with which the user interacts in order to give instructions to the computer – it interprets user commands

command-driven A type of human computer interface (HCI) in which the user must enter commands

communications channel The medium through which information is transmitted from a sender (or transmitter) to a receiver, for example, category 5 cable

compact flash A form of solid-state storage used in digital still cameras

compilation error A compilation error is an error which is detected during the process of compilation (or translation) of the program into the object code before it is run. Compilation errors are usually syntax errors

compiler A compiler translates a high level language program, the source code, into machine code, the object code

complete installation Installing all of a software package onto a computer system

complex condition A condition consisting of two or more simple conditions

comprehensive testing Comprehensive testing means that all your programs should be tested as thoroughly as possible

compressor Utility software which reduces the size of a file

concatenation Concatenation is joining two strings

conditional loops There are two types of conditional loop: test at start and test at end. Test at start may never be run if the condition is not met. Test at end is always run at least once

context-sensitive help system A system which provides a different type of help depending upon what it assumes the user is trying to do

control bus The control bus is made up of the read, write, clock, interrupt, non-maskable interrupt and reset lines

control characters Control characters control certain operations of the computer system

control line One of the wires which makes up the control bus, for example, address, data, reset, interrupt, clock

control structure There are three basic control structures used in procedural languages. These are sequence, selection and repetition

control unit The control unit controls all the other parts of the processor and makes sure that the program instructions of the computer are carried out in the correct order

corrective maintenance Corrective maintenance is fixing bugs or mistakes which were not discovered before the software was released

counting occurrences Counting occurrences is used to count how many times a value appears in a list

cross-compiler A cross-compiler takes a high level language program as source code, and can produce object code for more than one type of processor

cross-platform Software which works on more than one platform, e.g. Windows and Macintosh

customised installation A software installation which may be tailored to suit a user's requirements, perhaps to save on backing storage space

data bus The data bus carries data to and from the processor, main memory and any other devices attached to the data bus. The data bus is bi-directional

data bus width The number of wires in the data bus. Also the word size

data compression Data Compression means reducing the size of a file in order to save backing storage space. There are two types of data compression, lossy and lossless

data flow The movement of data (or the data flow) between subprograms is implemented by using parameters

data format conversion Data format conversion involves changing the data received from the peripheral into a form that the processor can understand and vice versa

data transfer rates The speed of data transferred between devices, normally measured in bits per second

data types The data types stored by a program include a number, a character, a string, a date, a file, an array, a sound sample and a video clip

debugging Debugging is the process of finding and correcting errors in a program

declarative language A declarative language states "what to do" rather than "how to do it", using facts and rules

defragmenter A defragmenter program defragments a disk, gathering all the free space on the disk together and reuniting scattered file fragments

design Design involves the careful planning of a solution to a problem using a recognised design methodology, for example, top-down design using an appropriate design notation, such as structure diagrams or pseudocode

design methodology Design Methodology is the approach that the programmer takes to the design of the solution, for example top-down design

design notation Design Notation is the way of describing or representing the design of a program. Pseudocode and Structure charts are two design notations

directories An area on a backing storage medium, such as a disk, where files may be stored. Also called a folder on some systems

disc editor A disc editor is a utility program which allows the user to edit data directly on the surface of a disk, by-passing the normal loading and saving features of the operating system

documentation Documentation of a program includes a user guide and a technical guide. All other stages of the software development process also need some form of documentation

double precision arithmetic Using additional bytes to store a number on a computer system, for example, increasing the number of bytes used to store the mantissa

DRAM Dynamic Random Access Memory. A type of RAM whose contents must be constantly refreshed

dry run Testing a program by hand without using a computer system (hand testing). To carry out a dry run you would begin by making a list of all the variables in the part of the program you are going to examine. This is called a trace table, and as you go through the program, it allows you to write down how the values of the variables change at each line

dual platform Software which is capable of running or being installed on two platforms, for example, *Adobe Photoshop* is dual platform

dumb terminal A dumb terminal has no processor and no local storage devices, just a screen and a keyboard

efficiency Efficient software is when the software does not require excessive resources, such as memory, or backing storage space, in order to run

element Each part of an array is called an element

elements of computer memory The elements of computer memory are registers, cache, main memory and backing storage

email filter A program which re-directs email to specific folders or blocks email according to pre-set rules

email worm A worm which is attached to an email message

emulator A utility program which imitates another type of computer system, for example, *Virtual PC*

EPROM Erasable Programmable Read Only Memory

error reporting Error Reporting is the communication and explanation of errors in the software to the user

Ethernet A widely used standard type of local area network

Ethernet disks A type of backing storage which is attached to an Ethernet network. Also called Network Attached Storage (NAS)

evaluation An evaluation is when the software solution is reviewed against suitable criteria, such as comparing the solution with the original software specification

event-driven language An event-driven language is provided with a program which helps you to design the user interface by placing graphics objects on screen. The action of clicking on or selecting a screen object is called an event, and the event is detected by the program, hence the name event-driven language

exceptional test data Test data which should be rejected by the program under test

execution error Another name for a run-time error, which only shows up when a program is run. Overflow and division by zero are two examples

exhaustive testing Testing which involves all of the possible sets of test data and all of the program pathways

expander The opposite of a compressor. Used to recreate the original data from its compressed form, for example, *unZip* or *UnStuffit*

exponent Part of a floating point number which contains the power to which the base must be raised

extended ASCII ASCII which uses eight bits instead of seven bits. Allows 256 different characters to be represented

extreme test data Test data which is on the limit or boundary of what is acceptable by a program under test. Also called boundary data

facts and rules The facts and rules described in a declarative language program are known as the knowledge base. When a query is entered, the declarative language looks for a solution contained in the knowledge base

fetch-execute cycle (summary of) The processor sets up the address bus with the required address; the processor activates the read line; the instruction is transferred from memory to processor by using the data bus (fetch); the instruction is decoded; the instruction is executed

field testing Field testing is allowing users (other than the people who wrote the program) to test the program

file management system The File Management System is concerned with the efficient use of the computer's backing storage devices and media, in order to store data

file server A file server provides central disk storage for user's programs and data on a network

file virus File viruses are so-called because they attach themselves to files. They either replace or insert malicious code into the files. The types of files that are usually infected are those with the extensions .COM and .EXE

firewall Software or hardware which attempts to prevent illegal access to a computer system connected to a network

Firewire IEEE 1394 – a high speed serial connection with maximum data transfer rates of 400 and 800 Mbps. Also called *iLink*

fixed loops A loop which is carried out a set number of times

Flash ROM A solid-state storage medium used in flash cards

floating point Floating point is a method of representing real numbers using a mantissa and an exponent

FLOPS Floating Point Operations Per Second. A measure of the performance of a computer system

flow chart A type of design notation, which uses boxes, linked by arrows

formal parameters Parameters which are contained in a procedure or sub-program definition

formatting of input/output Formatting of input/output is arranging the position or appearance of the data on the screen when input or output is taking place

forms dialogue interface A type of HCI in which data is entered into boxes

free process A process which could run if it was given the processor's time

function A function is a subprogram which returns a single value to a program

gateway computer A gateway computer allows an Intranet to connect to the Internet

GIF Graphics Interchange Format. A standard file format for storing images, with a maximum of 256 colours

global variables Global variables may be used anywhere in a program but local variables are defined only for use in one part of a program (a subprogram)

graphical design notation A design notation which uses lines and boxes to show the structure of a program, for example a structure diagram

graphics card A circuit board in a computer system which is responsible for the generation and display of graphics

hacking The process of gaining entry to a computer system or file, usually illegally

hand testing This is the process of going through the program code manually, in order to find mistakes

hardware platform A hardware platform is a particular combination of processor and operating system

heuristic detection A 'rule of thumb' used by anti-virus programs

heuristics Heuristics allow rules to be set up to detect new viruses that have not been seen before – for example – if it looks like a virus, and behaves like a virus, then it probably is a virus

hierarchical filing system A filing system which has a top level or root directory and one or more sub-directories

holographic storage A high capacity storage technique, which can store data in a number of layers on a storage medium

hotspot (wireless) A hotspot is an area where wireless network signals may be received, and a computer may connect to the network

hub A hub is a multi-port repeater

identifiers The name of something in a program. For instance, the name of a variable, like counter

IF The IF structure is suitable for use when a single selection (or a limited number of selections) is to be made

iLink Another name for *IEEE 1394* or Firewire

imperative languages Another name for procedural languages

implementation Implementation is changing the program design into a computer language and the production of internal documentation

in parameters Data structures (such as variables) which are only passed into subprograms to be used are known as in parameters

in/out parameters Variables which are passed into a subprogram and are changed or updated are referred to as in/out parameters

independent test group A group which tests software independently of the company which wrote the software and is able to provide an unbiased opinion

infinite loop A loop which never stops and may cause the computer system to 'hang'

input validation Input validation may be used to check that data input is within a certain (acceptable) range

input/output management The Input/Output Management system is the part of the operating system which communicates directly with the peripherals and handles the transfer of data between the peripherals and the processor

installer A program used to place software onto a computer system's hard disk

integer data Integer data is a subset of real data which includes only whole numbers, either positive or negative

integer variables A variable which can only hold either positive or negative whole numbers, without a fractional part

interface An interface is the hardware and associated software needed to allow communication between the processor and its peripheral devices and to compensate for any differences in their operating characteristics

interface functions The functions of an interface include buffering, data format conversion, voltage conversion, protocol conversion and the handling of status signals

internal documentation Internal documentation is comment lines which may be inserted in program code to provide a description of what the code does

Internetwork An Internetwork is a collection of two or more Local Area Networks

interpreter An interpreter translates and runs a high level language program one instruction or statement at a time. No separate object code is produced. Interpreted programs run slower than compiled programs because each line must be translated every time the program is run

interrupt An interrupt is a signal to the processor from a peripheral device

Intranet An Intranet is a private network belonging to a company or organization, for internal use only, although it may be geographically widespread

iteration Iteration is revisiting or repeating one or more steps in the software development process in order to improve the solution

JPEG Joint Photographic Experts Group – JPEG uses lossy compression which means that some data is lost

jukebox A jukebox can be used to hold a number of CD-ROMs at once, or to make backups of network data on multiple recordable disks

kernel The kernel is the part of the operating system responsible for managing processes and handling any interrupts

knowledge base Part of an expert system which contains the facts and the rules

least significant bit (LSB) The bit with the smallest place value (1)

lexical analysis Part of the process of compilation. In the lexical analysis stage, each recognised keyword in the source code is changed into a token

linear search Linear search is used to find an item of data (the target value) in a list

linker A linker is used to join a module from a software library to a program

linking error A linking error is when a program is incorrectly linked to a subroutine or module library

Local Area Network (LAN) A local area network (LAN) covers a small area such as a room or a building

local variable Local variables are defined only for use in one subprogram

logical data see Boolean

logical error Logical errors are mistakes in the design of the program. Logical errors only show up when you run the program and you can spot them because the program does not do what it is supposed to do, for instance, it produces the wrong results

logical operators These include AND, OR and NOT, and are used to link two or more conditions to create a complex condition

lossless compression Lossless compression means that none of the original data is lost

lossy compression Lossy compression involves sacrificing some of the data in order to reduce the file size

MAC address A MAC address is a Media Access Control Address provided by a NIC

machine code The computer's own language, written in binary

macro Programs written using a scripting language are often called macros. Once programmed, a macro may be activated by clicking on a button or by selecting from a menu. A macro is a set of keystrokes and instructions that are recorded, saved, and assigned to a single key or a combination of keys. When the key code is typed, the recorded keystrokes and instructions are carried out

macro virus A virus which can infect applications such as Microsoft Word or Excel, which allow the creation of macros

mail server A network server which provides a mailing service to clients

main memory Main memory consists of a number of storage locations, each with a unique address. Main memory consists of Random Access Memory (RAM) and Read Only Memory (ROM)

maintainability Maintainability is how easy it is to correct or update the software in future

maintenance Maintenance involves making changes in the form of corrections or updates to the program at some time in the future and is made easier by good practise in software development

malware A general term for software which can damage a computer system. Short for MALicious softWARE. Viruses, trojan horses and worms are all forms of malware

mantissa In floating point number, the mantissa determines the precision of the number

manual testing Testing a program by hand without using a computer system (hand testing)

maskable interrupt A maskable interrupt may be ignored by the processor

memory address register A register in the processor which is connected to the address bus

memory data register A register in the processor which is connected to the data bus

memory management system The Memory Management System controls where programs and data are placed in main memory. The Memory Management System keeps track of the total amount of main memory available, and which programs and data are currently loaded

memory read operation The steps involved are: the processor sets up the address bus with the required memory address; the control unit of the processor activates the read line on the control bus; the contents of the particular storage location in memory are released onto the data bus and are copied into one of the processor's registers. If it is an instruction, it is decoded and executed (carried out)

memory resident monitoring Anti-virus software which stays in the computer's memory and constantly checks the computer for the presence of viruses

Memory stick A type of solid-state storage, used in digital cameras

memory write operation The steps involved are: the processor sets up the address bus with the required memory address; the processor sets up the data bus with the value to be written to memory; the control unit of the processor activates the write line on the control bus; the value on the data bus is transferred to the required storage location in the computer's memory

menu selection interface A type of HCI in which choices may be made from menus

menu-driven see menu selection interface

mesh topology A topology which has multiple direct connections between all of the nodes

MIDI Musical Instrument Digital Interface

minimal installation Installing only enough of a software package onto a computer system to allow it to run

MIPS Millions of Instructions Per Second (MIPS). A measure of the performance of a computer system

mirroring Using two hard disks to hold exactly the same data

modular design Modular design is a method of organising a large computer program into self-contained parts called modules. Top down design and bottom-up design are both forms of modular design

modularity Modularity means that when a program is designed and written, it is divided into smaller sections called subprograms or sub-routines

module High level procedural languages use two types of modules or subprograms. These are procedures and functions

module libraries Module Libraries are pre-defined routines which support and speed up the software development process. Using a module library speeds up the whole software development process because time is saved in design, implementation testing and documentation

most significant bit (MSB) The largest place value in a number

Multimedia card A type of solid-state storage used in digital cameras

multiple outcome selection A program control structure which is best implemented by using a CASE statement

multi-port repeater a hub

multi-processor A computer containing more than one processor

multi-programming A type of operating system which can process more than one program, apparently at the same time

multi-tasking See multi-programming

multi-user It is common to have many simultaneous users on a mainframe computer – a mainframe is a multi-user or multi-access system

nanosecond 10^{-9} seconds

nested loops Loops which are contained inside other loops

network A network is two or more computers linked together in such a way that programs, data and messages may be exchanged between them

network cloud A network cloud is a collection of hotspots or areas within the range of wireless base stations

network interface card (NIC) A network interface card is a small circuit board that is fitted inside a computer system to allow it to communicate with a computer network

network operating system An operating system designed to allow network access. A network operating system provides secure login

network topology The network topology is the way in which the nodes or workstations on a network are connected together

node Each computer on a network may be referred to as a terminal, workstation or node. Nodes in a local area network are relatively close together and can be connected by using wires, fibre optic cable or wireless technologies as the transmission medium or communications channel

node failure The consequences of node failure are directly related to the network topology

non-maskable interrupt An interrupt which cannot be ignored by the processor

normal test data Test data which is within a range that the program under test should accept

numeric data Numeric data – may consist of real type data or integer type data

numeric variables A variable which can hold a number which may have a fractional part

object An object is the item of data which is involved in the process

object attributes Object attributes are used to describe an object in vector graphics, for example, centre coordinates, pen colour, line width

object code Object code is a machine code program produced as the result of translation

objects and operations An object is the item of data which is involved in the process, and an operation is a process which is carried out on an item of data

one-dimensional arrays One-dimensional array. An array with only one subscript

operation An operation is a process which is carried out on an item of data

optical fibre An optical fibre is a communications medium which is made of thin strands of glass. It is capable of very high data transfer rate and is immune to interference from electrical signals

OS compatibility A program is said to be OS compatible when it is capable of running under a particular operating system

out parameters Variables which are only passed out of subprograms are known as out parameters

overflow error This is an example of a run-time error when a storage location is too small to hold a number

page description language A page description language is a high level language used to describe the page set up and objects to be sent to a printer

parallel data transmission Parallel data transmission sends each bit which makes up a character simultaneously along separate data lines

parallel interface A parallel interface is one which uses parallel data transmission, sending each bit which makes up a character simultaneously along separate data lines

parameter A parameter is information about a data item being supplied to a subprogram when it is called into use

parameter passing (in, out, in/out) Parameters can be passed either by value or by reference. When a subprogram is used, the calling program must pass parameters to it – this is parameter passing

parity Parity is an example of a protocol used during data transmission. Parity is used to check for errors. One bit in every byte of data is reserved as the parity bit. Parity may be even or odd

parsing Checking the language statements against the rules or grammar of the language. This is part of the syntax analysis stage of compilation

pathname A pathname is the method or route used to find a file in a hierarchical filing system. John.work.files.letter1 is an example of a pathname

PCI Peripheral Component Interconnect is a type of interface standard

PCMCIA Personal Computer Memory Card International Association – an international standard for interfaces

peer-to-peer network Every workstation on a peer-to-peer network has a similar status in the hierarchy, each having its own local storage devices for programs and data

perfective maintenance Perfective maintenance is adding new features to a program

peripheral node A node on the outside of a star topology

personnel involved in the software development process Personnel involved in software development are the client, systems analyst, project manager, programmer and independent test group

phishing Phishing is an attempt to trick someone into giving away personal information using the Internet by pretending to be a well-known company

polymorphic viruses Viruses which can change their signature to avoid detection by anti-virus programs

portability Portability is the ability of software to be used on a computer other than that for which it was originally designed

precision of floating point numbers Increasing the number of bytes used for the mantissa will increase the precision of the number being stored

pre-defined function A function which is already supplied to the user as part of the programming language

print server A print server allows all of the client stations to use a printer controlled by it. A print server may incorporate a spooler program to temporarily store data in transit to the printer on a fast backing storage device like a hard disk drive

printer buffer A buffer is an area of memory used for the transfer of the data between the computer and a peripheral, in this case, a printer

printer driver A program which takes the codes in a document and translates them into the appropriate code for the printer in use. A type of device driver

procedural language A procedural language is one in which the user sets out a list of instructions in the correct sequence (an algorithm) in order to solve a problem

procedure A procedure is said to produce an effect or carry out an operation. A function returns a single value to a program

program design The process of planning a solution to a problem

program maintenance Program maintenance is changing a program, often some time after it has been written

program or structure syntax error A program or structure syntax error happens when you have made a mistake in the structure of your program, such as incorrect use of a control structure

program pathway A route in a program which is determined by a selection control structure

programmer A programmer writes code, working to a software specification

project manager A project manager is in charge of the software development process for a particular program

PROLOG A high level declarative language

PROM Programmable Read Only Memory

protocol A protocol is a standard set of rules that enables the connection, communication, and data transfer between computers or between a computer system and a peripheral

protocol conversion Protocol conversion is changing from one protocol to another. Protocol conversion is one function of an interface

pseudocode One design notation is pseudocode. Pseudocode is ordinary language used to define problems and sub-problems before they are changed into code in a high level language

RAID Redundant Array of Inexpensive Disks

RAM Random Access Memory holds its data as long as the computer is switched on

read line Part of the control bus. The read line is used in the memory read operation and in the fetch-execute cycle

readability Readability is how easy it is for another person to understand your program code

read-write head The read-write head is the part of the hard disk drive which reads and writes the data to and from the surface of the disk

ready process A process which could run if it was given the processor's time

real data Real data includes ALL numbers, both whole and fractional

real variables Variables which are capable of holding real numbers

recursion A type of loop used in a declarative language

reference parameter Parameters are passed by reference when the parameter requires to be passed in to a procedure, updated and then passed back out of the procedure again

registers The registers are a group of storage locations in the processor which are used to hold data being processed, instructions being executed and addresses to be accessed

relational operations Relational operations use relational operators to compare data and produce a Boolean answer of true or false. Relational operators include = and >

reliability Reliability is how well software operates without stopping due to design faults

repeater A repeater is a device which boosts or amplifies a signal on a cable

repetition Repetition is doing something over again e.g. in a loop, either conditional or fixed

replication Replication is copying. Used in spreadsheets to copy a formula between cells

reset line The reset line on the control bus is used to return the processor to its initial state

resolution The quality of the picture is determined by the resolution of the graphics available. The smaller the size of the pixels, the finer the detail that can be displayed on the screen

resolution independence When a picture is created using a vector graphics package, the resolution of the screen has no effect on the resolution of the printout. The picture will be printed out at the full resolution available on the printer

resource allocation Resource allocation is the way of managing which resource is available for use at any one time by a process

resource sharing A benefit of a Local Area network is that resources such as printers may be shared between all of the machines

RGB colour Representing colour by using pixels in groups of three, one each for Red, Green and Blue

ring topology A topology which has nodes connected in the form of a circle

robustness Robustness is the ability of software to cope with errors during execution without failing

root directory The main directory at the top of a hierarchical filing system

rounding error An error introduced as a result of rounding a number

router A router is a device which links two or more networks. A router looks at the destination addresses of the packets of data passing through it, and decides which route each packet should take

running process A process which has the processor's time

run-time error A run-time error is an error which shows up during program execution. These include overflow, rounding, truncation and division by zero

run-time version A limited version of one program that enables you to run another program. To run a program written in Visual Basic, for example, you need the runtime version of Visual Basic. This allows you to run Visual Basic programs but not to write them

sample data Sample data – consists of digitally recorded sound data (e.g. MP3) and video data (e.g. a video clip – MPEG)

scheduler The scheduler makes the decisions as to which process from the queue is given the processor's time

scope The scope of a variable is the range of statements for which a variable is valid. The scope of a global variable is the whole program. The scope of a local variable is a sub-program

screen object An object used in an event-driven language program, linked to code. Clicking on a screen object is an event, and this causes the code to run

scripting language A language which may accompany an application package. A scripting language uses the commands from within the package to automate a series of tasks, or to provide new functions which are not available in the packages menus

SCSI Small Computer Systems Interface

selection Selection is making a choice e.g. control structure + condition(s)

semantics The semantics of a particular instruction is its meaning or its effect

sequence Sequence is the order in which things are done

serial data transmission Serial data transmission sends the bits for each character in the data one after another along the same data line

server A server is a computer that handles requests for data, email, file transfers, and other network services from other computers

simple condition A condition made using only one relational operator, for example, age=18, average_temperature < 15

single stepping Going through a program one line at a time, usually in order to find mistakes. A feature of a trace facility

single user operating system A single user operating system is only capable of being used by one person at a time

software development personnel Project manager, systems analyst, programmer, independent test group and the client

software development process The software development process is a series of seven stages for the development of software; Analysis, Design, Implementation, Testing, Documentation, Evaluation and Maintenance

software hierarchy The software hierarchy starts at the bottom with the simplest form of software which is closest to the processor, namely machine code. The hierarchy continues through assembly language, high level language, and fourth generation language, to application packages

software library A software library is made up of a number of sub-programs, called library modules, which are stored on disk

software specification The precise definition of a problem

solid state storage devices A solid-state storage device contains no moving parts. Examples of solid-state storage devices include flash cards and USB flash memory

source code Source code is a high level language program, before translation

spam email messages Unsolicited electronic mail

spooling Saving data temporarily to fast backing storage before sending it to a peripheral device such as a printer

spyware Spyware is a type of computer program which can record the user's keystrokes, like passwords and forward them to another computer

SRAM Static Random Access Memory SRAM is faster to access than DRAM, and does not need to be constantly refreshed

stand alone program A stand alone version of a program is independent of the translator program and may be run on its own

stand-alone computer A stand-alone computer is one which is not connected to a network

standard algorithms Standard algorithms include input validation, linear search, counting occurrences and finding minimum and maximum

standard file formats Standard file formats have been developed to ease the transfer of data between application packages. Each type of application software has its own set of standard file formats. Some examples of standard file formats are GIF (Graphics Interchange Format), JPEG (Joint Photographic Experts Group) and TIFF (Tag Image File Format)

star topology A topology consisting of a single central node and a number of peripheral nodes, all connected directly to the central node by separate communications channels

statement syntax error A statement syntax error is misspelling a keyword, like typing PRUNT instead of PRINT or WRITLEN instead of WRITELN

status information The purpose of status information, provided by an interface, is to show whether or not a peripheral device is ready to communicate, that is, receive or to send data

stepwise refinement Stepwise refinement takes each step and breaks it down as far as possible, until each step can be turned into a single line of program code

storage location An item of data is stored in memory in a storage location. Each storage location has its own unique address in the computer's main memory

stored program A computer operates by fetching and executing instructions from a stored program

string operations String operations include joining strings, known as concatenation, and selecting parts of strings, known as substrings

string variables A structured variable, which holds one or more characters

structure chart A graphical design notation using lines and identical boxes

structure diagram A graphical design notation using lines and differently shaped boxes

structure syntax error A (program or) structure syntax error happens when you have made a mistake in the structure of your program, such as incorrect use of a control structure. This type of syntax error may be detected by examining or proof reading a structured listing

structured listing A structured listing is a formatted display or printout of the program code

sub-directories A directory which is beneath the root directory in a hierarchical filing system

sub-problem part of a problem identified in the top-down design process, and produced as a result of stepwise refinement, for example, a procedure or a function

sub-program See sub-problem

sub-routines See sub-problem

subscript Each element in an array is identified by the variable name and a subscript

substrings Substrings is selecting parts of strings, in COMAL, name$(2:5)

supercomputer A supercomputer is the fastest and most powerful type of computer, used for intensive mathematical calculations. It has many parallel processors and can process data simultaneously

switch A switch operates like a "smart" hub, dividing a network into separate segments, one for each machine. Workstations connected via a switch benefit because there are no collisions between signals to reduce the speed of the network

syntax The syntax of a programming language is the way in which you give instructions to the computer

syntax analysis During the syntax analysis stage, the language statements are checked against the rules or grammar of the language

syntax error A syntax error is when the rules of the programming language are broken

system error A system error occurs when the computer system (rather than just the program that you are working on) stops working properly. Windows™ users will no doubt be familiar with the so-called "blue screen of death"

systematic testing Systematic testing involves using a test plan

systems analyst A systems analyst observers, clarifies, and models an existing system to assess its suitability for computerisation. At the same time, the systems analyst will look for ways in which to improve the system

technical guide A technical guide explains how to install the software on to a computer system. It lists the type of computer system(s) upon which the software will run, and the installation requirements

terminal A terminal has no processor and no local storage devices, just a screen and a keyboard

terminated process A process which has finished

terminator The terminator on a bus network catches stray signals, and prevents them from interfering with other signals on the bus

test data Test Data is a set of data used to make sure that your program actually solves the problem it is supposed to (i.e. meets the software specification). Test data is made up of normal, extreme and exceptional data

test plan A test plan outlines what you are trying to test and how you are going to do it – for example: what program (or module) is being tested; what the program (or module) should do; list suitable test data; expected results from the test data

test report A test report summarises the results of testing a program

testing Testing is to ensure that a piece of software performs correctly (i.e. meets the software specification)

text editor A text editor allows source code to be entered and edited

TIFF Tag Image File Format. A standard file format for the storage of bit mapped images

time slicing When the processor divides its time between each process. Each process is given a slice of the processor's time, and the processor swaps processes in and out at very high speed so that it appears to be doing many tasks at once

top-down design Top-down design involves looking at the overall problem and breaking it down into a series of steps

topology The way in which the nodes on a network are connected together

trace facility Many programming languages have a trace facility, which allows the programmer to follow the path through the program at the same time as it is being run. A trace facility allows the user to go through the program one line at a time. This is called single stepping

trace table A list of all the variables in the part of a program under examination

translator A translator converts a computer program from one language to another (for example, from a high level language to a low level language). Examples: Compiler, Interpreter

translator programs Compilers and interpreters are types of translator programs

transmission media The media which carries the data, for example copper cable, optical fibre or wireless

trojan (horse) A Trojan is a program that appears to be safe, but hidden inside is usually something harmful, like a worm or a virus

true colour True colour is represented on a computer system using 24 bits per pixel, giving a total range of 16,777,216 different colours

truncation error Truncation means shortening a number to a given number of decimal places. A truncation error is the difference between the original number and the truncated number

two's complement A method of representing integer numbers in binary. To change a binary number into its negative counterpart, change all the ones to zeros, all the zeros to ones, and add one

two-state machine A computer system is known as a two-state machine because the processing and storage devices in a computer system have one feature in common – they have two states only. These two states are "on" and "off" and are represented using the digits 1 for "on" and 0 for "off"

Ultra-Wideband (UWB) UWB follows the IEEE 802.15.3 specification, with data rates of over 400 Mbps with a range of up to 10 metres in a Wireless Personal Area Network (WPAN)

Unicode Unicode is a method of representing a character using 16 bits, which is designed to be able to represent all the world's character sets

uninstaller A program which removes software from a computer system

UPS Uninterruptible Power Supply

USB Universal Serial Bus – a type of computer interface

USB flash memory There are two types of USB flash memory, according to the type of interface being used, USB 1 and USB 2

user guide A user guide explains how to operate the software once it is installed

user interface User interface looks at the nature of the HCI, help screens, instruction screens, visual appeal, screen layout and prompts for the user

user-defined function A user-defined function is a function which is created within a program rather than being already present or pre-defined as part of the normal syntax of a programming language

user-friendly An interactive computer system which helps the user by giving clear prompts, menus and help screens when needed

utility program A utility program is a type of systems software designed to perform an everyday task, like formatting a disk

UTP Unshielded Twisted Pair – it is a type of copper network cable

value parameter Parameters are passed by value when a parameter is passed into a procedure but does not require to be passed back out again

variable A variable is the name that a programmer uses to identify a storage location

variable type error An error in a program when a value of the wrong type is assigned to a variable, for example, a numeric variable cannot hold a character

vector graphics Vector packages work by drawing objects on the screen. Vector graphics are stored as list of attributes, rather than a bit map

virtual memory A method of using backing storage space to hold data instead of RAM

virus A virus is a program which can destroy or cause damage to data stored on a computer system. A virus infects other host files and is distributed along with them

virus checker An anti-virus program

virus code actions Viruses act differently according to how they are programmed. The actions that the program code in the virus may carry out when run include: replication, camouflage, watching and delivery

virus infections Viruses may infect files, the boot sector on a disk, or a document which contains a macro

virus signature A virus signature is a characteristic pattern or sequence of bytes that is part of a virus. If a virus scanner finds such a pattern in a file, it notifies the user that the file is infected

volatile memory Memory whose contents are erased when the power is switched off, for example, RAM

voltage conversion Voltage conversion by an interface is required when a peripheral operates using a different voltage from that used by the processor and its associated components on the motherboard of the computer

VRAM Video Random Access Memory

warchalking Warchalking symbols are used to identify hotspots where a wireless connection may be made

watching A technique used by a virus which waits for an event, such as a date, to trigger an action

web filter A program which prevents access to specific web sites or pages

web server A web server is a computer that provides World Wide Web services to a network

WiFi WiFi is the Wireless Fidelity Alliance standard for wireless networking

WiMAX Worldwide interoperability for Microwave Access

WIMP environment A type of human computer interface which uses Windows, Icons, Menus and Pointers

wireless hotspot An area where wireless network signals may be received, and a computer may connect to a network

wireless network interface card Most laptop computers are fitted with wireless network interface cards in order to access networks without a physical connection

WLAN A wireless local area network

word A word is the number of bits that can be processed by the processor in a single operation. Each storage location can hold a quantity of data called a word

worm A worm is a program which can make copies of itself and spread between computers without having to be attached to a file

write line Part of the control bus, used to send a signal from the control unit to the main memory

WYSIWYG page editing What You See Is What You Get – used in web authoring software

Index

Page numbers in italics indicate illustrations not included in text page range.

Answers

Chapter 1

1. Convert numbers to decimal
   a. 1011 = 11
   b. 1001 1111 = 159
   c. 1010 1010 = 170
   d. 1111 1110 = 254

2. Convert numbers to binary
   a. 122 = 0111 1010
   b. 193 = 1100 0001
   c. 256 = 0001 0000 0000
   d. 1023 = 0011 1111 1111

3. Convert numbers to two's complement
   a. +6 = 0110   −6 = 1010
   b. +25 = 0001 1001   −25 = 1110 0111
   c. +92 = 0101 1100   −92 = 1010 0100
   d. +120 = 0111 1000   −120 = 1000 1000

4. Express numbers using a binary point
   a. 0.25   = 0.01
   b. 7.375   = 0111.011
   c. 15.53125   = 1111.10001

5. Convert the following real numbers into binary using floating point representation. Assume that 16 bits is available for the mantissa and 8 bits for the exponent.
   a. 27.5 = 0000 0000 0011 011.1
      = .1101 1100 0000 0000 × $2^{0000\,0101}$
   b. 134.125 = 0000 0100 0011 0.001
      = .1000 0110 0010 0000 × $2^{0000\,1000}$
   c. 4200.25 = 0100 0001 1010 00.01
      = .100 0001 1010 00010 × $2^{0000\,1101}$

6. a. The largest binary number a nibble can hold is 1111.
   b. The range of numbers that can be held in a nibble is from 0000 to 1111, or 0 to 15 in decimal, making a total of 16 different numbers.

7. Calculations carried out using numbers represented by floating point may not always give the correct answer because of the limited storage available for the number in the computer's memory. If the number is too large to fit in the space available, part of the number will be lost, for instance by rounding or truncation errors.

8. The effect of increasing the number of bits used to store the exponent is to increase the range of the numbers that may be stored.

9. If four bytes are used for the mantissa and one byte for the exponent, then
   .1111 1111 1111 1111 1111 1111 1111 1111
   × $2^{1111\,1111}$
   may be stored (ignoring two's complement)

10. User's own program

11. a. A character is a symbol or letter on the computer keyboard.
    b. A character set is a list of all the characters a computer can process and store.
    c. A control character does not print on the screen in the normal way. It is used to control certain operations of the computer system.

12. a. ASCII stands for American Standard Code for Information Interchange.
    b. ASCII can represent 128 different characters.
    c. ASCII is a 7 bit code and 2^7 = 128.
    d. Use an 8 bit code because 2^8 = 256.
    e. i. 'e' = 101
       ii. 'E' = 69

13. a. Unicode is a method of representing text using 16 bits, which is designed to represent all the world's character sets.
    b. Unicode can represent more characters than ASCII (65,536 compared to 128).

14. a. 56 bits per character for bitmap
    b. 7 bits per character for ASCII
    c. 16 bits for Unicode
    d. ASCII is the most efficient method of storing this character

15. Bit mapped graphics have a direct relationship between the pixels displayed on the monitor and the contents of the computer's memory.

16. Vector graphics are stored by using a list of attributes for each graphic object in the image.

17. a. True colour on a computer screen is when 24 bits per pixel are used for the colour depth, giving over 16 million different colours.
    b. 24 bits

18. **a.** Resolution is the quality of the picture.
b. Resolution independence is the ability of a graphics package to print out at the full resolution of the output device, e.g. printer.
c. Vector graphics are resolution independent.

19. **a.** i, iv, vi
b. ii, iii, v, vii

20. Draw two overlapping shapes and try to separate them. If the two shapes separate successfully then it is a vector package. Try to zoom in on the graphic and edit the pixels. If this is possible, then it is a bitmapped package.

21. A page description language is a high level language used to describe the page set up and objects to be sent to a printer.

22. Example *Postscript*™ program to draw a square of size two inches:

```
1. 0     0     moveto
2. 144   0     lineto
3. 0     144   lineto
4. closepath fill
5. showpage
```

23. **a.** a 640 × 480 = 307200 pixels ; total pixels 256 colours = 8 bits ; bit depth 307200 × 8 = 2457600 bits = 307200 bytes = 300 Kilobytes
b. 1 megapixel = 1024 × 1024 pixels; total pixels 16 bits; bit depth 1024 × 1024 × 16 = 16777216 bits = 2097152 bytes = 2048K = 2 Mb
c. 4 × 6 × 600 × 600 pixels ; total pixels = 1.0299 Mb
d. monochrome = 1 bit ; bit depth 4 × 6 × 600 × 600 × 1 = 8640000 bits = 1080000 bytes = 1054.6875 Kilobytes

24. 8 bits means that 256 different colours or shades of grey may be stored.

25. **a.** green
b. blue
c. black
d. white

26. **a.** increased by 8 times to 2 Mb
b. same at 512 Kb
c. increased by 16 times to 8 Mb

27. Data compression is reducing the size of a file in order to save backing storage space.

28. Data compression is used on bit-mapped graphics files because of the large amount of storage space that uncompressed files take up.

29. **a.** Lossy compression involves sacrificing some of the data in order to reduce the file size.
b. Lossless compression means that none of the original data is lost.
c. Lossy gives the smaller file size.
d. i. lossless
ii. lossy

30. **a.** JPEG
b. TIFF

31. **a.** 448.03 Kb
b. Figure 1.11 has a compression ratio of 2.3:1 and figure 1.12 has a compression ratio of 5.6:1.

32. **a.** 8.1 Mb
b. 8 megapixels
c. This reduction shows the image has been compressed with a compression ratio of 5.3:1. The likely reason for this is that a compressed file format such as JPEG has been used in order to save storage space on the camera's flash card.

Chapter 2

1. The arithmetic and logic unit, the control unit and the registers. The control unit in the processor controls all the other parts of the processor and makes sure that the program instructions of the computer are carried out in the correct order. The arithmetic and logic unit carries out the calculations and performs the logical operations. The registers are a group of storage locations in the processor which are used to hold data being processed, instructions being executed and addresses to be accessed.

2. A set of wires which carries data between the processor and the other components.

3. Address bus, data bus and control bus. The address bus carries the address information from the processor to the main memory. The data bus carries the data to and from the processor and the main memory. The control bus is a series of separate lines: read, write, interrupt, non-maskable interrupt, clock and reset.

4. **a.** Address bus
b. Data bus
c. Control bus
d. The number of wires in the bus

e. i. An increase in the number of storage locations which may be addressed

    ii. An increase in the quantity of data which may be carried by the bus

5. a. A binary number used to identify a storage location

b. The method of identifying a storage location

c. A place in memory where an item of data is stored

d. The number of bits that can be processed by the processor in a single operation

6. a. A device attached to a processor which keeps the operation of the components in step with one another

b. The rate at which the clock produces pulses

c. One complete pulse

d. A method by which a peripheral can attract the processor's attention

e. An interrupt which cannot be ignored

7. When an interrupt occurs, the processor saves a copy of what it is doing at that moment, runs a program to deal with the interrupt, and then reloads its original task and continues what it was doing before the interrupt occurred.

8. To return the computer to its initial state as if it had just been switched on.

9. The instruction is carried out.

10. a. The processor sets up the address bus with the required memory address. It does this by placing a value in the Memory Address Register. The control unit of the processor activates the read line on the control bus. The contents of the particular storage location in memory are released onto the data bus and are copied into the processor's Memory Data Register. If it is an instruction, it is decoded and executed (carried out).

b. The processor sets up the address bus with the required memory address. It does this by placing a value in the Memory Address Register. The processor sets up the data bus with the value to be written to memory. It does this by placing the value in the Memory Data Register. The control unit of the processor activates the write line on the control bus. The contents of the Memory Data Register are transferred to the required storage location in the computer's memory.

11. Total addressable memory = Number of storage locations x size of each storage location

12. a. 1

b. 2

c. 4

13. a. Registers, cache, main memory and backing storage

b. Registers, cache, main memory and backing storage

14. Two types of main memory are RAM and ROM.

a. Random Access Memory and Read Only Memory

b. When the computer system is turned off, then the contents of RAM are lost.

15. Two types of RAM are Static RAM (SRAM) and Dynamic RAM (DRAM).

a. SRAM gives faster access than DRAM. SRAM does not need to be constantly refreshed.

b. DRAM is less expensive to buy than SRAM.

16. a. A relatively small amount of memory between the processor and the main memory

b. Video random access memory

17. To reduce the chance of them being copied

18. Flash ROM

19. Clock speed, MIPS, FLOPS, and application-based tests

20. Data bus width, use of cache memory and rate of data transfer to and from peripherals

21. a. None, because the quantity of memory actually installed has not increased.

b. Increase, because the quantity of data which can be transferred by each 'fetch', will increase.

22. The clock speed of the bus will slow down the processor, causing a 'bottleneck'

23. a. More data and programs may be held in RAM, and it is much faster to access RAM than hard disk

b. Cache memory holds frequently accessed instructions and it is faster for the processor to fetch instructions from the cache than from main memory

24. Most programs do not require the maximum amount of main memory in order to run. Providing more main memory would increase the cost of the computer above that of competitor's machines.

25. a. You could say Sarah was correct because it will take less time to process instructions on the machine with the higher clock speed. However, Mary's computer may have other differences, like a wider data bus or a larger cache which could improve its performance despite its slower clock speed.

b. An application based test would show which machine was faster, if any.

26. Increasing clock speeds, increasing memory and backing storage capacity.

Chapter 3

1. Five functions of an interface are buffering, data format conversion, voltage conversion, protocol conversion and the handling of status signals.

2. a. Handling of status signals, for example, ready or paper out

b. Buffering, for example holding characters temporarily

3. A serial interface is one which uses serial data transmission, sending the bits for each character in the data along the same data line.

4. A parallel interface is one which uses parallel data transmission, sending each bit which makes up a character simultaneously along separate data lines.

5. a. The address and data buses use parallel data transmission.

b. The control bus and the universal serial bus (USB) do not use parallel data transmission.

6. A protocol is a standard that enables the connection, communication, and data transfer between computers or between a computer system and a peripheral.

7. Parity is an example of a protocol used during data transmission. Parity is used to check for errors. One bit in every byte of data is reserved as the parity bit.

8. Odd parity would be useful to check for errors like 0000 0000 0000, since a continuous sequence of '0' would become 1000 0000 1000 0000 and so on, using odd parity. Similarly, 1111 1111 1111 1111 ….Would become 0111 1111 0111 1111 …….

9. Three standard interfaces are USB, IEEE 1394 and SATA.

10. The use of interface standards by a computer manufacturer means that their computers will be able to connect to peripherals using the same standards. The use of interface standards by a peripheral manufacturer means that their peripherals will connect to a computer which uses the same standards.

11. A buffer is an area of memory used for the transfer of the data between the computer and a peripheral.

12. A spooler is a program which uses fast backing storage such as a hard disk for the temporary storage of print jobs.

13. A spooler using a hard disk drive is more appropriate when large documents or a large number of small documents have to be sent to a printer. RAM in a buffer has a limited capacity.

14. The likely speed of a spooler using a hard disk drive will be slower than a buffer using RAM because the speed of access to a hard disk drive is much slower than RAM.

15. Switching off background printing would mean that the user would have to wait until printing was complete before continuing with a task.

16. A printer server uses a spooler.

17. a. A solid-state storage device is one which has no moving parts.

b. Flash ROM is the storage medium used in solid state storage devices.

c. In this context 'solid' means that there are no spaces containing moving parts in the device.

d. Solid-state storage devices are much more robust than hard disk drives.

18. This device is a flash card reader.

19. Development trends in backing storage devices include increased capacity, increased read and write speeds, reduced physical size and lower cost per unit of storage.

20. Trends in interfaces include increasing interface speeds and wireless communication between peripherals and CPU.

21. Two methods of wireless communication between peripherals and the CPU are WiFi and Bluetooth.

22. a. Digital video camera

b. Network switch

c. Digital still camera.

Chapter 4

1. A network is two or more computers linked together in such a way that programs, data and messages may be exchanged between them.
2. A stand-alone computer is one which is not connected to a network.
3. A local area network (LAN) covers a small area such as a room or a building.
4. A network interface card is a small circuit board.
5. The purpose of a NIC is to allow the computer to communicate with a network.
6. A MAC address is a *Media Access Control Address provided by a NIC*.
7. 2^{48}
8. A wireless local area network
9. WiFi
10. A wireless network interface card
11. A wireless base station
12. An area where wireless network signals may be received.
13. (a) university campus (b) outside a building with a WLAN
14. A client-server network is a method of organisation in which client workstations make use of resources available on one or more servers.
15. A peer-to-peer network is when every workstation has a similar status in the hierarchy, each having its own local storage devices for programs and data.
16. Increased security over peer-to-peer – each user must log in to server, different users can be given different levels of access to data.
17. If the file server is not working then users cannot access their data, client–server is more expensive than peer-to-peer – it is necessary to buy a server and server software.
18. A wide area network covers a large geographical area.
19. A mainframe computer is a very large computer system, which can process a very large amount of data at high speed.
20. A dumb terminal has no processor and no local storage devices, just a screen and a keyboard.
21. Mainframe has dumb terminals – each network station has its own processor. Mainframe does all of the processing – each network terminal does its own processing. Mainframe is multi-user. Network of computers is single user.
22. A supercomputer is the fastest and most powerful type of computer, used for intensive mathematical calculations. It has many parallel processors and can process data simultaneously.
23. The network topology is the way in which the nodes or workstations on a network are connected together.
24. A communications channel is the connection between two nodes on a network.
25. Copper wire
26. A bus topology:

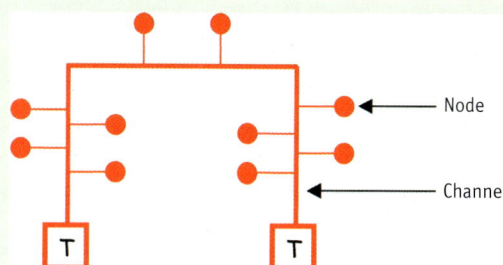

27. The terminator catches stray signals and prevents them from interfering with other signals on the bus.
28. A mesh topology would be very costly to implement on a LAN because of the multiple connections required. It would also be technically difficult in a single room – if there were 20 computers, each computer would have to have 19 connections for a fully connected mesh.
29.

Failure	Star	Ring
Node	Network down if central node down – otherwise no effect on rest of network	Failed node can be bypassed to maintain integrity of ring
Channel	No effect on rest of network	Network down

30. A repeater is a device which amplifies a signal on a cable.
31. A hub is a multi-port repeater.
32. A switch is like a 'smart' hub which divides a network into separate segments, one segment for each connected machine.

33. Workstations which are connected via a switch benefit because there are no collisions between signals to reduce the speed of the network.

34. A router is a device which links two or more networks. A router looks at the destination addresses of the packets of data passing through it, and decides which route each packet should take.

35. File, print and web

36. Redundant Array of Inexpensive Disks

37. Using two hard disks to hold exactly the same data.

38. Uninterruptible Power Supply

39. a. File server
    b. To provide central disk storage for user's programs and data on a network

40. A spooler stores data temporarily while it is in transit to the printer, on a fast backing storage device like a hard disk drive.

41. Print server

42. In order of when the print jobs were sent into the queue, or by giving priorities to some users over others.

43. A jukebox can be used to hold a number of CD-ROMs at once, or to make backups of network data on multiple recordable disks.

44. A LAN

45. Unshielded Twisted Pair – it is a type of copper cable.

46. There is no point in printing a document if you have to travel a distance to collect it.

47. An Intranet is a private network belonging to a company or organization, for internal use only, although it may be geographically widespread.

48. The main purpose of an Intranet is to share company information and computing resources among employees.

49. An Internetwork is a collection of two or more local area networks.

50. Higher bandwidth and wireless communication

51. Asymmetric Digital Subscriber Line

52. The maximum distance for 512 Kbps ADSL is 5.5 km, falling to 3.5 km for 2 Mbps.

53. A network cloud is a collection of hotspots or areas within the range of wireless base stations.

54. Warchalking symbols are used to identify hotspots where a wireless connection may be made.

55. WiFi is the Wireless Fidelity Alliance standard for wireless networking

56. IEEE 802.11b has a maximum bandwidth of 11 Mbps and operates at a typical range of 20–30 metres.

57. Bluetooth is the name for IEEE 802.15.1 wireless standard, with a range of up to 10 metres and a bandwidth of 1 Mbps.

58. WiFi has a greater range (20–30 metres) over Bluetooth (10 metres).

59. Advances in computer hardware and improved network related software

60. Data transfer rates are also increasing, for instance, 10 Mbps Ethernet is being replaced by 100 Mbps. This improvement in bandwidth allows larger files to be transferred in less time.

61. Browsers and network operating systems.

62. The laws which apply to the misuse of networks include the Copyright, Designs and Patents Act, the Computer Misuse Act and the Data Protection Act.

63. Using multiple copies of commercial software without an adequate license

64. Hacking is gaining/trying to gain unauthorised access to a computer system.

65. a. A skilled hacker who uses his or her ability to pursue their interest illegally
    b. A honeypot is a system which is deliberately left open to attract the activities of black hats, in the same way as bears are attracted to honey.

66. Spyware is a type of computer program which can record the user's keystrokes, like passwords and forward them to another computer.

67. Phishing is an attempt to trick someone using the internet by pretending to be a well-known company into giving away personal information.

Chapter 5

1. The operating system is a program that controls the entire operation of the computer and any devices which are attached to it.

2. The operating system runs in a computer all the time from the moment it is switched on until the computer is switched off.

3. It is not always necessary to load the entire operating system on start-up for a disk-based operating system.

4. a. Interpreting user's commands (takes the instructions from the user and passes them on to the rest of the operating system), file management (controls the organisation of backing storage), memory management (controls where programs and data are placed in main memory), input/output management (communicates between the computer system and the input and output devices), managing processes (controls processes and handles interrupts)

    i.   You issue the command to the CLI, SAVE *myfile*, either by entering the instruction or by choosing from a menu.

    ii. The kernel suspends the current CLI process, and passes the request to the FMS.

    iii. The FMS requests the I/O system to read the disk's catalog track, and loads a list of the filenames.

    iv. If the filename is present on the disk, then the FMS passes a warning message to the CLI to inform the user, otherwise

    v.   The MMS passes the file to the I/O system.

    vi. The I/O system places the file on disk.

    vii. The kernel allows the CLI process to resume, and you again have control of the computer.

    b. The disk may be full.

    c. CLI

5. The bootstrap loader loads the rest of the operating system from disk when the computer is switched on.

6. a. A disk formatter
    b. An anti-virus program

7. a. No
    b. Because some RAM is used up to hold the operating system.

8. To load the operating system from disk on start-up.

9. In ROM.

10. Resource allocation is the way of managing which resources are available for use at any one time by a process.

11. When the current process in the processor becomes blocked, or terminates, then the scheduler is able to allocate a free process to the processor, until that process terminates or is blocked.

12.

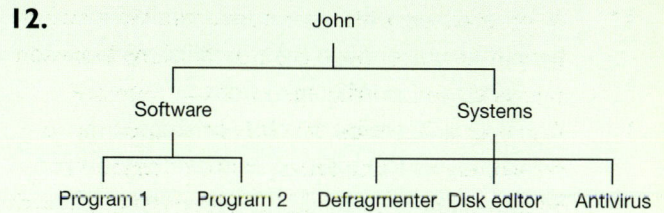

Figure 5.16 *Hierarchical filing system answer*

13. A utility program is a type of systems software designed to perform an everyday task, for example, transferring data from one backing storage device to another.

14. a. Virus checking software should be able to detect the occurrence of a virus infection and remove it from a computer system.
    b. A disc editor allows the user to edit data directly on the surface of a disk, by-passing the normal loading and saving features of the operating system.
    c. A defragmenter program defragments a disk, gathering all the free space on the disk together and reuniting scattered file fragments.

15. a. If your disk became slow to access
    b. See figure 5.6.

16. JPEG, GIF and TIFF

17. a. Joint Photographic Experts Group
    b. Graphics Interchange Format
    c. Tag Image File Format.

18. a. 16.7 million
    b. 256

19. a. Compatible software is software which works on a particular computer system.
    b. Software compatibility issues include: memory requirements, storage requirements and OS compatibility.
    c. The user should be able to tell whether the software is compatible with their computer system before buying it.
    d. Operating system, processor, clock speed, RAM requirements, Backing storage requirements, any peripheral requirements, for instance, monitor resolution.

20. a. TIFF
    b. TIFF files are very large.
    c. GIF
    d. GIF only allows 256 colours.
    e. JPEG offers variable compression.
    f. JPEG allows the user to balance file size against quality required.

21. **a.** Not enough disk space for installation

b. Either not enough RAM or incompatible version of operating system

c. File management system – change disk catalogue; I/O management system – write new catalogue to disk

22. A virus is a program which can destroy or cause damage to data stored on a computer system.

23. File virus, boot sector virus, macro virus.

24. A worm is a program which can make copies of itself and spread between computers without having to be attached to a file.

25. A Trojan is a program that appears to be safe, but hidden inside is usually something harmful, like a worm or a virus.

26. **a.** A worm can make copies of itself and spread between computers without having to be attached to a file, unlike a virus, which infects other *host* files and is distributed along with them.

b. Trojan horse is disguised as another type of file, but a virus is attached to, or becomes part of, another file.

27. Replication, camouflage, watching and delivery

28. **a.** A checksum is performed on an uninfected program. Repeating the calculation on a suspect program allows the anti-virus software to test if the program has been changed, and if so, it will issue a warning that the program may be infected with a virus

b. A virus signature is a characteristic pattern or sequence of bytes that is part of a virus. If a virus scanner finds such a pattern in a file, it notifies the user that the file is infected.

c. Heuristics allow rules to be set up to detect new viruses that have not been seen before – for example, if it looks like a virus, and behaves like a virus, then it probably *is* a virus.

d. Anti-virus software which stays in the computer's memory and constantly checks the computer for the presence of viruses.

29. **a.** A blended threat uses a variety of techniques to increase the spread and the severity of virus infection, typically a virus, a worm and a Trojan horse may be involved in a blended threat infection.

b. The 'I Love You' virus

30. Delete it immediately without opening it.

Chapter 6

1. The software development process is a series of seven stages for the development of software Analysis, Design, Implementation, Testing, Documentation, Evaluation and Maintenance.

2. Iterative as applied to the software development process means revisiting parts of the process in order to correct mistakes or improve the solution.

3. **a.** analysis
b. analysis
c. implementation

4. The process of planning the solution to a problem is called design.

5. Internal documentation is comment lines which may be inserted in program code to provide a description of what the code does.

6. Field testing is allowing users (other than the people who wrote the program) to test the program.

7. **a.** The pre-release version of a program is called the beta version.

b. The software company distributes this version so that the program can be tested on as wide a variety of hardware as possible, in order to improve the chances of finding mistakes in the code.

8. A test report summarises the results of testing a program.

9. An evaluation is when the software solution is reviewed against suitable criteria, such as the original software specification.

10. Questions for the evaluation stage are:
- Is the software able to cope with errors during execution without failing? (robustness)
- How well does the software operate without stopping due to design faults? (reliability)
- Can the developed software be used on a computer other than that for which it was originally designed? (portability)
- Does the software require excessive resources in order to run properly? (efficiency)
- How easy is it to correct and/or update the software in future? (maintainability)

11. Program maintenance is changing a program, often some time after it has been written.

12. Student's comments on their own program.

13. One design methodology is top-down design. This involves looking at the overall problem and breaking it down into a series of steps.

14. Bottom-up design begins with writing modules or procedures.

15. One design notation is pseudocode. Pseudocode is ordinary language used to define problems and sub-problems before they are changed into code in a high level language.

16. Design methodology is the approach that the programmer takes to the design of the solution. Design notation is a way of describing a program design.

17. The purpose of test data is to check whether or not the software meets the specification, or does what it is supposed to do.

18. Three types of test data are normal, extreme and exceptional.

19. Appropriate set of test data for two of the given problems.

20. Exhaustive testing involves testing a program with all of the possible sets of program inputs that it is designed to handle.

21. a. A structured listing is a formatted display or a printout of the program code.
    b. A structured listing can aid the programmer by helping her to spot mistakes in the structure of the program, such as unclosed loops.

22. a. A run-time error is an error which shows up during program execution. These include overflow, rounding, truncation and division by zero.
    b. A linking error is when a program is incorrectly linked to a subroutine or module library.
    c. A syntax error is when the rules of the programming language are broken.

23. a. A logical error can be detected if the program runs, but does not do what it is expected to do, for instance, produces the wrong results.
    b. An example of a logic error is: count% = count%+0

24. COMAL for MacOS has a trace facility and a check syntax facility.

25. Hand testing is reading through a printout of the code in order to find mistakes.

26. An error from the operating system could be 'printer jammed'.

27. Portability is of economic importance because of the cost of software development. If a developer does not have to produce different versions of software to run on different computers then a great deal of money can be saved.

28. a. A hardware platform is a particular combination of processor and operating system.
    b. Windows XP, Intel Pentium, IBM desktop computer

29. Efficiency is desirable because it means that the software does not require excessive resources in order to run.

30. The software specification may have to be enforced in a court of law if the software meets the specification but the client refuses to pay.

31. The software development team would have wasted time and money and would have to start the software development process over again.

32. Project manager, systems analyst, programmer, independent test group and the client.

33. The systems analyst

34. Making observation notes, using questionnaires, interviewing the client, examining information sources.

35. The project manager

36. The client

37. Top-down design and bottom-up design

38. Pseudocode is said to be language independent because it uses ordinary English terms rather than the special keywords used in high level languages.

39. A structure diagram, plus appropriate drawing (see figure 6.9)

40. The terms used are in:, out: and in-out.

41. The choice of language, the computer platform and the requirement for specific hardware features.

42. The name of the program or module, what the program or module should do, the test data and the expected results from the test data.

43. This can be true if it is impossible to test all the program pathways.

44. Testing.

45. Any two from:
- Examine the source code, object code, test plan and results of testing already carried out by the software developer;
- Document additional tests to be carried out if appropriate;
- Re-test the software, repeating all the original tests and performing any additional tests;
- Document any errors found and communicate these to the software developer for correction;
- Receive corrected code from the developer;
- Repeat all tests on the corrected code.

46. Debugging is the process of finding and correcting errors in a program.

47. Misspelling a keyword e.g. PRUNT instead of PRINT; FOR without a corresponding NEXT.

Sample answer to Analysis practice questions

Problem description

Write a program which will ask the user for two numbers and give their sum, product and quotient

Assumptions

Both numbers are integers (whole numbers)

The maximum number is 10

The minimum number is 1

The sum and product are integers and the quotient is a real (fractional) number

Input

Two integers within the range 1–10

Process

Sum, multiply and divide the numbers

Output

The sum and product as integers and the quotient as a real number

Chapter 7

1. Procedural, declarative, event-driven and scripting
2. A procedural language is one in which the user sets out a list of instructions in the correct sequence in order to solve a problem.
3. Data storage using variables of different types, Arithmetic and logical operations, Program control using sequence, repetition and selection, Subprograms or procedures, Data flow using parameters

4. When a program written in a procedural language is run, the sequence of instructions is followed from the beginning of the program to the end in the programmed order.
5. BASIC, COMAL and Pascal are examples of procedural languages.
6. A declarative language may be thought of as the opposite of a procedural language. Instead of giving a concise list of instructions set out in the correct order, a declarative language states 'what to do' rather than ' how to do it'.
7. Prolog
8. **a.** hot(tea)
   b. cold(ice cream)
9. Facts and rules make up the knowledge base in a declarative language.
10. Programs written in event-driven languages have no definite start or end. When the program is running, the user interacts with the event-driven language by selecting from a choice of screen objects.
11. It is much quicker to design a program with a graphical user interface when using an event-driven language.
12. The action of clicking on, or selecting, a screen object is called an event. The event is detected by the program, hence the name event-driven language.
13. Visual Basic
14. A scripting language allows the user to tailor an application package to carry out additional operations other than those provided in the original menus.
15. A macro is a set of keystrokes and instructions that are recorded, saved, and assigned to a single key or a combination of keys. When the key code is typed, the recorded keystrokes and instructions are carried out.
16. A macro may be created either by recording a sequence of keystrokes and mouse actions, or by entering a suitable script in an appropriate language into an editor.
17. The need for scripting languages arises from the requirement to be able to make changes to the commands or menus, or to automate tasks within an application package or an operating system.

18. The benefits of scripting languages are that they allow application packages to be enhanced with additional commands, automate tasks for an expert user and allow a beginner to perform tasks that they would not otherwise be able to undertake.

19. The main stimulus to the development of high level languages was the need to reduce the time taken for software development, when using machine oriented languages like machine code.

20. A translator is a computer program used to convert program code from one language to another.

21. Translators are used because it is very difficult to write programs directly in machine code. It is much easier for the programmer to write the program in a high level language and then have it changed into machine code by a translator program.

22. The function of a compiler is to translate a high level language program (source code), into machine code (object code).

23. Source code is a high level language program, before translation.

24. Object code is a machine code program produced as the result of translation.

25. An interpreter does not produce object code.

26. **a.** In the **lexical analysis** stage, each recognised keyword in the source code is changed into a token.

b. During the **syntax analysis** stage, the language statements are checked against the rules or grammar of the language.

c. The **code generation** stage produces the object code, which is a machine code representation of the source code.

27. **a.** Compiled – Pascal

b. Interpreted – COMAL.

28. Machine code programs are not portable because machine code is the computer's own language and is specific to the processor being used.

29. A cross-compiler takes a high level language program as source code, and can produce object code for more than one type of processor.

30. The function of an interpreter is to translate and run a high level language program one instruction at a time.

31.

Interpreted programs	Compiled programs
Run slow	Run fast
Report mistakes immediately	Report mistakes at end of compilation
Translate and run is a single process	Translate and run are separate processes
Cannot save translated version	Can save object code
Interpreter required to run the code	Compiler not required to run the code

32. A compiler is to be preferred over an interpreter if the code needs to be run fast (final version). An interpreter is to be preferred over a compiler when the code is being developed.

33. The source code is required if the program is to be maintained in the future.

34. Selling the source code would be giving away the programmer's expertise and would allow the user to change the program, or steal part of the code to be used elsewhere.

35. A stand alone version of a program is independent of the translator program and may be run on its own.

36. The programmer does not need to supply a translator program to accompany the code. Providing a translator would also increase the cost of the software.

37. A module library is part of a software library. A software library is a collection of software held permanently accessible on backing storage. A software library will typically include complete programs, a module library and a set of machine code routines, which may be loaded into user programs when required.

38. **a.** The design has already been done when the module was created in the first place.

b. A programmer would not write a procedure to sort numbers each time this was required in a new program, the procedure would simply be loaded from a module library.

c. All of the modules in a module library are already tested and known to be free from errors, so these modules do not need to be tested again.

d. Each module in a module library is already fully documented.

39. A text editor allows source code to be entered and edited.

Chapter 8

1. a. The syntax of a programming language is the way in which you give instructions to the computer.

b. The semantics of a particular instruction is its meaning or its effect.
picDisplay.Print "Hello World !" and PRINT "Hello World !" display the same text. They have the same semantics but different syntax. The statement "number = 10" has the same syntax but different meanings (semantics) depending upon the language in use.

2. *number :+ 1* and *number ++ 1* have the same semantics but different syntax. They have the same effect, but are written differently.

3. Modularity means that when a program is designed and written, it is divided into smaller sections called subprograms.

4. A procedure produces an effect and a function returns a value.

5. a. A user-defined function is a function which is created within a program rather than being already present or pre-defined as part of the normal syntax of a programming language.

b. The SQR function is an example of a pre-defined function.

6. A reference parameter allows data from a procedure to be passed back out to a program.

7. a. An operation is a process which is carried out on an item of data.

b. An object is the item of data which is involved in the process.

8. a. Concatenation is joining two strings.

b. Substrings is selecting parts of strings.

9. a. Logical operators include OR and NOT

b. Arithmetical operators include + and −

c. Relational operators include = and >

10. Formatting of input/output is arranging the appearance of the data on the screen when input or output is taking place.

11. a. 38

b. 1820

12. Control, data storage and data flow

13. a. Sequence, selection and repetition

b. Sequence is the order in which things are done. Take in a number; find square of number; display answer – is a sequence which will only operate

when the statements are arranged in the correct order.

14. Age=18 – is a simple condition. Month >= 1 AND Month <= 12 – is a complex condition

15. The condition determines the course of action which should be taken, for instance, "switch heating on" OR "switch heating off" are two courses of action. The control structure is the framework which allows the choice to take place, for example IF average temperature is less than 15 degrees Celsius THEN "switch heating on".

16. a. A variable is the name that a programmer uses to identify a storage location.

b. Local variables are defined only for use in one part of a program.

c. Global variables may be used anywhere in a program.

d. The scope of a variable is the range of statements for which a variable is valid.

e. The kind of data which is being stored, for example, alphanumeric, numeric or Boolean.

17. a. A sub-program

b. The whole program

18. Selection and repetition

19. Array

20. Arrays are particularly useful for handling a set of data items in a program. Because an array uses a single identifier, each element of the array may be easily found using a subscript.

21. A parameter is information about a data item being supplied to a subprogram when it is called into use.

22. a. i. Parameters are passed by value when a parameter is passed into a procedure but does not require to be passed back out again to be used in another procedure.

ii. Parameters are passed by reference when the parameter requires to be passed in to a procedure, updated and then passed back out of the procedure again.

b. One exception to this rule exists for the array data structure only. When an array is being passed as a parameter, it is always passed by reference.

23. a. i. The purpose of sequence is to ensure that instructions given to the computer in the form of a computer program are carried out in the correct order.

   ii. The purpose of repetition is to allow statements in a program to be repeated as many times as is necessary.
   iii. The purpose of selection is to allow a choice to be made in a program, like changing the order or sequence of execution of program statements.
- **b.** Repetition
- **c.** A loop which is contained within another loop

24. **a.** A logical error
b. In this case it will lead to an infinite loop.

25. The amount of data to be processed need not be known in advance.

26. Using test at start means that the loop does not need to run if the condition is not met. Using test at end means that the loop must always run at least once – in order to reach the test condition statement.

27. **a.** To end a conditional loop with test at end
b.
1. loop REPEAT
2. take in a word
3. ask user to enter a word
4. UNTIL the word 'end' is entered

28. When a multiple outcome selection has to take place:

1. CASE destination OF
2. WHEN town
3. take credit card
4. WHEN pool
5. take swimming costume
6. WHEN beach
7. take bucket and spade
8. WHEN hillwalking
9. take rucksack + food
10. WHEN disco
11. take ID card
12. OTHERWISE
13. watch TV
14. END CASE

29. One example answer only for: Calculate the area of a circle given the radius as input (π^{r2})
1. Ask user for radius
2. Take in radius
3. Calculate area by using the formula π^{r2}
4. Display answer

30. It is necessary to describe the data flow in a program in order to work out how the parameters should be passed between the main program and any sub-programs and between the sub-programs themselves.

31. **a.** Grade 3
b.
```
CASE mark OF
WHEN >= 70
display grade 1
WHEN >= 60
display grade 2
WHEN >= 50
display grade 3
END CASE
```

32. UNTIL word$ = 'END' OR word$ = "end" – the purpose of the "OR" is to allow either "END" or "end" to stop the conditional loop

33. **a.** Output
```
99 bottles of beer on the wall.
    99 bottles of beer.
Take one down, pass it around.
    98 bottles of beer.........
..............
................
Take one down, pass it around.
    1 bottle of beer.
    1 bottle of beer on the wall.
    1 bottle of beer.
Take one down, pass it around.
    0 bottles of beer.
```
b. Practical work on computer in COMAL

34. Practical work on World Wide Web

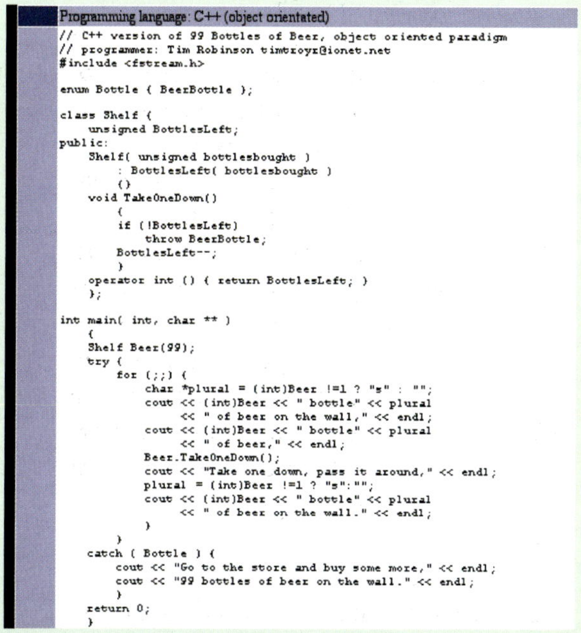
Programming language: C++ (object orientated)
```
// C++ version of 99 Bottles of Beer, object oriented paradigm
// programmer: Tim Robinson timtroyr@ionet.net
#include <fstream.h>

enum Bottle { BeerBottle };

class Shelf {
    unsigned BottlesLeft;
public:
    Shelf( unsigned bottlesbought )
        : BottlesLeft( bottlesbought )
        {}
    void TakeOneDown()
        {
        if (!BottlesLeft)
            throw BeerBottle;
        BottlesLeft--;
        }
    operator int () { return BottlesLeft; }
    };

int main( int, char ** )
    {
    Shelf Beer(99);
    try {
        for (;;) {
            char *plural = (int)Beer !=1 ? "s" : "";
            cout << (int)Beer << " bottle" << plural
                << " of beer on the wall," << endl;
            cout << (int)Beer << " bottle" << plural
                << " of beer," << endl;
            Beer.TakeOneDown();
            cout << "Take one down, pass it around," << endl;
            plural = (int)Beer !=1 ? "s":"";
            cout << (int)Beer << " bottle" << plural
                << " of beer on the wall." << endl;
            }
        }
    catch ( Bottle ) {
        cout << "Go to the store and buy some more," << endl;
        cout << "99 bottles of beer on the wall." << endl;
        }
    return 0;
    }
```

Figure 8.22 *99 Bottles of Beer in C++*

35. Repetition

Chapter 9

1. Design

2. a. Input validation
b. Linear search
c. Count occurrences
d. Find maximum / minimum

3. a. Pseudocode
b. In pseudocode, each line represents a line of code, so it is easy to see the relationship between the code and the design.
c.

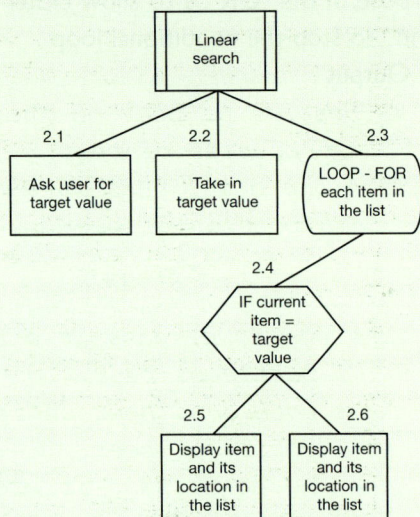

Figure 9.5 *Structure diagram for Linear Search algorithm*

4. Input validation

5. The linear search algorithm uses a Boolean variable, found. The counting occurrences algorithm uses a counter for the number of hits. Both algorithms compare each item in the list with the target value.

6. The search can stop when an item smaller (or larger) than the target item has been reached. This is an advantage when large lists are being searched.

7. There is no maximum number of attempted entries.

8.
```
4.1   READ in the first item from
      the list
4.2   set the maximum value to be
      equal to the first item
4.3   set the minimum value to be
      equal to the first item
4.4   loop - REPEAT
```

```
4.5   READ in the next item from
      the list
4.6   IF the current item is
      greater than the maximum
      value THEN
4.7   set the maximum value to be
      equal to the current item
4.8   END IF
4.9   IF the current item is less
      than the minimum value THEN
4.10  set the minimum value to be
      equal to the current item
4.11  END IF
4.12  end loop - UNTIL end of data
      has been reached
4.13  display maximum value
4.14  display minimum value
```

9. Depends upon chosen software development environment

10. a. Nothing
b. In COMAL:
```
FOR position% := 1 TO no_of_items%
  DO
    IF list% (position%) = target%
    THEN
      PRINT "Item found"
      PRINT "The item"; target%;
        "was found at position";
        position%; "in the list"
    ELSE
      PRINT "The item"; target%;
        "was not found in the list"
    ENDIF
NEXT position%
```

11.
```
2.1   ask user for target value
2.2   take in the target value
2.3   loop WHILE target value is
      less than 1 OR target value
      is greater than 100
2.4     prompt to re-enter target
        value
2.5     take in the data
2.6   end loop
2.7     loop - FOR each item in
        the list
2.8     IF current item = target
        value THEN
```

```
2.9      display found message
2.10     display item and its
         location in the list
2.11     END IF
2.12  end loop – NEXT item
```

12. Answer depends upon software development environment in use.

13. Zero may not be a value in the list, the list may consist entirely of negative numbers, or the minimum value may be less than zero (negative).

Appendix

1. **a.** Force quit the program by pressing a sequence of keys, or press the reset button.
    b. Free RAM is the quantity of RAM left for use after the operating system has been loaded.
    c. i. The program requires 256 Megabytes, leaving no room for the operating system to load.
       ii. Buy and install more RAM or use virtual memory.
       iii. Buy more RAM – advantage – new program will run – disadvantage – cost of RAM. Use virtual memory – advantage – no cost option – disadvantage – slows down computer.
    d. Use a printer spooler program, which temporarily saves print jobs to hard disk and allows the user to continue working, or buy a new printer with a large buffer, or install more RAM into the existing printer.

2. **a.** 3 megapixels
    b. One million pixels
    c. It takes the same quantity of backing storage space to store shades of grey as it does colour for each pixel.
    d. A solid-state storage device which uses flash ROM to store data.
    e. Each photograph is compressed, and so takes up much less than 7 Megabytes, in this case, around 1.4 Megabytes each (128/90).
    f. By connecting the camera to the computer using a (USB) cable, or put the camera's memory card into a card reader.

3. **a.** One million floating point operations per second.
    b. MIPs – millions of instructions per second.

c. A test which times how long it takes for an application program to complete a task, for example, spell check a 100 page document.

d. The type of application tested is not known.

e. Using the processor clock rate on its own is not a good measure of performance, because there are many other factors which influence the speed at which a computer system operates, for example, the width of the data bus.

f. The Panic chip, with its dual core, has two processors. The Paramecium chip only has one processor, albeit a larger cache memory. The Panic chip will give better test results than the Paramecium chip if the test programs are able to recognise the presence of, and take advantage of the two processors. If not, the results of the tests will be much harder to predict.

4. **a.** Every workstation on a peer-to-peer network has a similar status in the hierarchy, each having its own local storage devices for programs and data.
    b. i. A mainframe terminal is a screen and a keyboard with some RAM. It has no processor.
       ii. The mainframe terminal cannot operate unless it is connected to the mainframe computer.
       iii. James should choose a laptop computer because it will be able to be used anywhere in his house, OR he should choose a desktop computer because it is likely to have a larger screen than the laptop, and he may prefer using a mouse to using a trackpad.
    c. i. A hub is a multi-port repeater.
       ii. The company should buy switches because workstations which are connected via a switch benefit because there are no collisions between signals to reduce the speed of the network.
    d. i. The network topology is the way in which the nodes on a network are connected together.
       ii. If one channel on a star topology fails, then only one node is affected. If the channel on a bus network fails, then the whole network cannot operate.

e. i. Hardware – file server. Software – file server software.

ii. Client-server allows centralised control of backup, peer-to-peer – users are responsible for their own backups.

f. A wireless base station

5. a. i. A bit-mapped graphics package

ii. 'ideal for digital camera or scanner output'

b. The software can open files and create files in many different standard data formats.

c. JPEG, GIF, TIFF, BMP

d. A scripting language

e. The user can load scripts from the library rather than having to write them themselves.

f. True colour is 24 bit colour, 8 bits per pixel (RGB), 16.7 million different colours.

g. The users can be kept informed of software updates and special offers. The company can benefit from user feedback about its products, and can send advertising about its products to users on a mailing list.

h. i. Graphics Interchange Format

ii. GIF files are much smaller than TIFF files, and so will download faster from the Internet.

6. a. No CD-ROMs or packaging need be created, no delivery costs. The company will save money.

b. A utility program is a type of systems software designed to perform an everyday task, for example, formatting a disk.

c. Helen's computer's hard disk is faulty.

d. Encryption is putting data into a code so that it cannot be read by unauthorised persons.

e. A decompressor.

f. A text editor or word processor.

g. The files are too large to fit on a floppy disk.

h. A CD writer.

i. A start-up disk is one which may be used to start up the computer when it is switched on.

j. A copy of the operating system program.